SO-FIN-711

LIVES IN LETTERS

Princess Zinaida Volkonskaya
and her correspondence

Princess Zinaida Volkonskaya, née Beloselskaya.
Louis Berger, around 1829

LIVES IN LETTERS

Princess Zinaida Volkonskaya
and her correspondence

BAYARA AROUTUNOVA

Slavica Publishers, Inc.

Slavica publishes a wide variety of scholarly books and textbooks on the languages, peoples, literatures, cultures, history, etc. of the former USSR and Eastern Europe. For a complete catalog of books and journals from Slavica, with prices and ordering information, write to:

Slavica Publishers, Inc.
PO Box 14388
Columbus, Ohio 43214

ISBN: 0-89357-251-9.

Copyright © 1994 by Bayara Aroutunova. All rights reserved.

All statements of fact or opinion are those of the authors and do not necessarily agree with those of the publisher, which takes no responsibility for them.

Printed in the United States of America.

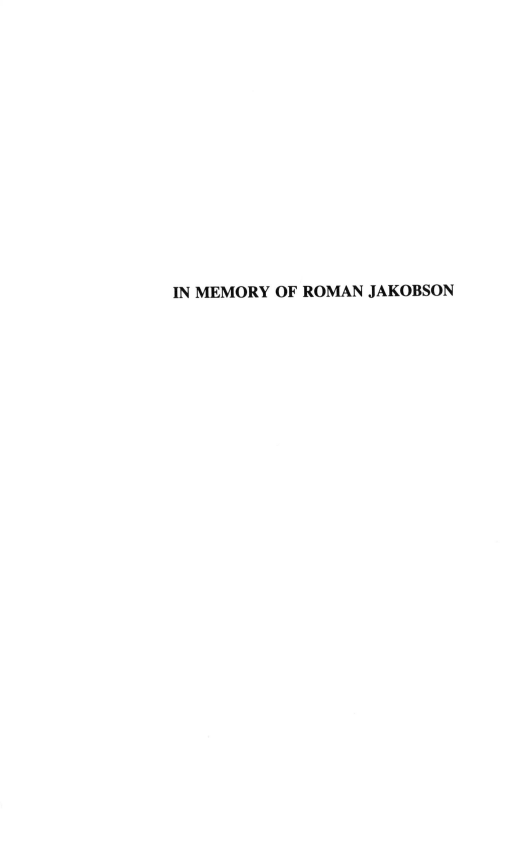

IN MEMORY OF ROMAN JAKOBSON

CONTENTS

Acknowledgments
Notes on Editing the Manuscript
On Transliteration
The Question of Dating
List of Abbreviations
Introduction... 17-41

Letters Written to Princess Z.A. Volkonskaya

Letter from Mme. de Staël 43-48
Letter from E.A. Baratynsky 49-52
Letter from I.I. Kozlov.. 53-59
Letter from M.I. Glinka.. 60-69
Letter from A.I. Turgenev 70-74
Two Letters from P.A. Vyazemsky............................... 75-85
Three Notes from V.A. Zhukosvky............................... 86-91
Fifteen Letters from Tsar Alexander I........................... 92-132
Seven Letters from Cardinal Ercole Consalvi.................. 133-152

Letters to Prince A.N. Volkonsky

Introductory Note 154
Letter from P.A. Vyazemsky..................................... 155-158
Three Letters from Ya. N. Tolstoy.............................. 159-170
Letter from I.S. Turgenev to A.P. Golitsyn 171-175
Endnotes 177-198
Index 199-204
Illustrations 205-224

Lives in Letters

Acknowledgments

The archive of the Russian Princess Zinaida Volkonskaya, acquired by Harvard University in 1967, is presently in the manuscripts collection of Houghton Library. Professor Roman Jakobson, who became acquainted with this archive when it was still in Rome, encouraged me to undertake a study of its materials. This publication represents the first volume of my study and is devoted to the letters from the Volkonskaya Archive. The second volume will treat her life and work as well as the unpublished literary contributions of the contemporaries, among whom were not only Russian, but also French and Italian writers.

While working on this book, I received valuable help form many colleagues and friends which I feel honored to acknowledge. First comes my gratitude to the late Roman Jakobson, my teacher and inspiration of many years, who generously helped me with his advice and guidance. I am most grateful to my colleagues who shared their time and knowledge in long, helpful conversations with me: Paul Benichou, Jean Louis Bruneau, Donald L. Fanger, George H. Williams, and the late Wiktor Weintraub. My work on this book was also aided by Rodney G. Dennis, the Curator of Manuscripts in the Harvard College Library.

In Rome, I received generous assistance coming from various sources, and I am grateful to my Italian consultants for the helpful attitude. The late Baron Basil Lemmerman, a knowledgeable collector, who had acquired this archive from one of the Volkonskys' heirs, the Marchese Vladimir Campanari, and later transferred it to Harvard University, made available to me his large library and collections which were the sources of the most valuable information. He also gave me permission to use reproductions of his paintings for illustrations to my book. I should also like to extent thanks to the present owner of a part of Lemmerman's collection, Savo Raskovic, who showed interest in my work and offered me some illustrative materials. I am much indebted to Sister Fabiola from the Order of the Precious Blood in Rome, who unsparingly helped me with much needed information and documentation. The assistance given to me by the competent librarians at the library of the Vatican cannot be left unmentioned. Last, but by no means least, comes the helpful support I received from the Holy Office of the Vatican for which I am deeply grateful to the office of Cardinal Samorè.

At Harvard University, throughout the period of my research on the Volkonskaya Archive, I was assisted by the kind and erudite staff of Houghton Library whose help I value highly.

My work on this volume was greatly facilitated by competent assistance from those who helped me to prepare this manuscript for publication, and I am much indebted to them all: Donald Anderson, Christine Brousseau, Caroline Butler, Cathleen Clover, Catherine Edmonds, David Keily, Federica Lamperini, Lucinda Leveille, Jana Orlen, Cynthia Vakareliyska, and Catherine Tridon.

I am also grateful to the Harvard Clark Fund which supported my research and preparation of this book for publication.

A long overdue expression of my thanks goes to Charles Gribble, the publisher and editor of Slavica, for his patience, helpful attitude, and interest in my work. I express gratitude to Dean S. Worth for his support and encouragement.

All manuscripts and pictures marked as belonging to Houghton Library are published by the permission of the Houghton Library, Harvard University.

Cambridge, Massachusetts

Notes on Editing of the Manuscript

Initially I intended to present all the materials of the Volkonskaya Archive in one volume. In the course of my work, however, it became evident that it would be advisable to place the most interesting letters in a separate volume. Because of the great variety of people, events, and places appearing in the manuscripts, I have supplied each group of letters with an introduction and detailed commentary. It has to be noted that if a lesser-known figure is important in the context of a particular letter, he may receive more detailed treatment than a personality well-known to the reader.

Having thoroughly considered the question, I decided to translate only the Russian texts into English, leaving those written in French untranslated. All letters are presented in their original language without any editorial changes. I have made no attempt to conform the language of the manuscripts to the standard language of the period or to the contemporary literary usage. If the texts had mistakes or inconsistencies in grammar, I did not correct them. In several cases, the French of Volkonskaya's Russian correspondents has been briefly analyzed in the commentaries. Proper and geographical names are also left as they were spelled. I have made emendations only in cases when authors either used unclear abbreviations of left out words or letters. The reconstructions of these omissions as well as my reading of illegible words are placed in brackets.

If a letters was not signed, or if its date or place of writing was not indicated, I used its content, language, style, and various extracontextual connections in attributing authorship and establishing other missing information. In the commentaries, I have described in detail the searches leading to the establishment of the needed data.

The Question of Dating

The problem of dating Russian materials is complicated by the fact that the Russians used the Julian calendar ("old style") until 1918. In the eighteenth century, this calendar fell eleven days behind the Gregorian calendar used in the Western world; in the nineteenth century, this difference was twelve days.

In our text, the new Gregorian style of dating will be used: 1) when dealing with Western writers and the events of European history, and 2) whenever it was followed by Russians abroad or in their foreign correspondence. We preserved the old Julian style when dealing with Russian authors and events. Thus, Pushkin was born on May 26 and died on January 29 (the Julian dates are still used in Russian sources); and the battle of Leipzig, described in the letter of Alexander 1, was fought on October 4-7 (as he dated it) and not on October 16-19 (as is found in Western documentation).

Since this study deals with letters, we followed the dates as they appeared in the manuscripts. Hence, we are using both Julian and Gregorian dates if this practice was followed by the author or if it proves helpful for establishing the date, place, or authorship of a manuscript. We realize that this system is somewhat confusing, but unable to find a better solution, we tried to follow it consistently. There were some cases when the authors, particularly those living abroad, used a system of dating inconsistently. We preserved there usage, commenting on this in our notes.

On Transliteration

The transliteration of Russian names and places in this book follows the system customarily used in English publications, the one most likely to be familiar to the non-specialist reader to aid him in pronunciation (System I): Pushkin, Delvig, Vyazemsky, Tolstoy, Chaadaev, Volkonskaya, Shcherbatov, Zhukovsky, archkiv. In the endnotes and bibliography, Russian citations and documentation not integrated into English sentences are transliterated in accordance with the international standard scholarly system (System II): Puškin, Del'vig, Vjazemskij, Tolstoj, Čaadaev, Volkonskaja, Ščerbatov, Žukovskij, arxiv. In the case of non-Russian names, the original spelling is preserved (Goethe, Stendhal, Mérimée), unless differently spelled by the author. In quoting letters, diaries and memoires, our aim is to present the text without changes. Therefore, the name of Zinaida Volkonskaya may appear also as Zeneida, Zénèide, Volkonsky, Volhonsky, Wolkonskaya, Wolkonska, etc., according to the spelling used by the author of the given manuscript.

Consistent adherence to these principles in bibliographical notes, however, results in a sometimes awkward use of both systems: in the same note, both types of transliteration may be used. Russian words and names with English sentences will be spelled according to System I (''In his letter of May 12, 1832, Prince Vyazemsky writes . . .'') though in the next sentences, where only the source is given, the transliteration follows System II (Vjazemskij, *Zapisnaja Knižka*). The titles of books, articles, and poems, if introduced in two languages, are first given in Russian transliteration with English translation offered in brackets.

Abbreviations

BBP	Biblioteka poeta. Bol'šaja serija, vtoroe izdanie. (Leningrad: Sovetskij pisatel').
CGADA	Central'nyj gosudarstvennyj arxiv drevnix aktov SSSR.
CGALI	Central'nyj gosudarstvennyj arxiv literatury i iskusstva.
GIZ	Gosudarstvennoe izdatel'stvo.
GIXL	Gosudarstvennoe izdatel'stvo xudožestvennoj literatury.
IORYAiS	Izvestija otdelenija russkogo jazyka i slovesnosti Akademii Nauk.
Izd. ANSSSR	Izdatel'stvo Akademii Nauk SSSR (Moscow-Leningrad).
LN	*Literaturnoe Nasledstvo* (Moscow-Leningrad, Akademija Nauk 1931-).
MS, MSS	manuscript, manuscripts
n.a.; n.b.	not after; not before
n.d.; n.p.	no date; no place
PSS	polnoe sobranie sočinenij
A.S. Puškin, *PSS*	A.S. Puškin, *Polnoe sobranie sočinenij* (Moscow- Leningrad: Akademija Nauk SSSR, 1937-1959), I-XVII.
RA	*Russkij arxiv* (Moscow: 1863-1917).
RS	*Russkaja starina* (St. Petersburg: 1870-1918).
SiN	*Starina i Novizna* (1897-1917).
Tip.	tipografija
VE	*Vestnik Evropy* (St. Petersburg: 1866-1918).
P.A. Vjazemskij, *PSS*	P.A. Vjazemskij, *Polnoe sobranie sočinenij* (St. Petersburg: 1878-1896), I-XII.
OA	Ostaf'evskij arxiv knjazej Vjazemskix (St. Petersburg: 1886-1903).
( )	Parenthetic remarks in my own text as well as those by the authors of the letters appear in parentheses.
[ ]	Square brackets, on the other hand, have been reserved for two purposes: the reconstruction of illegible or abbreviated text, and the supplementation of facts established by me, such as places, dates, names or attributions.

"Correspondence for me is as alive as the spoken word."
Madame de Staël to François de Pange.

"I was born for letters, nowhere do I pour out myself as in letters."
P.A. Vyazemsky to A.I. Turgenev.

The poem A.S. Pushkin dedicated to Princess Volkonskaya.
Harvard University, Houghton Library

INTRODUCTION

"The Queen of Muses and of Beauty"
A.S. Pushkin to Volkonskaya

The letters to the Russian Princess Zinaida Volkonskaya cover almost thirty years of Russian and European history: 1812-1838. This was a period marked by crucial political, social and cultural developments. The letters in the Volkonskaya Archive carry the reader through the waves of war and peace: they witness the struggles of the Napoleonic wars, the victory and subsequent upheaval during peacetime in Europe and Russia, and the growing influence of Roman Catholicism which was competing with that of the Russian Orthodox church. It would be hardly an exaggeration to say that the most important events of the early nineteenth century are eloquently reflected on the pages of these letters.

The personal relationships and everyday life of broad circles of society were also mirrored in letters to Volkonskaya. The letters offer important information about people, events, and the cultural environment. In many cases they supply the reader with new facts. In the orbit of Princess Volkonskaya's turbulent life were the most outstanding people of her time. They were from different countries, and some of them from different social classes and cultural circles. Among Volkonskaya's correspondents were no lesser figures than Tsar Alexander I, the Prime Minister of the Vatican, Cardinal Consalvi, the French author Mme. de Staël, and writers representing the Golden Age of Russian letters. The diversity of Princess Volkonskaya's correspondents reveals the complexity and multitude of her interests, as well as the wide range of contacts she established while in Russia and during the years of her tireless wandering about Europe.

These letters supply the reader with rich information and can serve as a guideline which we shall follow in introducing the life of Zinaida Volkonskaya. This brief outline, however, could hardly portray the Princess in all her complexity, as the person she actually was.[1] Thus, the text of the letters may help to fill in some gaps and to show her as she was seen by those who were closest to her.

Zinaida Alexandrovna Volkonskaya, née Beloselskaya, was born on December 3, 1789 in Dresden,[2] where her father, Alexander Mikhaylovich Beloselsky-Belozersky (1752-1809), was an envoy extraordinary to the King of Saxony. A man of encyclopedic erudition, thoroughly cultivated in the best tradition of the eighteenth century, a minor writer and important art collector, the Prince succeeded in impressing Kant with a serious philosophical tract and long letters.[3] He had a decisive influence on the development of the young Zinaida, guiding her reading, studies in art, music, and languages. Russian, however, was neglected for years, becoming a second language that she never truly mastered. Her mother, Varvara Yakovlevna, née Tatishcheva (1764-1792), died early, leaving three young daughters. The Prince remarried in 1801, and his second wife, Anna Grigorievna, née Kozitskaya (1767-1846), took charge of the family affairs after his sudden death in 1809.

In 1808, Zinaida was introduced to the court and became lady-in-waiting to the Dowager Empress. Her beauty and artistic talents were immediately noticed. When Queen Luise of Prussia arrived in St. Petersburg in December 1808, the young Princess was assigned to her. Two years later, Zinaida's stepmother arranged for her to marry Prince Nikita Grigorievich Volkonsky (1791-1844),[4] who belonged to the highest Russian aristocracy and was very wealthy. The Prince was weak, superficial, insignificant intellectually, and rather indifferent to his young wife. Ever since her wedding on February 3, 1811, Zinaida suffered from depression. This condition was aggravated after the delivery of her son on November 11 of the same year, taking the form of a severe post partum depression.

We learn about this depression from the letter of Mme. de Staël of August 27, 1812.[5] Evidently she knew that Princess Volkonskaya was an influential figure at the court: the Tsar was her admirer and godfather to her son Alexander. The contact with the Russian ruler in whom she wanted to infuse her hatred of Napoleon, was of great importance to Mme. de Staël. This may explain why she was so eager to meet with the Princess. We see from this letter that Mme. de Staël knew of Volkonskaya's psychological trauma and its physical manifestation, the scar on her lip, which she had bitten during one of her nervous fits.

Volkonskaya's attempts to write occasional verses in French began in her early youth. At that time, she did not hesitate to send to the famous author the poem "To Mme. de Staël, returning Corinne to her." In the Stroganov collection there were more French poems by Princess Zinaida written around the same period.[6]

The autumn of 1812 was marked by a national disaster: Napoleon's invasion of Russia. The initial Russian defeats were followed by an upswing in patriotism and a successful offensive on the broad front. In February, when the French troops had already been driven from Russia, the Tsar invited Princess Zinaida with her small son and her sister-in-law, Princess Sofia Volkonskaya, to accompany the imperial suite, which was then stationed in Kalisz. On May 14, 1813, the Tsar wrote the first of fifteen letters to Princess Zinaida. The thirteen years which elapsed between the writing of the first and the last letters were for both of them a period of great personal change.[7] Their relationship went through several distinct stages, and Alexander's letters reflect clearly this development.

The new experience, the new closeness to the Tsar cured Volkonskaya, at least temporarily. Alexander was quite taken by the Princess and was truly devoted to her at that time. Our commentaries to these letters follow the subtle indications which confirm that the Tsar was indeed romantically involved with Zinaida.

The first six letters show the development of the romance. During the height of military activities, when he did not have time to answer the most urgent inquiries from Petersburg, the Tsar was still able to write long epistles to Zinaida. In the letters from Toeplitz and Leipzig of October 1813, Alexander discusses the political situation, gives detailed descriptions of the battles, and accompanies them with statistical data. But the main subject of the first set of letters remains his feelings for Zinaida, which are expressed in long emotional declarations.

Although the relationship is presented only in Alexander's voice, the letters characterize their addressee as well. We can hear Zinaida's echo: first more or less reserved, then receptive to the Tsar's avowals, even reproaching him for his not too frequent visits, and later, for his lack of attention. Then came the practical matters: Zinaida never hesitated to ask Alexander to promote her husband's career and, on different occasions, to help her friends and acquaintances. We show in our notes that the Tsar often expresses irritation at these interferences.

Since March 1813, Volkonskaya stayed in Kalisz and Toeplitz, visited Weimar, where she met with Goethe, and then went to Prague for a longer time. Zinaida occasionally saw her husband, an aide-de-camp assigned to the Tsar, who often used him to deliver letters to her ("courrier ordinaire" as Alexander ironically called him.). While the victorious armies were moving further west, the Princess undertook a short tirp to Italy where Alexander's letter from Leipzig reached her in October 1813. At the end of December, she was already back north, first in Basel and then in Schaffhausen, where she received a long letter from the Tsar, the seventh of his communications. The text of this letter indicated clearly the beginning of a new phase in their relationship. It does not yet have the cool tone characteristic of the second period, but shows greater reserve and detachment when compared with previous letters. Unmistakably, the romance was over. Some of the possible reasons for this rupture are discussed in our commentaries.

The Princess did not take the end of the relationship lightly. Her contemporaries remained discreet about the affair, but her altered way of life proves that she had undergone a deep change. During her years of wandering after 1814, she not only sought amusements, but also became involved in some serious work.

The end of the war found Volkonskaya in Paris. She plunged into the endless celebrations that marked the victory over Napoleon. She also established contacts with numerous salons, refreshing old friendships and establishing new ties. Her husband was also in Paris, but their relations were far from idyllic.

On June 1, 1814, the Princess went to London to join the imperial suite. During the celebrated meeting of the "three kings," the Tsar was in his best form. Alexander in London " . . . was admirable — and he was much admired by the English people."[8] In English society, he behaved like a young man, dancing and flirting with beautiful women, but continued to spend much of his time with his sister Catherine. Volkonskaya met the Tsar on social occasions, but the affair was over. While in London, the Princess took in a child that supposedly had been found on the pavement in front of her door. Named accordingly "Pavey," he became a playmate of her son, and stayed with them from then on.[9]

On June 29, 1815, the Princess was back in Paris, from where she proceeded to Vienna, well ahead of the beginning of the Congress. Soon after her arrival, she delivered a son christened "Grigory", who soon died. In the Volkonskaya Archive, there is a short poem "Helas! ainsi que moi cette pauvre hirondelle.," in which she laments the death of the child, accusing herself of neglecting her responsibility. Perhaps she felt guilty because throughout the pregnancy she had corsetted herself tightly before going to social events. But the sombre mood of the first stanza ends with an optimistic exclamation: "Let's run away from pain, / let's throw ourselves into spring!"[10]

During the Vienna Congress there were no letters from the Tsar. Alexander was absorbed with the amusements of the "Congrès dansant", as Prince de Ligne called it: "The Emperor of Russia dances almost continually He is a magnet for women . . . is always in a state of infatuation."[11] Volkonskaya took part in many social affairs, but remained a marginal figure, distant from the Tsar. She occupied a prominent place in a different way: by attending the theater, opera and concerts, by visiting the most interesting salons, where she sometimes sang, and by meeting regularly with the many outstanding people participating in the Congress.

After the end of the Congress, Volkonskaya and her son went to Italy, reaching Rome in early April 1815. During her three months there, she established close contact with Roman artistic circles, attended opera, concerts and museums, and began to study the city that later became so important for her.[12] It is most likely that during this Roman visit she met a handsome young Michelangelo Barbieri, an amateur painter and average tenor, whom she took back to Russia as her secretary.

As much as she enjoyed Rome, Volkonskaya was nevertheless drawn to Paris, and returned there in the early summer of 1815. On July 10,1815, after Napoleon's second defeat, Paris was the meeting place of the rulers of the victorious states that formed the Holy Alliance. The Princess appeared again in the suite of the Tsar, but did not go back to Russia. She remained in Paris, where she gave vocal recitals, sang in private operas, and championed the music of her friend Rossini, who was then almost unknown in France, by staging his *L'Italiana in Algeri*. She was praised for her acting by the famous actress Mlle Mars, who was quoted as saying: "What a pity that such a talent is being wasted on the society lady."[13] The Princess dedicated a poem in French to Mlle Mars whom she admired greatly.[14]

Volkonskaya felt completely at home in the Paris salons, where she befriended, among others, Queen Hortense, Mlle. de Cochelet, and Sosthène de La Rochefoucauld. When the French colonel La Bédoyère (1786-1815), who had joined forces with Napoleon after his flight from Elba, was condemned to death for treason, Zinaida united with other members of the French aristocracy in an attempt to save his life. Then suddenly she received a letter, dated May 12/24, 1816, from Tsar Alexander. In his first communication in almost two and a half years, the Tsar reproached Volkonskaya not so much for the "affair de La Bédoyère" as for her "frivolous" way of life in Paris. He also asked her to return to Russia. This request, which should have been understood as an order, did not prompt the Princess to change her plans.

Only in March of 1817 did Princess Volkonskaya return to Russia. First she stayed in Petersburg, then went to Revel (now Tallinn) for the summer.[15] In October, she continued on to Moscow in order to participate in ground-breaking ceremonies for the Church of Christ the Savior, which was erected to commemorate the liberation of Moscow. While in Moscow, the Princess stayed at the Beloselskys' residence on Tverskaya, where on October 8 she received a short letter from the Tsar, who wrote that he would like to visit her that evening. This note is too short and its contents too neutral to allow us to make any observations about the nature of that meeting.

The entire court was in Moscow at that time, and society gossip was flourishing. The news about Zinaida's companion, the attractive Signor Barbieri, had reached Moscow, and she was condemned for compromising herself with this "Monsieur de compagnie," as he was called.[16]

Four months later, in March 1818, Volkonskaya decided to move to Odessa, "the Russian Italy" on the Black Sea, known for its good climate and pleasant way of life. The prominent educator, Abbé Nicole, who was famous for his Petersburg lycée, had established a similar institution in Odessa. This was the main attraction for Volkonskaya, who wanted to entrust the Abbé with the education of her son Alexander. In September 1818, before the formal education of the young Prince had begun, Nicole presented the Princess with a general twelve-year *curriculum*, to commence in September of 1819.[17] She herself added a section dealing with Russian subjects.

Odessa, however, was not Italy: although she knew how to entertain herself and was pleased with Barbieri's company, Volkonskaya soon became disappointed in the city of her choice. As the poet Batyushkov observed, Odessa was quite pleasant during good weather, otherwise, "I find here rain, mud, and boredom."[18] Odessa's bad weather inspired the Princess to write a seven-couplet poem entitled "The Mud of Odessa," which depicted the atmosphere of the city and its inhabitants.[19] At that time she had already decided to leave inhospitable Odessa for a longer stay in Italy. We know that while she was in Odessa, she obtained from Governor Langeron a passport for her maid, Avdotia Naumova, whom she sent well ahead to accompany the shipment of heavy baggage to Rome.[20] In the early summer of 1819, Volkonskaya left Odessa for good and started on the long trip to Petersburg. On the way, she stopped at the estate of the Repnins in Poltava.[21] At that time, her husband, Prince Nikita, was in London engaged in the not too glamorous task of purchasing thoroughbreds for Russia. As Alexander Bulgakov remarked, it was Zinaida who managed to send him away so far.[22]

In July 1819, Volkonskaya arrived in Petersburg. Her first prose work, *Quatre nouvelles*, was published at that time.[23] She did not stay long, however: apparently she was hurrying to Italy, where her baggage had already arrived. Her first long stop was in Warsaw, where she arrived on September 20, 1819. The reason for going to Italy via Poland was that Tsar Alexander and his entourage were then in Warsaw where the social life was thus quite animated. Volkonskaya and her singing were acclaimed in the salons of the Polish capital. Prince Vyazemsky compared her with the famous Borgongio.[24] As for her literary efforts, the Prince, a discriminating critic, remained indifferent if not skeptical.[25] We will see that the Princess no longer hurried to Italy. Apparently she took pleasure in leisurely travel. Only four months later did she reach her destination.

In February 1820, the Princess was in Milan, from where she left on March 3 for Naples. This information comes from a letter from Stendhal and is followed by an interesting note: "Mme Volkonsky, quite a remarkable woman, without any affectation, sings contralto like an angel ... She is rather ugly [sic], but has a pleasant kind of ugliness, and she composes beautiful music."[26] Zinaida, then thirty, was invariably described as one of the most beautiful women wherever she happened to be. But her beauty obviously failed to impress Stendhal: perhaps he did not find her attractive because of her pallor and the scar on the lip.

Volkonskaya arrived in Rome in May 1820. This time she stayed in Italy for three years. She immediately engrossed herself in the artistic life of the old city, establishing close contact with Russian and local artists, becoming a member of the Accademia Filarmonica, and resuming her serious study of Rome. At the same time, she started composing the opera *Giovanna d'Arco*, based on an Italian libretto adapted from Schiller. She published the work in 1821, appeared successfully in the title part, and was later painted by Bruni as Joan of Arc. The Princess was also admired for her acting talent. In several Roman salons and in her own residence, she not only performed opera, but also gave reading recitals. Her dramatic talent and singing were particularly noticed in Rossini's *Tancredi*, which she performed in Rome.[27]

On January 22/February 3, 1821 Volkonskaya received a letter from the Tsar who was at the Congress in Laybach at that time. This was the first communication in the third set of letters, written at a time when the romantic relationship was over and Alexander again felt close to the Princess. He writes of his unfailing friendship, stressing that he is thinking of her very often. The next, shorter letter from the Tsar reached her in Rome a year later, on December 13/25, 1822. It is much cooler and shows the Tsar's irritation with "so many papers," obviously dealing with requests that he had received from her.

In October 1822, the Princess went to Verona to take part in the festivities of the new Congress. She was at once noticed in society and admired for her voice and acting. There too, she sang opera and recited French tragedy. Volkonskaya's most important success came with her performance in Paisiello's *La bella Molinara*, Alexander's favorite

opera, which she staged herself to surprise him. The reports of her success in Verona reached her friends in Paris. "You found yourself on the
truly large theater," wrote Duc de La Rochefoucauld, "but you should
enjoy success on a smaller stage as well."[28]

Now we face another voluminous corresponcence with the Cardinal
Ercole Consalvi, the Vatican Secretary of State. Their acquaintance
would later develop into a rather unusual friendship. The seven letters
from Cardinal Consalvi are important in that they shed light on Volkonskaya's three years in Rome. Moreover, they help to show the conflict
in Zinaida's inner life, so well hidden under her glittering facade, and to
outline the reasons that would later bring her to the Catholic Church.
This correspondence started in October 1820, soon after Volkonskaya's
arrival in Rome. The first letter, dealing with the question of clearing her
baggage from customs, is rather business-like. In the following letters,
we learn about her social life in Rome. Later, the Cardinal's letters
become longer and much more personal, his expressions of admiration
and devotion much more emphatic. We learn from these letters about
many important events in the Vatican State, and finally about Consalvi's
own sad end.[29]

After three years in Rome, Volkonskaya became restless. Now it was
Paris which drew her away from Rome. From Consalvi's letter we know
the exact date of her departure: June 22, 1823. On August 4 and October 10, 1823, the Cardinal wrote emotional letters, asking her to return
for the winter to Rome. The Princess, however, stayed in Paris, from
where she would later go directly to Russia.

Again, the correspondence and the memoirs of that period offer information about Volkonskaya's activities in Paris. Actually, she continued
the same life she had led in her earlier stay in Paris and during her three
years in Rome. Good music and dramatic recitations were again heard
in her salon. The famous Mlle Mars became one of her frequent guests.
Perhaps more attention was now paid to literature and political discussions. The letters of Sosthène de La Rochefoucauld, for example, show
that Volkonskaya was again involved in politics. But she also found time
to continue her literary efforts, concentrating on writing prose in French.
Barbieri had been with her all this time — hidden in the background, but
still very much present. Meanwhile, Prince Volkonsky appeared on the
scene only once or twice since Zinaida went abroad. Her return to Russia
was long overdue, but she kept postponing the inevitable homecoming.

Then in June 1824, just a year after her arrival in Paris, Volkonskaya
received a letter from the Tsar, this time from Russia. It was a long and
cordial letter. Alexander was ill and the political situation in Russia was

very complex; nevertheless, he spoke kindly about her most recent request concerning her husband. In passing, the Tsar suggested that he expected Zinaida to be already in Russia. It now seemed that there was no way out. The Princess, however, was reluctant to interrupt her pleasant and productive way of life, and she stayed in France part of the summer, not far from Paris in Château Brou.

Late in July 1824, Volkonskaya finally arrived in Russia. A letter from the Tsar was waiting for her there. Her husband was in Moscow at that time and knew nothing of her whereabouts.[30] During the first four months the Princess chose to stay in St. Petersburg. This time, however, the court and society life did not attract her much. She had grown during the last ten years: the range of her interests had become remarkably wide; she was determined to fill the gaps of her not too systematic education in order to be able to accomplish some serious work. While continuing to write her own prose and poetry in French, she started to study first under the guidance of the Swiss historian and linguist André Mérian,[31] and then with the Russian orientalist, Gulianov. Society had not accepted Zinaida's new image, and she was criticized for her independent behavior. One of Volkonskaya's outstanding contemporaries, the diplomat Kozlovsky, commented on her present situation: "The mocking of these cold, ignorant souls should not take you off your road. The high society has its merits, but not if it has to handle serious matters. One can be only sorry for them ... Preserve for your friends the source which refreshes and renews whatever it touches."[32]

While in Paris, Volkonskaya had started writing her longer novel *Tableau slave du cinquième siècle*,[33] which was published there in 1824. She used several historical sources for this novel, although not too critically, and this led to many inaccuracies. Her interest in early Slavic history could be explained at least partly by her father's preoccupation with the roots of the Beloselsky-Belozerskys, which were older than those of the Romanovs.[34] The novel was favorably reviewed in France. It was praised for the absence of Romantic exaggerations and for its elegant style: "If Madame is not French, she deserves to be: her works have enriched French literature."[35] At about the same time, Volkonskaya was working on a longer poem in French from the Scando-Slavic past, *Olga*, which was never completed: only fragments were later published.[36]

By the end of November 1824, Princess Zinaida had moved to Moscow, where she established herself in the Beloselskys' palatial residence on the Tverskaya (now ulitsa Gor'kogo, 14). Experienced in creating salons in several countries, and perfectly suited to being the center of attention, she began receiving on Mondays in her spectacular residence, which was spacious enough to accommodate more than one hundred guests. The palace had a private theater with a stage, over which hung the inscription *Ridendo dicere verum* ("speak the truth while laughing"), with portraits of Cimarosa and Molière on both sides.

It would be no exaggeration to say that during the next four years the salon of Zinaida Volkonskaya played an important role in the history of Russian culture. We leave the description of this salon to Prince Vyazemsky: "The house of Princess Zinaida Volkonskaya had been a gathering place for all remarkable people . . . Here were the representatives of the high society, dignitaries, beautiful women, young people and those of mature age, the intellectuals, the professors, the artists. Everything there carried an imprint of serving arts or ideas."[37] Later, after the Princess had left Russia, Vyazemsky recalled: "There is no music here anymore as it had been during her days in Moscow. Then music entered all our pores, *on était saturé d'harmonie.*"[38]

To list the visitors of Volkonskaya's salon, one must name all the important people of that time: Pushkin, Mickiewicz, Baratynsky, Vyazemsky, Odoevsky, Venevitinov, Melgunov, Shevyrev, Chaadaev, and both Kireevskys to mention only a few. When Pushkin came to Moscow on September 8, 1826, he was introduced to the Princess by Sobolevsky. She conquered him the very first day by singing his elegy transposed to music by Genishta ("Pogaslo dnevnoe svetilo"). During his stay in Moscow, Pushkin visited Volkonskaya so frequently that her house became subject to surveillance.[39] Here Pushkin met Adam Mickiewicz, whose poetry and improvisations he admired so much.[40] On October 29, 1826, the Princess wrote to Pushkin, pleading with him to return to Moscow: "Return to us. The Moscow air is easier to breathe."[41] She added to this letter the Italian libretto of the opera *Giovanna d'Arco*, which she had translated from German, and a portrait of her in the title role by Bruni.

At the end of March 1825, Princess Zinaida went for a short time to Petersburg. On Easter Sunday, April 2, she received a very affectionate letter from the Tsar. This last letter was followed by their last meeting on the same day. Two days later, he left the capital.

While in Petersburg, the Princess also visited the blind poet Kozlov. The letter which he sent to her later to Moscow sheds light on this friendship and also introduces the important literary events of the time.[42]

We cannot fail to mention a constant guest at Volkonskaya's gatherings, Dmitry Venevitinov. One of the most promising young poets, a translator of poetry and philosophical works, he was himself a philosopher whose achievements were surprising for a man of his age. At twenty, he had been completely captivated by the Princess and was desperate because of her indifference. He died at the age of twenty-one holding in his hands the ring Zinaida had given him and imagining in his delirium that this was their wedding. Venevitinov dedicated to Volkonskaya several poems that were very good, even for the time of the Golden Age of Russian poetry.

On December 1, 1825, Tsar Alexander died in Taganrog. The Princess took his death very hard. She mourned it in her first Russian poem "Aleksandru Pervomu" and also composed a cantata for vocal performance. The Alexandrine Age had ended. Less than two months after his death, the Decembrist uprising took place in Petersburg. Zinaida's brother-in-law, the hero of the Napoleonic wars and the Tsar's personal friend, Sergey Volkonsky, was one of the main participants. He was arrested, court-martialled for treason, and sent to Siberia. His young wife Maria, née Raevskaya, decided to follow him there. Before starting this long journey, she stopped in Moscow to see the Princess, who enveloped her with love and attention. On the eve of Maria's departure, Volkonskaya invited close friends to a remarkable concert which she intended as a parting gift.[43] Pushkin also came: he had known Maria before her marriage and was very fond of her.

Pushkin continued to visit Volkonskaya. In 1827, before leaving Moscow, he sent her a copy of his new long poem, *The Gypsies,* which was accompanied by his famous poem dedicated to her.[44]

Soon after the departure of Maria Volkonskaya, Zinaida's salon resumed its usual activities. Again, literary readings and discussions, recitals, plays, and operas gave the Princess creative joy and distraction. Her theater and musical activities in her salon were highly regarded, particularly her own performances such as in *Tancredi.* She attracted to her salon the best amateurs of Moscow, among them, Count Mineato Ricci and his wife, née Lunina.[45] A new romance started but, unlike the affair with the modest and uncommitted Barbieri, Zinaida's involvement with Count Ricci became quite serious. In 1827, Barbieri yielded to Ricci, who a year later would leave his wife and go with Zinaida to Italy. This new romance was certainly noticed and gossiped about.

It was, however, a difficult time for the Princess. A new psychological crisis began. Confused, afraid of death and punishment for her sins, she turned for help to the Russian Orthodox Church. She chose as her priest an educated theologian, the Archmandrite Pavsky.[46] Two of his letters in the Archive allow us to reconstruct the content of her letters, the thoughts and apprehensions that troubled her. But all the simplistic solutions offered by Pavsky obviously failed to help. The contact with

Cardinal Consalvi was too vivid in her memory. And the beauty and atmosphere of the Catholic Church was too impressive to resist. She was already on the road to Rome.

One of Pushkin's letters to Vyazemsky shows in what light he now viewed Princess Volkonskaya. When Pushkin was in Moscow in 1829, he was nervous and often irritated. Volkonskaya's salon and her "literary dinners" began to annoy him. Once he even read "The Poet and the Mob" when asked to recite his poetry. This may explain the passage about the Princess in this letter: "I am resting from these damned dinners at Zinaida's. God should grant her neither bottom nor covering, i.e., neither Italy, nor Count Ricci."[47] Here Pushkin is playing with the Russian idiom, "Ni dna, ni pokryŠki," which actually means "bad luck," giving each of its constituents a literal meaning. The whole passage hints at Volkonskaya's decision to go to Italy, and to go with Ricci. Pushkin's acerbic remarks about Volkonskaya, however, cannot be taken out of context. In the preceding sentence, he ironically praises Petersburg's high society soirées: ". . . We are created for routs since they request nothing: neither intelligence nor gaiety, nor general conversation, nor politics, nor literature."

Before finishing with the Moscow period, it is appropriate to take another look at the literary production of the Princess. Her novels in French were followed by shorter works in French and Russian, published in the literary journals of Moscow and Petersburg. Some of the works written at that time appeared only after her departure from Russia in 1829.[48] Volkonskaya's earlier works had already earned her recognition: in 1826, she was elected an honorary member of the Society of History and Russian Antiquities.

The Princess decided to move to Italy, but she had not yet converted to the Catholic faith, as is sometimes assumed. On December 3, 1828, Volkonskaya's birthday, her close friends assembled at her house to wish her farewell. This occasion, both happy and sad, was witnessed in memoirs and in poems written by Baratynsky, Pavlov, and Shevyrev, among others, and even by I.V. Kireevsky, who usually did not write poetry.

After leaving Moscow, the Princess had to go to Petersburg to wind up her affaires and to obtain the Tsar's agreement to her going abroad. Having overcome all obstacles, she left Russia on February 28, 1829.[49] She was joined by her sister Maria Vlasova, her son Alexander and his tutor Stepan Shevyrev, Vladimir Pavey, four servants, and Barbieri, who was leaving both Russia and the Princess at the same time.

True to her traveling habits, Volkonskaya did not rush directly to Rome. On May 5, 1829, after a month in Berlin, she visited Goethe in Weimar together with Shevyrev and Rozhalin, the Russian translator of *The Sorrows of Young Werther*.[50] Then she proceeded to Dresden and Munich, and from there to Italy. She described this journey in the last issue of her *Travel Notes*. After a summer in Pisa and Iscia, Volkonskaya finally went to Rome. She first settled in the Palazzo Ferucci, at Monte Brianza 20. Although she had been suffering from a bout of depression in Iscia, she kept up her usual lifestyle. The events held at her salon were recorded in the letters and diaries of her contemporaries. Sergey Sobolevsky, for example, quipped to Shevyrev: "You and your Princess manage even in summertime to entertain yourselves with balls and mascarades."[51] As Shevyrev wrote from Rome, the Italians were now singing Russian airs: "You know that with her, even the deaf would be joining in song."[52]

In the first years of this period abroad, Volkonskaya was acutely interested in all that was going on in Russia. In her letters to Vyazemsky, she showers him with questions about her Moscow friends and about Pushkin and his *Literary Gazette*, copies of which she asked him to send her: "This reading is precious to all, but particularly to those who are in Rome, far from our native land."[53] During 1830-31, Volkonskaya became actively involved in a project which she herself had initiated: the establishment of a fine arts museum at the University of Moscow. The museum was to acquire reproductions of outstanding works of art, representing different periods and countries. Although the project was received enthusiastically both in Russia and abroad, it was doomed because of a shortage of funds. Volkonskaya's efforts, however, were rewarded eighty years later, when Ivan Tsvetaev founded the Moscow Museum of Fine Arts (now the Pushkin Museum).

The Princess was in close contact with Russians who visited Rome. Alexander Turgenev arrived there in 1832 and saw her quite often. In a letter to her, he discusses literary matters, writes about her prose, and invites her and Maria Vlasova to contribute materials to Pushkin's issue of *The Northern Flowers*.[54] During the same year, on his way through Rome, the composer Glinka visited Volkonskaya, and she later invited him to take part in music-making at her salon.[55]

Volkonskaya continued writing in Rome, but she abandoned all literary activities after 1836. Some of her earlier works were published in Russia after she had left the country. Others, which had been written later in Italy, appeared in print in Russia at about the same time.[56]

Prince Alexander's departure in 1832 to study in Switzerland and then in Russia was another difficult emotional experience for the Princess, who was parting from her son for the first time. In May of the same year, on her way either to or from Geneva, she fell ill and had to stop in Botzen (now Bolzano). She suffered a recurrence of her previous nervous condition, which took the form of a severe mental breakdown. Prince Vyazemsky was so worried about her that in the space of two weeks he wrote five letters about her condition to his wife. It was first assumed that Volkonskaya was going through the same state of "temporary madness" that she had suffered in 1811. It turned out that this second attack was much milder. Nevertheless, as she had done twenty years ago, she bit through her lips and tongue while in an uncontrolled state. In one of his letters, Vyazemsky wrote: "Zinaida called for a priest and went somewhere to seek a Greek father, to whom she made confession and from whom she received communion, which helped to quiet her down." In another letter, the Prince reported to his wife that on July 18, he had learned that Volkonskaya had recovered and returned to Rome.[57] A penchant for mysticism, as well as an increased attachment to Roman Catholicism, began to dominate the Princess' spiritual outlook and soon all other aspects of her life as well. We doubt, however, that she actually converted before the end of 1835 or in 1836. The notes in her *Scritti spirituali* do not indicate the conversion date: they only describe the experiences which led to it.[58] Her turning to a Greek Orthodox priest in Bolzano, described by Vyazemsky, is a clear indication that the Princess had not yet converted to Catholicism before July of 1832.

Except for two visits to Russia, the Princess now spent most of her time in Rome. After her recovery from mental illness in 1832, she resumed her regular way of life. Her salon still attracted many visitors, but now the majority were artists and writers rather than society figures. Among the artists, the closest to Volkonskaya were Karl Bryulov, Fyodor Iordan, Josif Gaberzetter, Orest Kiprensky, and Horace Vernet. She was visited as well by the Italian poet Giuseppe Belli, who dedicated to her a poem written in the Roman dialect.[59] Sir Walter Scott also met with the Princess while he was in Rome and dedicated a poem to her.[60]

On December 12, 1834, Prince Vyazemsky arrived in Rome with his family, seeking a better climate for his daughter, who suffered from tuberculosis. His longtime friendship with Volkonskaya is presented vividly in a long letter which he sent her from Hanau, as well as in a second letter sent from Florence.[61] During this time the Princess moved to the Palazzo Poli and completed construction of a beautiful villa in Lateran (now Via Wolkonsky), which even today occupies a place in the history of Roman culture.[62]

On May 8, 1834, a new law in Russia placed the estates of all Russians living abroad under trusteeship of the state. Prince Nikita, concerned about his son's financial security, set about arranging the transfer of his own estate to Alexander. The financial situation finally prompted Volkonskaya to go to Russia. Alexander was given leave from Warsaw, where he was stationed, and he joined her on the way to Petersburg. On June 23, 1836, Princess Volkonskaya was presented to the court. "She was well received, but the general consensus was that she had greatly changed," wrote Sofia Volkonskaya.[63] Princess Zinaida's own reactions were complex and rather negative. Still, she could not resist making music: on July 16 there was an informal concert at Anna Venevitinova's, where she sang, accompanied by the composer Glinka at the piano. Together with the painter Fyodor Bruni, she also attended Peterhof festivities. The Princess was detained in Petersburg after Alexander fell ill, and was able to spend only a few days in Moscow. She then returned for a brief stay in Petersburg, and, after arranging her affairs, left Russia on the first of October.[64]

On the return trip, the Princess made a long detour, stopping for a month in Paris. In early November, on her way to Rome, she stayed for a few days in Langre to meet with theologians at the famous Grande Séminaire.[65] Several facts support the conclusion that Volkonskaya was converted in late 1835 or early 1836. After the traumatic experience in Petersburg, the Princess was now prepared to make the last step on the road to the Catholic faith. Our assertion is confirmed by other data. Volkonskaya's name (given as "Zenaida Venconschi") as well as the names of her sister Maria Vlasova, Vladimir Pavey, and five servants appear in the 1836 church register of the Parish of Sts. Vincenzo and Anastasio. All were listed as residing at Via Poli 88. It is clear that they all had converted about that time, since each was listed as being Roman Catholic and as having been administered Holy Communion.[66] It is significant that Volkonskaya's name does not appear in pre-1836 parish records. It is not unusual that the actual date of the conversion remained unknown even to the family of those converted. "I cannot say with certainty when my mother and sister had been converted to Roman Catholicism," stated M.D. Buturlin in his memoirs.[67] In any event, 1835 can be viewed as a transitional year in Volkonskaya's life. It is also important that after 1835, she gradually abandoned her musical activities and writing and became more withdrawn from society. And then the last, but not least in importance: a statement we received from the Vatican's

Santa Ufficia: without giving the exact date, it informs us that Zinaida Volkonskaya was converted in 1835.[68]

Once back in Rome, although Volkonskaya returned to her usual routine, her new religious philosophy began to manifest itself in everyday life. In March of 1837, Gogol arrived in Rome and was introduced to the Princess. During the first years of his stay, which was interrupted in 1839 and resumed in 1840, he was a frequent visitor at the Palazzo Poli and at the Villa in Lateran. He contributed a page to Maria Vlasova's album, in which he wrote that although he would like to inscribe something nice, nothing would come out of his silly head.[69] This witty, marvelously structured short text is an example of how a casual album entry can become a masterpiece. Gogol's relationship with the Princess cooled after the death of Josif Vielgorsky, who had been staying at the villa until his death on June 2, 1839: he could not forgive her for trying to convert the dying Vielgorsky to Roman Catholicism.[70] Nevertheless, when Gogol offered to give a formal reading of his new play *The Inspector General*, with proceeds to go to needy Russian artists in Rome, Volkonskaya offered the large hall at the Palazzo Poli. The performance was well organized and a sell-out, but for some reason was not a success.[71]

In December 1838, the Crown Prince, the future Tsar Alexander II, arrived in Rome. Volkonskaya gave a lavish reception for the Crown Prince and his entourage at the villa. It was recorded that during this visit she presented him with a petition for reunification of the Orthodox and Roman Catholic churches.[72] Accompanying the Crown Prince and his entourage was the poet Zhukovsky. In the Archive, there are three notes from Zhukovsky to Volkonskaya which cast light on this stage of their friendship, which was now marked by a certain coolness. Diary entries made by Zhukovsky during his first stay in Rome in 1832 indicate that at that time he had paid more frequent visits to the Princess, and his comments about her in these earlier entries are warmer than those in the later notes.[73] Apparently he was disappointed by her newly-acquired religious zeal.

Volkonskaya's second trip to Russia was her last. The immediate reason for the journey was to settle the family financial affairs. Their enormous fortune was in disarray, having been poorly managed and squandered by Prince Nikita, and now threatened by the new law on expatriates. She left Rome in December 1839 and arrived in Petersburg on February 23, 1840, after spending nearly two months in Warsaw waiting for her son, who was on diplomatic assignment. This time the reception by the Russian court was far from pleasant. The Tsar had learned about Volkonskaya's conversion and her activities in Rome, and attempted to persuade her to return both to Russian Orthodoxy and to Russia. Failing in this, he sent her an Orthodox priest. When Zinaída saw him, she went into a nervous paroxysm that ended in convulsions. Durnovo notes in his diary that the Princess had "another attack of her old illness, a kind of insanity: they are torturing her, and the Synod wants to confine her to a monastery."[74] At the end of April, the Tsar finally permitted Volkonskaya to go abroad, and on May 2, 1840, she left Russia forever. Prince Nikita Volkonsky, in contrast, was recalled to Russia. We turn again to Durnovo's diary entry, in which he notes: "They are afraid that his wife may tempt him to change his religion."[75]

Prince Volkonsky, the eternally absent husband, has been in the background up to now. It is time to turn our attention to him. What kind of person was he? What were his real feelings toward his wife? Both the Volkonsky family and high society liked to recount the legend that Zinaida's first nervous breakdown was caused by anxiety after Nikita had failed to write her for a long time. In fact things were more complicated: the marriage had been a failure from the very beginning. The beautiful, intelligent and wealthy Zinaida had actually been Prince Volkonsky's second choice after Princess Lobanova had turned him down.[76] It would be difficult and probably irrelevant to establish who first began to be unfaithful. We know of Zinaida's romances, and it is known that Nikita had several as well. But more important than the infatuations and occasional affairs were the Prince's personality and his attitude towards his wife. All who knew him characterized Nikita as weak-willed and averse to activity. "He was the embodiment of laziness,"wrote Sergey Volkonsky.[77] It took great effort on Zinaida's part to have him promoted to the rank of general. Prince Nikita also failed to impress English society when he was in London: "... a magnificent Highness, but the English don't find him any cleverer on that account."[78] As for Nikita's feelings toward his wife, Durnovo summed them up neatly: "Nikita Volkonsky does not love Princess Zinaida."[79]

It is appropriate at this point to return to Volkonskaya's romance with Count Miniato Ricci where we left it — in 1828, when the Count separated from his wife and went to Rome, followed shortly thereafter by the Princess. Ricci had qualities attractive to Zinaida: he was handsome, energetic and had a beautiful voice. He was highly cultivated, a second-rate poet, a translator with mixed results of great poets such as Derzhavin, Pushkin and Zhukovsky. While in Rome, he spent much time with the Princess and was known to be her *amministratore*. Greetings were sent to him in all letters that the Princess received from Russia. In

1835, however, the Count became afflicted by a serious eye disease which changed his life. The romance with Zinaida was transformed into a warm platonic friendship surprisingly soon after their move to Rome. Perhaps the reason for this transformation was the religious fervor that had overcome Volkonskaya. Still, after 1838, when he was already ill and physically changed, Ricci continued to be very attached to the Princess.[80]

After returning from her last trip to Russia, Volkonskaya took the next step following her conversion: she drastically changed her way of life. If during the 1830's her circle included the Roman Catholic philosophers and writers Lacordaire and Lamennais, the theologian Gerbet, and the linguist Cardinal Mezzofanti, she was now surrounded by clergy who worked directly with the people: missionaries, organizers of Orders and schools, and founders of Roman Catholic societies. Gerbet continued to guide her spiritual life, but new figures appear as well: the missionary Abbé Luquet, Dom Guéranger, and Archimandrite Vladimir Treletsky, among others.[81]

Music was no longer heard in the house that had attracted so many artists in the past. Those who used to attend her salon were surprised by this change. Andrey Muraviev, for example, wrote in an article that Volkonskaya "has reached the extreme limits of fanaticism and is now constantly surrounded by clergy."[82] When Tsar Nicholas I visited Rome, Volkonskaya's name was not even mentioned. She attended neither the reception for him given by her brother-in-law, Prince Pyotr Volkonsky, nor the gala opera performance in his honor which featured one of her salon guests, the singer Ivanov.[83]

Prince Nikita Volkonsky moved to Rome in 1841 and became very attached to his wife during the last four years of his life. Before his death in Assisi on December 6, 1844, he was converted to Roman Catholicism by Abbé Gerbet. Maria Vlasova had already been converted, and Vladimir Pavey succumbed easily to Volkonskaya's influence, not only converting, but also serving at the Papal Court. Zinaida's son, Prince Alexander Volkonsky was never close to conversion. His mother, however, did not lose hope: "My son is not yet a son of The Son, although he has a good Catholic wife . . ."[84]

After her husband's death, Volkonskaya decided to break with the past: she left her palatial residence and moved to a more modest, sober place on the Via degli Avignonesi. As Archmandrite Treletsky writes, her house was now a gathering place for "people known for their piety, missionaries, and those who have distinguished themselves with important deeds benefiting the Church."[85]

On April 30, 1847, Volkonskaya's spiritual father, Vincenzo Palloti, introduced her to Maria De Mattias, the founder of the women's branch of the Order of the Precious Blood, which had been established in 1836 by D. Gaspar Bufallo. De Mattias had known of the Princess since 1845, when Don Giovanni Merlini had asked her to meet the Russian convert. When they finally met in 1847, Maria De Mattias became an important influence on Volkonskaya, providing direction and inspiration for her later activities. The extent of this influence is revealed in a voluminous correspondence that covers the period from December 2, 1845 to November 1861.[86] Maria De Mattias, for example, inspired the Princess to found a school for girls. This school became the Princess' favorite project. In December 1847, she received Papal permission to open the school in her own house on the Via degli Avignonesi. The first enrollment of forty students doubled the next year. The Princess recognized the need for a second school and threw herself into this new project: the second school opened on the Via Rasella the following year, had to be later closed and then reopened in 1854. The next school she founded was St. Joseph's for boys, which offered instruction in crafts and agriculture. The Princess used her own funds for all of these projects. From her correspondence with Maria De Mattias we learn about her successes and difficulties. At great financial sacrifice, Volkonskaya took on an obligation to contribute one thousand *scudi* in a single year. Her son Alexander helped her financially more than once.

In 1847, Volkonskaya became involved with the issue of Church reunification. She worked actively with the Oriental Society, of which Gerbet, Luquet and Treletsky were the founding members.[87] When Dom Guéranger came to Rome, he brought the idea of liturgical revival to the Princess. Another project in which she participated was the effort to convert Jews. Volkonskaya was respected and supported by Pope Pius IX, to whom she described her projects minutely in long letters.[88]

Did this intense life in the spirit of Roman Catholicism bring Volkonskaya fulfillment? She clearly gave all her spiritual and physical energy to the new faith and its realization in practical deeds, but not without occasional relapses into depression. We know that her spiritual father and confessor of the last decade, Don Merlini, helped her: "... whenever she was ill or overcome by dark moods, Merlini visited her often."[89] Nevertheless, the Princess went to extremes. From her *Scritti Spirituali* we learn that on November 7, 1853 she took vows of poverty at the Franciscan tertiary in Naples. Her previous trip there in August of 1852 had prepared her for this decision. Volkonskaya realized these vows to the full extent, carrying out all her obligations and using what remained of her enormous fortune to continue charitable work.

During the last years of her life, the Princess lived in near-poverty, giving away her money and sharing her personal belongings. In fact, her last act of charity was the cause of her death: on a cold winter day, she offered her own warm cloak to a poorly-clad woman. As a result, she developed pneumonia and died on February 5, 1862. She was buried together with her husband and her sister Maria Vlasova in the Church of Sts. Vincenzo and Anastasio near the Fontana di Trevi. This church is famous as the burial site of the hearts of twenty-three Popes.

The Roman Catholic faith helped the Princess to find her place in the world. Since her youth, she had striven to express herself creatively, have an active life, but her position in society was more of an obstacle than an asset. It also did not help that she was a woman: it had put her in the center of society, but restricted opportunities for serious work. An image from Volkonskaya's *Travel Notes* expresses her thoughts on this: "Notice the similarity between a woman's most precious adornment and teardrops. Are pearls not created to remind our sex, even when festively attired, of our fate?"[90]

During the last third of her life, Princess Volkonskaya was a dedicated Catholic. She gave all of herself to the Catholic Church, and served it with impassioned devotion, energy, and resourcefulness. Volkonskaya is still remembered and revered by the Order of the Precious Blood in Rome, where her letters and diaries are preserved.

It would be unjust to say that Volkonskaya lived a double life: that of a society lady and of a dedicated servant of the Catholic Church. Closer to the truth would be to assert that she lived two lives, one leading to another. The inner contradictions of her early life in society gradually led to the crucial changes that brought her to conversion and to total dedication to her new religion. This total dedication, however, did not completely transform her attitude towards life. The past against which she struggled was still partly present, at least during the first decade after her conversion. Volkonskaya herself was aware of this rather elusive connection. She realized that in the Catholic Church she found the seeds of her earlier, and still present, love of beauty and harmony: "I was always sensitive to the beauty of nature. This did not leave me: it only took the form of prayer. When I am listening to the singing of birds, I am thinking of St. Rose, who said that their singing, or even the buzzing of the insects seem to her a hymn to the Creator."[91]

The letters in the Volkonskaya Archive not only shed light on the people and events of five decades of the nineteenth century, but also illuminate many puzzling aspects of the fascinating life of Princess Zinaida Volkonskaya.

Having followed Princess Volkonskaya's life and placed the letters written to her within a chronological framework, we shall now see how different addressers and their communicative goals determine not only WHAT is written to her, but also HOW it is presented.

It is difficult to classify these letters according to their subject matter because most of them combine different types of communication. Thus, the strictly personal letters from Alexander I touch on private affairs, as well as political and governmental issues; those from the year 1813 devote many pages to the description of military actions. In his long personal letter, Prince Vyazemsky, who counted on the Princess' help, shares many of his problems with her. He does not digress to literary matters, but several sections in his letter could be, on their own merits, treated as a literary text. The personal letter from Mme de Staël, although it does not include any literary and political issues, is most likely politically motivated. Letters from the writers Kozlov and Alexander Turgenev deal with literary questions, but also touch upon personal matters. The poet Zhukovsky and the composer Glinka combine in their letters the task of conveying various information with observations on literary and musical life. Volkonskaya's involvement with Roman Catholicism is revealed in her correspondence with Cardinal Consalvi. Although the dominant subjects in the Cardinal's letters are religion and the affairs of the Vatican, political events and the social life of the time find treatment here as well. All letters, with the exception of three notes from Zhukovsky, are written in French. Evidently, Volkonskaya's correspondents followed the language spoken in her salon. Even such masters of Russian epistolary style as Vyazemsky and Alexander Turgenev wrote in French to the Princess. The reasons for this were not only that Russian was a second language for her, but also that the usage of French in Russia followed an accepted behavioral code of her social milieu. Even during the war with Napoleon, which prompted the Russian people to turn to their native language, French continued to be widely used. While fighting the French armies, the Tsar conducted his private correspondence in French: in his fifteen letters to Volkonskaya he does not insert a single Russian word.

Russian and French continued to coexist, their usage determined by the type of communication and the social environment. Interesting information in this respect can be obtained from Pushkin's letters of the years 1828 through 1831.[92]

The use of French in epistolary communication depended on the sex of the correspondents as well. Pushkin's correspondence with men was carried out mostly in Russian: out of 149 letters to men, only fifteen, sent to five addressees, were in French (10.07%). In one of these letters, written to the philosopher Chaadaev, the poet apparently refers to the difficulty of expressing abstract ideas in Russian when he writes: "I will be speaking to you in a language of Europe which is more familiar to me than my own."[93] It is quite different in the case of Benkendorf, who was charged by the Tsar with the supervision of Pushkin's behavior. Out of seventeen letters to Benkendorf, Pushkin wrote seven in French. Here the humiliated poet attempts to use French as a psychological shield to create an impression of equal standing. To women, however, Pushkin wrote consistently in French. In the same period, out of seventy letters to women, only five were in Russian (73), and those were addressed to his wife. Only one letter was written to her in Russian before the marriage, and the poet himself explains the reason for this shift: "I don't know how to scold in French . . ."[94] But even earlier, when their relationship was growing closer, Pushkin began to insert many Russian words and sentences in the letters to his bride. He used them to introduce Russian proverbs, idiomatic expressions, jokes, and intimate hints, thus making his letters more personal and colorful. All his letters to her after the marriage were written in Russian.[95]

Russian began to occupy an important place in correspondence of that time. More attention was assigned to style and language: writing letters now became a stylistic task. The great writers took pride in developing an unmannered light style, using puns, epigrams, and allusions, often with frivolous hints. The focal point of these experiments became the word. The struggle for the precise meaning and its semantic expansion called for a search for synonyms and the creation of neologisms as well as for manipulation of the meaning of the word in different tropes and figures.[96]

In the case of letters written to Princess Volkonskaya in French, the situation was quite different. Here, the stylistic task is moved to the background: primary importance is assigned to the content. Along with well-developed literary language, Russians writing in French acquired an elegant style perfectly suited for both light conversation and serious messages. The structure of these letters was also conventionally established. A tendency to hyperbolic exaggerations and pleasant gallantry went along with the light and witty style. Quotations, sententious expressions, literary suggestions, and maxims find their place in the poetics of French epistolary form.

Volkonskaya's Russian correspondents who wrote in French, however, did not take full advantage of this rich arsenal of devices. They used a neutral literary French which made their letters clear, pleasant, sometimes even elegant, but they did not risk embarking on stylistic experiments or exercising their wit on any frivolous puns and suggestions (the latter more characteristic of men's correspondence with men). The modality of personal communication with the Princess and the unwritten requirements of the social etiquette are inevitably reflected in the tone of the letters to her. It has to be noted, moreover, that the language and style vary from author to author. We include in our commentaries brief notes on the French used in these letters, showing that it was occasionally impaired by non-idiomatic usage and grammatical errors.

The letters to the Princess contain numerous literary quotations and allusions, but their sources are usually not indicated: each of her correspondents assumed that she was well-acquainted with the literary works referred to. Hence literary quotations were integrated into the text of the letters, and it has taken considerable effort to identify some of these references, particularly if they were paraphrased, as in the case of the letter from the poet Kozlov.

It has already been observed that two of Volkonskaya's correspondents can be singled out: Prince Vyazemsky and Alexander Turgenev. Well-versed in French, Vyazemsky wrote with a freedom and imagination manifesting a distinctly individual style. Our textual analysis of his first letter shows how changes in subject-matter are marked by changes in language and style. When finished with the sad part of his communication, the Prince allowed himself the pleasure of switching to what he called *naezdničestvo pera*, or "trick-riding the pen." Thus, the last section of this long letter exemplifies his mastery of playing with language. He generously resorted to puns, used subtle allusions and quotations, and even coined a word to achieve comic effect — all this to entertain himself and his addressee, to relieve the solemn tone of this letter.

Language and style, along with the content, played an important role in our search for the author of the unsigned, undated communication that we were able to attribute to Alexander Turgenev. Important also was the form of addressing Volkonskaya: instead of "Chère Princesse," the author used the more familiar "Chère Corinne," which suggested the name of the heroine of the famous de Staël novel. This too served as one of the clues for the letter's attribution, since it narrowed the number of possible authors to a small circle of Zinaida's intimate friends.

In numerous cases, when faced with the similar task of identifying people and facts mentioned in letters as well as explaining many other *lacunae*, we turned our attention to the diaries, memoirs and correspondence of the time. The necessary information was often found in the most unexpected places, and was not limited to the more predictable Russian sources.

Unlike their contemporaries corresponding in Russian, those writing in French could neither regard their letters as an important stylistic experiment with lasting literary merits nor assume that they were contributing to the development of the French literary language. Nevertheless, they approached writing letters in French as a serious, yet pleasant task. Most of Volkonskaya's correspondents wrote with the freedom typical of lively conversation — in fact realizing the principle promoted by Karamzin: "Write as we speak . . ." The spontaneous and casual attitude displayed in letters was, however, often deceptive. We have already seen what attention was paid to the selection of style and subject-matter, both determined by the interests and taste of the epistolary interlocutors. As in the case of letters written in Russian, preliminary drafts often preceded the final form of the letters written in French.

It is interesting to see how the recognized masters of epistolary form approached writing letters:

"I was born for letter," writes Prince Vyazemsky, "nowhere do I pour out myself as in letters. I don't stand out in conversation. I often notice that sometimes my voice lacks the strength to express my thoughts; my pen has more force and freedom. Conversation is like a dream when one wants to talk, but feels that something is suppressing one's words."[97] Fourteen years later, Vyazemsky makes another observation about his letters: "My letters are really devilishly clever, so that I am myself terrified. Isn't it an evil spirit that's writing them for me?"[98] In a letter to a friend in Germany, sent when the poet was writing more letters than poetry, he shows how highly he valued his epistolary craft: "Don't I have a secret hope that you will show my letter there to make it known in Europe how we Russians dash off letters to friends and family — casually, jokingly, without any preparation."[99]

Alexander Turgenev is another master of epistolary form. His erudition, wit, and style made his letters "a strong broth" which, as Vyazemsky observes, was so much needed in Russian literature. They were widely read, copied, and published. "His letters," writes Vyazemsky on another occasion, "are usually a model of style, of lively conversation.

They are entertaining in both their content and artistic form. And he has mastered the Russian language as only a few recognized writers have managed to master it.''[100] We have already seen how the person of the addressee was important in correspondence: it clearly determined both the content and the style of the letters. Those writing to the Princess knew that their interesting observations and stylistic sparkle would not pass unobserved.

Although Zinaida Volkonskaya did not excel in any of the areas to which she applied her talents, she was nevertheless in the center of the cultural life of her time. Her voice, much praised by Stendhal,[101] could have secured her a professional opera career, but we remember how she was scolded by the Tsar for her few appearances on the private stage in Paris. The same fate befell her acting talent. Her efforts in musical composition were interrupted after a few successful attempts. On the whole, Volkonskaya's literary works in prose and poetry could not be regarded as outstanding. In spite of certain limitations, the wide range of her interests and her impressive realization of some of them made Zinaida Volkonskaya a truly remarkable figure. Her importance was not limited to Russia: she indeed possessed what the French admire, what they call *esprit*. This attitude towards life was praised by Mme de Staël as a requirement for any person of culture: "In our contemporary time, one has to possess the quality of European *esprit*."

Princess Volkonskaya is still remembered in Catholic Rome. But in the history of Russia, and to a certain extent in European culture, she is still admired as "Tsaritsa muz i krasoty," "the Queen of Muses and of Beauty," as she was glorified by Pushkin. Whatever her own accomplishments and failures, Zinaida Volkonskaya stood firmly in the center of cultural life during the period of the Golden Age of the Russian literature.

LETTERS WRITTEN
TO PRINCESS Z. A. VOLKONSKAYA

LETTER FROM MADAME DE STAEL
TO PRINCESS Z.A. VOLKONSKAYA

In August 1812, while Mme. de Staël stopped in Petersburg on her way to England, she wrote an affectionate letter to Princess Volkonskaya, which had never been published in full.[1] This letter is the longest of those written during her sojourn in Russia, with the exception of the lengthy epistles to Alexander I, which were inspired by her hatred of Napoleon and her desire to incite the Tsar to action against him. These were the main reasons for her prolonged stay in Petersburg.

Toward the end of 1811, Anne Louise Germaine Necker, Baroness de Staël, realized that she was in effect imprisoned at her Swiss estate Coppet. Napoleon had resolved to isolate "cette véritable peste," who was poisoning his public image all over Europe. Mme. de Staël decided to flee to England, making the trip by way of Russia and Sweden. She left Coppet on May 23, 1812, just a month before France declared war on Russia. On July 14 Mme. de Staël crossed the Russian border. She was struck by "the image of infinite space, and the eternity needed to cross it."[2] Her acquaintance with Russia was based not only on conversations and encounters in her salon, but also on the reading of some historical sources.[3] Although this was not sufficient to raise her observations to the level of those she made about France, Italy, and Germany, some of them are too interesting to be neglected.

Before she reached Moscow, Mme. de Staël had already been moved by "something gigantic about this people, to whom ordinary dimensions do not apply."[4] Moscow, on the other hand, reminded her of an "Asiatic Rome."[5] The governor of Moscow, Count Rostopchin, gave a lavish banquet in her honor, where she met "the most enlightened men of science and letters."[6] These people, however, including the famous Karamzin, failed to interest her. "Having played with her *esprit* and shown her beautiful arms, Mme. de Staël left Moscow," Rostopchin later quipped in a letter to the Tsar.[7] Mme. de Staël, apparently, did not take the trouble to pay close attention to the Russian writers she met while in Moscow and Petersburg. She insisted that in Russia "pleasures of conversation do not exist," and that the only area where "men of genius can be found is the military."[8] She also asserted that the Russians were not able "to assimilate ideas that are in the least abstract."[9] Critical of the Russian tendency to imitate French literature and mores, she mentioned Russian literature only in passing.[10] As for the Russians, however, most of them knew Mme. de Staël's works and greeted her enthusiastically. Vyazemsky regretted having missed her while she was in Moscow, while Batyushkov observed that "she was ugly as a devil and intelligent as an angel."[11] The few critical voices were lost in the general acclaim.[12]

When Mme. de Staël arrived in Petersburg, the new capital built on a swamp impressed her as "a proof of Russian strength of will, which refuses to believe that anything is impossible."[13] All Petersburg wanted to see the author of *Corinne*, and a flood of invitations poured into the Hotel "Evropa" where she was staying. Counts Rumyantsev and V. Orlov, Prince A. Naryshkin, the Kutuzovs, the Suchtelens, and the Princesses Laval, Golitsyna, and Beloselskaya were among those with whom she met in their palaces and summer residences.[14] But the "Asiatic grandeur" of the capital did not impress her, and she rather reproached Petersburg society for its pursuit of pleasure and its excessive respect for fortune and rank. Mme. de Staël's ability to create a salon wherever she set foot manifested itself here as well: "Mon salon: Bentinck, Wilson, Zea, Bermudes, Teterborn, Stein, Dornberg, Arndt, Cathcart."[15] This mixed group, consisting mainly of English and German diplomats, formed her inner circle, where she felt completely in her element. Finally there came two meetings with Tsar Alexander I. The usually skeptical and acid-tongued Mme. de Staël expressed an unreserved admiration towards the Tsar, in whom she saw an antithesis to Napoleon. Accusing the latter of misrepresenting the Tsar's personality, she described Alexander as a man of remarkable intelligence and education "whose character is the constitution for the empire and whose conscience is its guarantee."[16] It is amusing that Mme. de Staël almost literally repeated Napoleon's evaluation of the Tsar.

Such were three and half weeks Mme. de Staël passed in Petersburg. The letter she wrote to Zinaida Volkonskaya during her stay offers only vague clues as to their personal relationship. It is not even clear whether they had ever met before, although their frequent trips to France, Italy, and Austria made it possible. As the letter states, Mme. de Staël knew Zinaida's husband, Prince Nikita, who had visited her in Coppet (see our note "e"). She also knew many of Beloselsky's friends, such as Prince Razumovsky, Uvarov, Kozlovsky, and Tyufyakin.[17] When she arrived in Petersburg, it did not take her long to discover Zinaida's reputation as an enlightened woman and learn of the Tsar's interest in her. The author of *Corinne* was eager to meet with the Princess, the "Corinne du Nord," as her friends called her. But in August 1812 Volkonskaya was seriously ill and avoided all contact with the outside world.[18] While visiting Princess Laval, Mme. de Staël had the opportunity to meet her sister,

Princess Beloselskaya, who was Zinaida's stepmother, and to learn more about the nature of this illness. We know that Mme. de Staël had sent (or lent) to Volkonskaya a copy of her famous novel *Corinne, ou l'Italie*, which had appeared in French in 1807 and was translated into Russian in 1809. The well-read Zinaida was certainly already familiar with this novel and probably had a copy in her library. Although the exact date is not known, it is likely that Mme. de Staël sent this book to the Princess soon after her arrival in Petersburg. Volkonskaya answered with a poem entitled "A Madame de Staël en lui renvoyant *Corinne*," which, along with some of the Princess' other manuscripts was found among the materials in the *Stroganov Academy*.[19] Volkonskaya's poem to the author of *Corinne* is imbued with nostalgia for Italy: "Corinne! je te suis dans les ruines sombres / Au pied de ces volcans qui enivrent leur fureur / Alors que ton pinceau nous trace tes douleurs . . ." ("Corrine! I follow you into the dark ruins / At the foot of these volcanoes spewing their fury / While your brush traces for us your suffering . . ."). She turns next to her own fate in the land where "le luth languit sans harmonie. / Aussi la fleur éclose au milieu des hivers / Exhale en s'entrouvant un vain souffle de vie." ("the lute languishes without harmony. / And the flower blooms in the middle of winter / Gasping in vain for a breath of life.") The Princess expresses her present state of deep depression and renounces her own poetic aspirations: "C'est à vous de chanter, à vous dont le génie / Sous un ciel libéral a pris un libre cours." ("Now you must sing, you whose genius / took full flight under a free sky.")

Four pages, 12½ x 20 cm, folded, of which three pages contain the text of the letter. On the fourth pages is the address, also written in the hand of Mme. de Staël: à Madame / Madame la Princesse Zeneíde Volkonsky / chez Madame la Princesse Beloselsky. We insert capitals and periods, which were consistently substituted by Mme. de Staël with dashes. Occasionally omitted dots of "j" and "i" as well as -*s* for plurals are inserted as well. *Unpublished in full.*

[n.p.] ce jeudi — 1812[a]
[St. Petersburg, n.b. August 8/20, n.a. August 15/27, 1812]

Princesse!

Votre lettre et votre présent m'ont fait une impression si vive et si profonde que je ne puis me consoler de ne pas vous voir. Tout le monde dit que vous êtes un ange mais je le sais à présent mieux que tout le monde.[b] Ne pourriez-vous pas me recevoir pour quelques minutes? Je sais que vous êtes pâle et que votre charmant visage est un peu altéré mais songez que je vous en aimerai davantage car vous saurez tout à la fois m'attendrir et me charmer.[c] Vous êtes malade à force d'âme — qui sait si je ne pourrais pas vous dire des paroles qui vous seraient douces![d] Enfin je ne veux pas être indiscrète mais ce me serait une grande faveur qu'un moment de vous. J'ai vu le Prince votre époux dans cette retraite de Coppet dont vous m'avez rendu le souvenir si présent. Il est devenu depuis le plus heureux des hommes, conservez-lui celle qu'il aime.[e] Songez que le Dieu de bonté qui vous a donné tant de moyens d'être aimée veut que vous jouissiez en paix des dons de la vie. J'ai le pressentiment que vous serez bientôt guérie: tant d'êtres sensibles sont liés à votre existence! Tant de bonnes prières sont adressées pour vous, qu'elles seront exaucées! Mais moi, qui sais vous connaître, ai fait tant de voeux pour vous, je voudrais bien en déposer quelques uns à vos pieds mêmes et vous dire que jamais je ne vous oublierai.

Agréez princesse et faites agréer à la Princesse Béloselsky mon tendre hommage

Necker de Staël
Holstein

a) The arrival of Mme. de Staël in Petersburg has been usually recorded as August 1/13, 1812, and her departure from the city as Monday, September 7/19, 1812.[20] There exists, however, information that contradicts these dates. A letter from Countess Gurieva dated "le Juillet 1812" indicates that Mme. de Staël had already arrived in Petersburg, whereas another letter of September 4/16, 1812 states that ". . . Madame de Staël had left the city."[21] If we accept this new dating furnished by Gurieva, who was living at that time in Petersburg, we can conclude that the letter to Princess Volkonskaya was written by Mme. de Staël either on Thursday, August 8/20 or on Thursday, August 15/27.

b) This is the second, or possibly even the third letter to Volkonskaya, since Mme. de Staël writes about the Princess' reply and her gift ("votre présent"). We have reasons to assert that this gift was an engraving representing a view of Coppet. The clue for this was found in the letter that Prince A.N. Volkonsky wrote to Bartenev, publisher of the *Russian Archive* and author of an article "About the Princess Z.A. Volkonskaya," which appeared there in 1867. Supplying Bartenev with the material for this article, Prince Volkonsky mentioned a letter which Mme. de Staël had written to his mother "in response to a gift she had received, a view of the estate in Coppet belonging to the famous writer."[22] Princess Zinaida was known to follow the example of her father, a connoisseur and collector of art, who showered his illustrious friends with gifts — engravings from his impressive collection. This assumption is supported by the text of out letter: "Your present . . . revived the memory of this retreat of Coppet." Here Mme. de Staël plays with three meanings of the word *présent*: "votre présent" (your gift), "à présent" (now, at present time), and "si présent" (so vivid).

c) Here we face a rather puzzling declaration of Mme. de Staël's full awareness of the Princess' condition. Apart from the explanations possibly received from Zinaida's stepmother, Princess Beloselskaya, and her aunt, Princess Laval, the most plausible source for Mme. de Staël's information would be the previously-mentioned poem by Volkonskaya.

d) This "maladie à force d'âme" refers not to an indisposition or even to a state of depression, but to a severe mental disturbance, which also recurred later in the Princess' life. We have learned from different sources that during the summer and early fall of 1812, Zinaida was seriously ill. A direct reference to the nature of this illness can be found in a letter of Lanskaya, who wrote from Petersburg on August 12, 1812 to a friend in Moscow, that if it were not for her faith in God, she would "go insane like Zinaida."[23] Mme. de Staël's hint that Zinaida's "beautiful face is now a little altered" confirms the time and circumstances of an injury which the Princess had suffered. Count M.D. Buturlin writes in his reminiscences that in 1812 "while temporarily insane, Zinaida bit her upper lip, leaving a scar, which remained there all her life." From the memoirs of the Countess de Boigne we learn that when she met with Volkonskaya in Paris on March 12, 1814, she was surprised by the change in her appearance. The Countess explains that in a fit of jealousy the Princess had bitten her lip, and that the resulting scar, still fresh, somewhat altered her face.[24] Mme. de Staël's letter confirms that this first injury may have occurred as a result of the uncontrollable fits accompanying the Princess' illness during the summer of 1812.

e) Prince Nikita Volkonsky's visit to Mme. de Staël in Coppet can be tentatively dated to 1808, when he was on his way to Russia after completing a diplomatic mission to Napoleon in Bayonne. Annoyed with Napoleon, whose parting gift he did not accept, considering it too modest, Prince Nikita may have desired to visit the Emperor's fierce enemy in Coppet — a trip which would not divert him too much from his route.[25] At this time Coppet was swarming with French and foreign visitors who came to pay their respects to the celebrated de Staël in her place of forced exile, ''cette retraite de Coppet,'' as she refers to it in this letter.

LETTER FROM
EVGENY ABRAMOVICH BARATYNSKY
TO PRINCESS Z.A. VOLKONSKAYA

The signed, unpublished letter from Evgeny Abramovich Baratynsky to Princess Volkonskaya indicates neither the date nor the place where it was written. To ascertain this information, a connection must be found between the facts set forth in this letter and the events of Baratynsky's troubled life.

It can be easily determined that the letter was written in Moscow. Between 1819 and 1825, when he was serving in the ranks, Baratynsky spent no more than two years in Russia, mostly in Petersburg, but the Princess was abroad during this period. It was only after his rehabilitation and subsequent promotion to the rank of officer that Baratynsky moved to Moscow, where Volkonskaya was living at the time (1824-1829). A closer look at this Moscow period helps to establish the date of Baratynsky's letter to the Princess.

On May 3, 1825, Baratynsky learned of his promotion, which gave him the right to travel and went to Moscow at once to see his elderly mother, who had been greatly distressed because of his expulsion from the page corps and a long period of military service in Finland.[1] Feeling obliged to stay with her, Baratynsky decided to move to Moscow, but when he eventually arrived in October 1825, he was lost and unhappy there since all his friends and literary contacts were in Petersburg. The first months in Moscow "poured poison not only into my heart, but also into my bones," he complained to his friend N. Putyata. A few months later he came to the conclusion that Moscow had become a new place of exile for him.[2] This depression finally resulted in physical illness.

On November 21, 1825, Baratynsky met Prince Vyazemsky, who already knew and admired his poetry, and who tried to help with his rehabilitation. Vyazemsky introduced Baratynsky to important figures in Moscow, and this opened the doors of the old capital's literary circles to him.[3] Baratynsky began visiting Pogodin, Khomyakov, and also the critic-publicist Polevoy, to whom he later entrusted the publication of his literary works. Toward the end of 1825, an important event in Baratynsky's life helped him to overcome his depression: he met Natalia Engelgart, whom he married on June 9, 1826. As he himself said, this marriage brought him happiness and inner peace.[4] Although he was still called "Hamlet-Baratynsky," the poet no longer felt himself an outsider in Moscow. His wife's avoidance of his literary friends did not isolate him from them. Within a few months of the wedding, he began to frequent the salons where Vyazemsky had introduced him. He attended the literary gatherings held by the prominent Moscow hostess Sverbeeva, and regularly visited the salon of Avdotia Elagina whose son, Vasily Kireevsky, became his close friend.

The salon of Zinaida Aleksandrovna Volkonskaya occupied a special place in Baratynsky's life during this period. Previously, while ill and avoiding society, he had not been a frequent guest in "the Palace of Muses," as Muscovites called her house on the Tverskaya. Now, however, he was enjoying the opportunity of meeting the most remarkable people of the time at this salon which became a source of inspiration for him. Baratynsky attended Volkonskaya's dinners, literary readings, and concerts. It was there that he established close contact with two great poets who had such an important influence on him, Pushkin and Mickiewicz. Before Pushkin left Moscow, Volkonskaya gave what she called a "literary dinner" in his honor, to which she invited Baratynsky as well as Vyazemsky, Sobolevsky, Khomyakov, Venevitinov, Pogodin, Raich, and Mickiewicz.[5] Baratynsky's admiration for Volkonskaya is expressed in a poem in which he laments her departure for Italy in February, 1829 — "Away from the Kingdom of Whist and Winter."[6] Collectively with Vyazemsky, Shevyrev, Pavlov, and I.V. Kireevsky, he composed another poem dedicated to the Princess on the occasion of her birthday on December 3, 1828.[7]

Volkonskaya's absence from Russia did not end Baratynsky's friendship with her. In the Princess' private library in Rome we came upon two volumes of Baratynsky's works bearing his hand-written dedications, which he had sent from Moscow.[8] In her letters from Rome, the Princess inquired about Baratynsky. Volkonskaya also sometimes served as an intermediary between the poet and their mutual friends. A letter of Januar 1, 1829 from Prince Vyazemsky to Alexander Turgenev informs him that he will be receiving a letter and some poems from Baratynsky through "Princess Zeneida."[9]

When in late 1843 the seriously ill Baratynsky set out with his wife on his first — and last — trip abroad, he immediately contacted Volkonskaya in Rome, who advised him concerning physicians and treatment in Naples.[10] The Baratynskys arrived in Naples in the early spring of 1844. The poet was overwhelmed with joy. Life "under the sky of Torquato" filled him with new inspiration. His last poem, "To my Italian tutor," is an ecstatic glorification of Italy and its beauty, voicing the desire to merge "the sleep of sweet bliss with the last, eternal sleep."[11] This line became prophetic. On July 11, 1844, Evgeny Abramovich Baratynsky died unexpectedly in Naples at the age of forty-four.

A page of yellowed paper folded in four parts, 12.3 x 21 cm. On the reverse side, traces of a green seal, and the following address written in faded black ink: "Madame/ Madame la Princesse de Volkonsky." *Unpublished.*

[n.p., n.d.]
[Moscow]
[n.b. November 21, 1825 - n.a. June 4, 1826][a]

Je suis pénétré de reconnaissance, Madame, pour tout ce que vous dites d'obligeant pour ma petite nouvelle.[b] Votre approbation serait plus que flatteuse pour moi, si je ne savais que vous êtes un critique aussi indulgent qu'éclairé.[c] Ce n'est que ma mauvaise santé que m'a empêché de me présenter chez vous et qui me privera encore demain de ce plaisir. Vous ne pouvez douter, Madame, que dès que je me sentirai en état de sortir, je m'empresserai de vous présenter mes respects: s'il en était autrement je manquerais en même temps à mon interêt et à mon devoir. J'ai l'honneur d'être

Madame
votre très humble et très
obéissant serviteur
Eugène Baratinsky

a) It was not unusual for Baratynsky to leave his letters undated: only two of his seventy recently published letters bear a date, and these two are official dispatches.[12] We have already established that the letter to Volkonskaya was written in Moscow. To determine the date, one must again consider the changes in Baratynsky's mental and physical condition. This letter in which he complains of poor health could not have been written earlier than November 21, 1825, when he first met Prince Vyazemsky, who introduced him to Zinaida Volkonskaya. It could not, however, have been written later than June 4, 1826, when, with his marriage, he had recovered from his illness and depression. Hence, tentative dating would cover a span of six months.

b) To determine what Baratynsky meant by the "little novella" he sent to Volkonskaya, one must examine his shorter works published between November 1825 and June 1826. Although his poem *Eda* appeared in a separate edition in 1826, and has a pronounced narrative character, it is doubtful that Baratynsky would call it a "novella." It is much more likely that he sent Volkonskaya his short story, "History of Coquetry," which was published in the literary journal *Northern Flowers* in 1825.[13] This work of only nine pages is a whimsical parable about the Goddess of Coquetry, a daughter of Venus. The plot of the novella, with its mythological setting, extends up to the time of the French Revolution, when the Goddess must change her strategy without abandoning her basic character: "One must call coquetry the politics of the fair sex." This short witty piece was very much to the taste of the Princess.

c) Even in light of the affected manners and exaggerated compliments that were fashionable at the time, Baratynsky's evaluation of Volkonskaya as a critic who was "as much indulgent as enlightened" shows that he had literary discussions with her and valued her opinions. His regard for her literary abilities is also expressed in the poems which he dedicated to her.[6,7]

LETTER FROM IVAN IVANOVICH KOZLOV
TO PRINCESS Z.A. VOLKONSKAYA

The following unpublished letter from the poet Ivan Kozlov to Zinaida Volkonskaya is significant in several respects. It sheds light on the relationship between the blind poet and the Princess, who occupied an important place in his life for many years, both as an understanding friend and as a source of poetic inspiration. At the same time, the letter itself is valuable because of its references to the contemporary literary scene and to the poet's own works. Of all the letters written in Kozlov's hand or dictated to his wife and daughter, only a small number have been preserved and published, and of these only a very few present any literary interest. The diary which he started in 1820 was interrupted suddenly on July 20, 1825, to be resumed only five years later.[1] Any information on the period between 1825 and 1830 is therefore of value to those interested in Kozlov the poet and the man.

In 1826, when the letter to Volkonskaya was written, Kozlov had already become blind and paralyzed. His adjustment to this condition was made possible by his involvement with family, friends, and literature. As Zhukovsky observed, "His misfortune made him a poet."[2] Kozlov never felt neglected or isolated. "Despite his blindness," joked Vyazemsky, "because he doesn't look at anything now, he knows all about what's going on in the city — like our hundred-legged and hundred-eyed Turgenev."[3] Beginning in 1825, Kozlov was constantly surrounded by his literary friends, among whom were Zhukovsky, Griboedov, Vyazemsky, Alexander Turgenev, and Baratynsky; they kept him well informed about what was happening in literature both in Russia and abroad.[4] Kozlov was an ardent music lover and took particular pleasure in listening to the performances of his friends including the composers Glinka and Dargomyzhsky, the pianist Szimanowska, and the singers Golitsyna, Barteneva, and Volkonskaya. The bedridden poet was visited frequently by many beautiful and spirited women, but he maintained the closest ties with Alexandra Protasova and Princess Volkonskaya.[5]

Although we do not have the exact date of their first meeting in Petersburg, Kozlov's poem to Volkonskaya of 1825 states that he vividly remembers her appearance: "Ja tol'ko pomnju, čto vidal / Pevicy obraz nesravnennyj. / O, pomnju ja, kakim ognem / Sijali oči golubye ..." ("I only remember that I saw / The incomparable image of the singer. / Oh, how well I remember / With what fire her blue eyes were shining ...")[6]

Their acquaintance could have taken place only before the Princess went abroad in 1813, or while she was again in Petersburg between April and September of 1817. It obviously could not have been after 1821, when the already paralyzed poet had completely lost his sight.

The friendship between Kozlov and the Princess covered two decades. After Volkonskaya moved, first to Moscow and later abroad, they did not meet for years, but their interest in each other never ceased.

In the spring of 1825, when the Princess visited Petersburg, she met with Kozlov several times. In his diary entry of April 14, 1825, the poet notes that when he received the first few copies of his long poem *The Monk* from the publisher, he gave the first to his wife and the second "to Princess Zinaida."[7] The diary gives a detailed account of his meeting with Volkonskaya two days later: "I went to the Princess Beloselskaya's residence to meet with Princess Zinaida Volkonskaya. This charming Zinaida showed such a touching tenderness towards me! I read the poem which I had dedicated to her. She enchanted me with the aria from *Paresi* and the song "Isolina Veluti." She sings marvelously: she has everything — voice, youth, soul . . . and she sang for *me*! I recited to her from memory my "Venetian Night." She spoke with such grace, this melodic Zinaida, a romantic Peri! I returned home with my heart filled with her . . . She promised me tender friendship forever." On April 18, the poet gave an exalted rendering of another encounter with Zinaida, who visited him with Princess Sofia Volkonskaya and her daughter Alina: "Zinaida shows such touching concern for me. Her friendship is a true happiness. I hope that our attachment will last all our lives."[8]

The previously mentioned poem to Volkonskaya, "They tell me: She is singing," gives a poetic impression of her vocal performance. Kozlov creates an irresistible image of the singer — her romantic appearance, her remarkable voice, and her spirited conversation: "I to, čto milo na zemle / Kogda poet ona — milee, / I plamennyj ogon' ljubvi, / I vse prekrasnoe svetlee." ("And what is dear on our earth / Becomes more precious when she sings, / And love's flaming fire /And all that is beautiful becomes more radiant"). Kozlov's *amitié amoureuse* for the Princess was nourished by their mutual love for poetry and music: "O, pomnju zvuk ee rečej / Kak pomnjat čuvstvo dorogoe; / On slyšitsja v duše moej, / V nem bylo čto-to nezemnoe." ("Oh, I remember the sound of her words / As one remembers a precious feeling; / It still resounds in my soul; / There was something heavenly in it").[9]

After Volkonskaya returned to Moscow, their "tender friendship" still continued. A letter of November 25, 1826, which we include below, is, however, the only remaining trace of their undoubtedly extensive correspondence. In 1828 Kozlov sent the Princess his translation of Byron's verses "From the Portuguese," for which Dargomyzhsky had composed music obviously intended for performance by Volkonskaya.[10]

The last meeting of Volkonskaya with the blind poet had probably taken place in early 1828, when Vyazemsky wrote to Kozlov about Volkonskaya's interest in his poetry and her forthcoming trip to Petersburg: "I recently read our sonnets at the academic dinner of the Princess Zenaida who was listening to them with great pleasure. She will speak of this to you herself, since she is about to go to Petersburg."[11] Zinaida's absence from Russia after 1829 did not break the thread of this long friendship. In Volkonskaya's Roman library there are several volumes of Kozlov's works.[12] We know that in late 1830 he sent his poem "The Madwoman" to the Princess, who already left Russia. Princess Zinaida's aunt, Countess Laval, conveyed the following message to the poet: "She charged me to thank you for your remembrance . . . she read the poem and particularly liked your description of the northern light."[13] Kozlov sent to Rome another poem dedicated to Volkonskaya, which remained unpublished until now: "Come, come. The nightingale's song." Here the poet complains that he lacks the wings which would allow him to fly after the Princess to the distant country of his dreams: "ne poletet' mne za toboj . . . Kuda vsegda zavetnye mečty/ I vse želanija stremilis'." ("It is impossible for me to fly after you . . . / To where my cherished dreams / And all my desires were always striving.")[14]

Two years before Kozlov's death, Volkonskaya sent him from Italy a poem beginning with the lines "Ty arfa stradan'ja, / Ty arfa terpen'ja — / Ty arfa ljubvi." ("You are the harp of suffering, / You are the harp of endurance — / You are the harp of love"). She laments the poet's suffering and appeals to his moral strength, promising him a reward in paradise: "Terpi, moja arfa. / Zvučis' ty nadeždoj, / Proročiš' ty raj." ("Endure, my harp. / You resound with hope, / You prophesy paradise.").[15] Kozlov answered with an emotional variation on Volkonskaya's theme: "Ty arfa trevogi, ty — arfa ljubvi . . ." ("You are the harp of anxiety, you are the harp of love"). He ended the poem with the glorification of his distant friend, using the image of a beaming star: ". . . A ty goriš' v nebe prekrasnoj zvezdoj, / Kak angel prekrasnyj, netlennyj!" (And you are burning in heaven like a beautiful star, / Like a beautiful and eternal angel!).[16]

Thus ended the poetic dialogue between Kozlov and Zinaida Volkonskaya.

A sheet of paper, folded in four, written on three sides, each 20.5 cm by 24 cm, in the hand of Kozlov's daughter Alexandra. Signed in the unsteady handwriting of Kozlov himself: Jean de Kosloff. *Unpublished.*

St Pétersbourg, le 25 Novembre 1826

Chère Princesse,

Agréez, je vous prie, mes remerciments pour l'aimable lettre que vous avez eu la bonté de m'écrire; je ne puis vous exprimer l'extrême plaisir qu'elle m'a causé, votre souvenir m'est si précieux! Et rêvant toujours à ce qui est si cher à mon cœur, je trouve dans les gracieuses expressions de votre délicate amitié un charme infini. Vos lettres, Chère Princesse, sont pour moi comme ces pots de fleurs que l'on place sur la fenêtre des prisonniers. Je dois aussi vous remercier beaucoup pour l'agréable connaissance de mr Vénévitinoff: il paraît avoir beaucoup d'esprit, beaucoup de connaissances et surtout une bonne et belle âme.[a] Il m'a remis votre Jeanne d'Arc, et croyez que vous serez pour nous deux un sujet intarissable de bien doux entretiens.[b]

Ma *Fiancée d'Abydos* a paru depuis deux jours; hier j'ai remis à la Princesse Bélosselsky un exemplaire avec une inscription de ma main, qui vous est adressée, et je vous supplie de recevoir ma jeune Turque avec votre grâce accoutumée.[c] La Princesse Bélosselsky m'a répondu par écrit, qu'elle vous ferait tenir votre exemplaire tout de suite, et vous m'obligerez beaucoup en m'accusant le reçu.[d] Je me suis bien promis de ne plus rien traduire; j'avais planté là ma *Fiancée* à la moitié de l'ouvrage, pour faire mon *Černec*, ensuite je l'ai achevé tout en écrivant ma *Princesse Dolgorouky*. Ce nouveau petit poème avance, je voudrais bien vous lire la scène de la jeune pélerine chez le prêtre qui ne la reconnaît point et lui raconte sa propre aventure.[e] J'ai beaucoup changé à la vision que vous connaissez déjà, je cherche à faire de mon mieux, et à moi aussi: *l'art de bien parler aux hommes me semble bien digne d'envie*; cette charmante citation d'un auteur que j'aime tant, vous dira qu'on m'a lu quelque chose qui m'a bien fait plaisir: il était impossible de choisir un plus beau sujet, ni de le commencer d'une manière plus brillante,[f] je vous en parlerai plus amplement dans ma prochaine lettre, espérant toujours une réponse à celle-là dans laquelle vous me direz ce que vous pensez de ma Zuleica; je vous recommande son portrait dans le Ier chant, le fatal combat et sa mort, ainsi que celle de Sélim dans le II[d], et surtout l'épilogue. Je suis fâché de ce que la censure m'a rayé le commencement du XXème fragment du IIe chant.^{g}

Mon Dieu! Comme la maladie de la bonne Princesse Sophie me trouble et m'afflige; je l'ai vue assez souvent pendant ce mois d'Août, j'allais chez elle le matin et nous causions beaucoup, je me suis fort attaché à elle: elle a l'âme bien pure et bien noble! C'est la manière dont elle a pris ses chagrins qui a provoqué ce mal si douloureux pour elle, si effrayant pour ses amis: j'espère que Dieu la tirera pleinement d'affaire; elle-même et sa charmante fille le méritent bien, espérons et beaucoup. Le billet d'hier de la chère P[rincesse] Aline est très satisfaisant, et j'en rends grâce au Ciel.^{h} Parlez-moi de vos occupations, Chère Princesse: que fait ce beau chant qui me vibre encore dans le fond de l'âme? On m'a lu des scènes de Godounoff, il y a des choses tout à fait dignes de Shakespeare, c'est un véritable génie.^{i}

Veuillez dire à Viazamsky que je lui enverrai son exemplaire par la poste prochaine.^{j} Ma femme et mes enfants se rappellent à votre souvenir, et moi, je suis de coeur et d'âme avec un respect sincère pour la vie^k

tout à vous
Jean de Kosloff

a) *Dmitry Venevitinov* (1805-1827). Poet, translator of Byron, Goethe, Schiller, E.T.A. Hoffman, as well as of philosophical treatises of Schelling and works of classical literature. Together with V. Odoevsky, Titov, Rozhalin, and Koshelev, Venevitinov was a founding member of the philosophical society "Lovers of Wisdom." The range of their interest was broad and included not only the German philosophers, but also French (Descartes) and English (Hume, Locke). The discussions of the group often took place in Volkonskaya's salon. Venevitinov, hopelessly in love with Princess Zinaida, dedicated his best poems to her. In October 1826, after being transferred from Moscow to St. Petersburg, he often met with Kozlov, to whom, as the letter indicates, he was introduced by the Princess. Among his articles was a review of Kozlov's poem *The Bride of Abydos*. I.V. Kireevsky admired in Venevitinov "the harmony of mind and heart."[17] Z.A. Volkonskaya placed a marble monument in memory of the young poet in her Roman villa and dedicated a poem to him: "Everything is pure, all is wise in his work, all — the form and the style." ("Le style et la forme de l'ouvrage, tout en est pur, tout en est sage . . .")[18]

b) Volkonskaya first translated Schiller's play *Die Jungfrau von Orleans* from German into Italian in Rome in 1821, with the help of the sculptor S.I. Galberg. She used it as the libretto for her opera *Giovanna d'Arco*, in which she herself sang the title role. Five years later, in Moscow, she returned to this work and began to translate it into Russian, but left the attempt unfinished. In October 1826, Volkonskaya sent Pushkin a few pages of this translation together with a lithograph of a portrait of her as Joan of Arc, by Fidel Bruni.[19] Venevitinov brought a copy of this work to Kozlov.

c) Kozlov translated Byron's poem *The Bride of Abydos* into French in 1819, dedicating it to Empress Elizaveta Alekseevna, and later translated it into Russian.[20] His rendering of Byron's "Turkish poem" came out in book form on November 24, 1826. Here Kozlov speaks of this first complete edition, which he had sent to Volkonskaya through her stepmother two days after its publication.

d) *Princess Anna Grigorievna Beloselskaya, née Kozitskaya,* (1767-1846), Prince Beloselsky's second wife whom he married in 1801. Though untitled, she was one of Russia's most sought-after heiresses; her wealth permitted the Prince to maintain his usual style of life and indulge in serious art collecting. At that time Zinaida's step mother lived in St. Petersburg in a palace on Nevsky, and was in constant contact with Kozlov, trying to help him in many ways — even copying his poems for him.

e) *The Monk, a Kievan Tale* was Kozlov's first long poem. Although it was influenced by Byron's *Giaour*, it established his reputation as an important poet. Fragments of *The Monk* appeared first in journals, and then, in 1825, the poem was published as a book, with a preface by Zhukovsky.[22] At the same time Kozlov was working on *Princess Natalia Dolgorukaya*, another long poem based on Russian history. He began this poem in 1824, assuring Delvig that it would be ready in a few months. As is evident from the letter, however, the poem still had not been finished by November 1826. It was published in an incomplete form in 1828. In this letter, the title of the poem in Russian was inserted in a different, wavering hand, which is most likely Kozlov's own.

f) Discussing the progress of his work on *The Monk*, the poet includes the following unidentified French quotation: "The art of knowing how to speak to people seems to me a quality much deserving of envy." The reference to a "beloved" author, who begins his work "in such a brilliant manner," sent us first to those writers whom Kozlov himself acknowledged as his favorites.[23] We came to the conclusion that the novel referred to is Benjamin Constant's *Adolphe*. The blind poet gives a free rendering of a passage which struck him as true to human nature. Constant begins his novel with a long characterization of Adolphe's father, who "exercised such an unfortunate influence on the formation of the character" of his son. Years later, however, he came to understand that the reason for this seemingly heartless behavior was inborn shyness, the inability to communicate, which "... chills our words, distorting all we attempt to say, and does not allow us to express ourselves in any way but with vagueness or bitter irony ..."[24] A similar reference to Constant appears in Vyazemsky's dedication of his translation of *Adolphe* to A.S. Pushkin: "Accept my translation of our favorite novel."[25]

g) Zuleika and Selim are the main protagonists in Kozlov's *The Bride of Abydos*. The lines deleted by the censor, which deal with the revolutionary spirit of the rebels, reappeared in the later editions of the poem.

h) *Princess Sofia Grigorievna Volkonskaya* (1785-1868), sister of Zinaida's husband, and wife of Prince Pëtr Mikhaylovich Volkonsky, who was at that time Minister of State under Tsar Nicholas I. In mentioning the difficult emotional experience which had caused the Princess' illness, Kozlov is referring to the arrest and subsequent Siberian exile of her brother, Sergey, who participated in the Decembrist uprising of December 14, 1825. Kozlov was much concerned over the illness of Princess Sofia. When she went a few months later for a cure to Bath Ems and then to Italy, the blind poet wrote notes to her, scribbled in his own hand, and asked their common friends to keep him informed of her condition.[26] Kozlov was also very fond of Sofia Volkonskaya's daughter, Alina, by marriage Durnovo (1804-1859), who was loved and respected by the foremost writers of the time for her intelligence and kindness.[27]

i) It is generally assumed that Pushkin's drama *Boris Godunov* was first read to Kozlov in 1827. Soon after the appearance of the first excerpts of the play, Prince Vyazemsky wrote to him: " I well understand what pleasure you have received from your acquaintance with Pushkin and company — I mean Evgeny Onegin and Boris Godunov. Your Princess certainly will be flirting with these gentlemen."[28] Our letter, however, proves that several scenes from *Boris Godunov* were read to Kozlov as early as the fall of 1826.

j) Prince P.A. Vyazemsky, then in Moscow, to whom Kozlov sent one of the first copies of his recently published poem *The Bide of Abydos*.

k) Kozlov's wife, *Sofia Andreevna*, née Davydova (?-1864), whom he married in 1809 when still a dashing officer. They had a son, *Ivan* (1810-1883), and a daughter, *Aleksandra* (1812-1903), who was Kozlov's secretary, reader, and constant companion.

LETTER FROM MIKHAIL IVANOVICH GLINKA
TO PRINCESS Z. A. VOLKONSKAYA

The letter that Mikhail Ivanovich Glinka wrote to Zinaida Volkonskaya on February 23, 1832, is of particular interest, since it is the only
known source which sheds direct light on the relationship between the
Russian composer and the Princess.[1] Volkonskaya herself was an
accomplished musician and for many years occupied an important place
in the musical life of Europe.

Before coming to Naples, where he wrote the letter to Volkonskaya,
Glinka traveled in Germany and Italy. This was his first trip abroad,
which he officially justified by his need for medical treatment. The
composer's real aim, however, was to become acquainted with German
and Italian music. He left Russia on April 25/May7, 1830, accompanied
by Nikolai Ivanov, a young and promising singer, whose trip was
financed by Glinka's father.

Glinka's first stop in Italy was in Milan, where he and Ivanov lived
for almost a year. This was a happy and productive time. Glinka completely immersed himself in Italian music, attending concerts and opera
performances at La Scala and Carcano, meeting frequently with many
Italian musicians, playing chamber music, taking voice lessons, and
studying composition. His knowledge of Italian, which he had begun to
learn in 1828, allowed him to establish close contact with many Italian
musicians.

Glinka's memoirs give a detailed analysis of the performances he
attended, including penetrating characterizations of such composers as
Bellini, Donizetti, and Pollini.[2] The first of these had an important influence on him, and the last became his mentor and confidante.[3] Shterich
and Sobolevsky, two old friends from Russia, visited Glinka in Milan
and spoke of his "italianization." "Maestro russo" became widely
known, and his new compositions in the style of the Italian *sentimento
brillante* were frequently performed in Italy.[4] Only recurring bouts of
poor health marred the happiness of this first year abroad. Speaking of
his nervous sensibility, Glinka called himself "a touchy mimosa ...
with a quadrille of diseases," and noted that he had been treated by at
least twenty-four doctors.[5]

On September 24/October 6, 1831, Glinka and Ivanov left Milan for
Naples, attracted by the musical life there. In early October they reached
Rome, where Glinka's arrival had been preceded by rumors of his death,
and this made the "resurrected" composer's welcome especially warm.

In his memoirs Glinka gives only a brief account of the two weeks he spent in Rome:

"At that time Princess Zinaida Volkonskaya was living there. Shevyrev, whom I had met at Melgunov's in Moscow in 1828, now a well-known professor at Moscow University, was then the tutor of the Princess' son. During my stay in Rome, he was my *cicerone* and showed and explained to me all the important sights."[6]

Although it may seem surprising that this is the only entry referring to his Roman visit, it should be remembered that Glinka did not record these events until 1854, twenty-three years after they had actually occurred. Many facts may have become obscured in the composer's memory or simply forgotten. "If I recall correctly," "perhaps," "I assume," and occasional question marks appear on many pages. This may well be the explanation for the occasional surprising omission of important material. For example, he does not even mention his meeting with the already famous Berlioz, which the latter related in his article on Glinka. According to Berlioz, they met in Rome in 1831 at one of Horace Vernet's soirées, where "several Russian songs he (Glinka) had composed were beautifully sung by Ivanov. I was particularly struck by their marvelous melodic turn of phrase, so completely different from what I was used to hearing up until then."[7]

The German composer Felix Mendelssohn was also in Rome at that time, but makes no mention of Glinka. In fact, Mendelssohn remained totally unimpressed by Roman musical life. Apparently music in Rome left Glinka indifferent also, since in the concise biographical notes which he prepared in 1854 for Fétis' *Biographie universelle des musiciens*, he makes no reference to his Roman sojourn, although he devotes considerable space to his stay in Naples.

Had Glinka previously met Princess Volkonskaya, with whom as our letter suggests, he was in close contact during his first Italian trip?[8] There are, indeed, no direct references to an earlier personal acquaintance in Russia. When the Princess was living in Petersburg, the future composer was still a youth at boarding school; but there are reasons to believe that they later met in Moscow either in 1826 or in 1828, possibly at both times.

Glinka's notes on these years are again rather scanty. In his entries for 1826 he does not even mention the trip to Moscow, which was significant because Pushkin's presence in the old capital that fall had caused general excitement in artistic circles. Again, only the long interval between these events and their recording can explain such omissions. Dealing with this period, Mikhail Pogodin recounts Pushkin's reading of

his new play *Boris Godunov*. He describes the literary gatherings at the
Kireevskys' and the Vyazemskys' as well as the informal meetings at the
Venevitinovs' and the Sobolevskys': "Glinka arrived — he was closer
than the others to Melgunov and Sobolevsky, and music entered our
life."[9] Since Princess Volkonskaya moved in the same Moscow society
and used every chance she had to meet with Pushkin, it is very likely
that Glinka was introduced to her on one of these occasions. Moreover,
music played such an important part in the Princess' life that it is difficult to believe that their mutual friends would fail to introduce to her the
young composer, whose outstanding talent was already recognized.
Glinka devotes just a few lines to his trip to Moscow in the spring of
1828, mentioning only his host Melgunov, and the Adagio in B major he
completed while there.[10] He does not even mention Shevyrev, whom,
according to his later notes, he met in Moscow that year. The Princess
must have known of Glinka's works, since there were many people to
bring them to her attention. First, there was N.A. Melgunov, Glinka's
oldest and closest friend, who had presented him to literary Moscow.
Translator, journalist, music critic, and minor composer, he belonged to
the inner circle of Volkonskaya's salon and continued to correspond with
the Princess after her departure for Italy. It is inconceivable that Melgunov, who admired Volkonskaya as a musician, would not share with
her his enthusiasm for Glinka's compositions. Then, A. Sobolevsky and
V.F. Odoevsky were other possible links, the first being Glinks'a close
friend, the second, a writer and music lover, a more recent Petersburg
acquaintance. In a joint letter to Sobolevsky, Prince Odoevsky and D.
Venevitinov expressed their admiration for Glinka as "a rare and
extraordinary musician."[11] Venevitinov, deeply in love with Volkonskaya, and Odoevsky, one of her friends, most likely brought this outstanding new talent to the attention of the Princess.

There is a reference to Volkonskaya's singing couplets to the text of
the poet N.F. Pavlov at a musical soirée held by Count Soymonov, a
Moscow music lover, whose house concerts were of high artistic quality.[12] Years later, Pavlov asked the journalist A. Kraevsky to publish this
composition: "Send to *The Morning Dawn* (*Utrennjaja zarja*) my couplets and the romance. The latter, to Glinka's music, had been published
only once . . ." Pavlov's letter to Kraevsky, when published, contained a
footnote: "Couplets sung by p. Z.A. V-ja in Moscow at the soirée held
by C. Soymonov, and the romance were published in Vladislavlev's
Almanac *Morning Dawn* for 1840."[13] It is not clear who wrote the
music for the couplets: Glinka or the Princess herself. It is also uncer-

tain that Volkonskaya performed Glinka's romance as well, but it is noteworthy that their names were linked in this publication by their mutual friends.

Among the books and music from Princess Volkonskaya's library we came upon a leatherbound collection of musical compositions, entitled *Lyric Album for 1829*, which had been published in Petersburg by M.I. Glinka and N.I. Pavlishchev. It consists of sixteen vocal and piano pieces, of which three romances and two works for piano are by Glinka. On the title page there is the inscription:

Offert à ma très chère tante par son très affectionné neveu.
G. V[olkonsky]
à Rome le 16 avrile Vendredi 1830[14]

This album was offered to the Princess by her nephew Grigory Petrovich Volkonsky, then twenty-two years old. An ardent music lover and an amateur singer with an impressive basso profundo, he knew Glinka from Petersburg. Hence, this album reached Volkonskaya in Rome well ahead of Glinka himself, who arrived there in the fall of 1831.

As we already mentioned, Glinka's entry in his diary about this first Roman sojourn was surprisingly brief. We know, however, that he visited Volkonskaya, and probably more than once. Ten days after having left Rome for Naples, in a letter to Shevyrev, Glinka extended his thanks to the Princess for her warm reception: "Our deepest respect to the Princess Zinaida Aleksandrovna and all the others. Thank them for us for their kind reception."[15]

On November 1, 1831, Glinka and Ivanov left Rome for Naples. In his memoirs the composer devotes almost a full page to a description of the Neapolitan countryside: "I was enraptured and could not admire enough the majestic beauty of the landscape."[16] Only ten days later, however, he wrote to Shevyrev that "Naples, in spite of its extraordinary beauty, is *antipatico* to me ... It reminds me of Petersburg ... I found little of Italy there." He also complains of the climate, and assures Shevyrev that he will have to leave very soon.[17]

In spite of the fact that his attitude towards Naples did not improve, as is demonstrated by a letter to Shterich, Glinka did not leave the city as soon as he had planned. In December he gradually began to appreciate the diversity of the local musical life.[18] Although spoiled by his earlier Italian experiences, Glinka became more and more impressed by the high caliber of concerts, opera, and theater that he found there. His memoirs give accounts of performances in the Fondo, San Carlo, and Nuovo theaters, as well as in his favorite small playhouse, San Carlino, where commedia dell'arte was performed in the *vago dialetto napolitano*.[19] He also met the great composers Bellini and Donizetti, and worked with the renowned Nozzari and Fodor-Mainvielle, formerly famous singers and now excellent voice teachers, "to whom, more than anyone else, I am obliged for my singing."[20] A brilliant pianist, Glinka also loved to sing. Although he had an unremarkable voice, whenever he sang, his audience forgot his limitations: "Anyone who heard Glinka realized that one could be a stunning and majestic singer without having any of the physical requisites for it."[21]

Social life in Naples turned out to be much more pleasant than Glinka had expected. He met the great Russian painter Karl Bryulov, who became his lifelong friend and later collaborated on the stage settings for his operas. This friendship also brought the composer closer to the local artistic society. Among the Russians then in Naples, Glinka often visited Zinaida's sister-in-law, Princess Sofia Grigorievna Volkonskaya, Grigory's mother. It was her hospitality that reconciled him to this "detestable" place: "Otherwise we could have perished in this huge and alien city."[22] Glinka postponed the second visit to Rome until his return journey to Russia. Volkonskaya's circle in Rome in which music played such an important part was certainly of interest to him: Zinaida succeeded in transplanting there the atmosphere of her Moscow salon. Her house soon became a point of attraction to writers, artists, and musicians. The Princess' Russian friends, with whom she maintained a constant correspondence, when in Rome, felt completely at home there.[23]

On February 17/29, 1832, Glinka, again ill and depressed, finally left Naples. This time he would stop in Rome for just a few days, as he had announced in his apparently delayed response to Princess Volkonskaya's letter.

Four years later, Glinka met Volkonskaya again, this time in Petersburg, where she was visiting in the fall of 1836. At a reception held by the Venevitinovs, Princess Zinaida sang and Glinka accompanied her on the piano. "The Princess is still singing well in spite of her age. Glinka played marvelously," commented Pavel Durnovo, who attended the reception.[24]

A folded page of well-preserved, slightly yellowed paper, 14 cm x 17 cm, written on three of the four sides. On the postmarked envelope, Volkonskaya's address, written in Glinka's hand: "Son excellence / Madame la Princesse / Zéneïde de Volkonsky / Hôtel de l'ambassade de Russie / Rome.'' *Published.*

Naples, le 23 février 1832.

Veuillez bien me pardonner, Madame la Princesse, de n'avoir pas jusqu'à présent répondu à la lettre dont vous avez eu la bonté de m'honorer. Il m'a été impossible de prendre une résolution quelconque avant d'avoir reçu des nouvelles d'un de mes amis qui ne me sont parvenues qu'hier.[a]

Je m'estime fort heureux de pouvoir venir vous remercier en personne de vos bontés. Je quitte Naples dans quelques jours pour aller à Milan.[b] Ma santé a souffert du climat inconstant d'ici au point que j'ai entièrement abandonné mon clavecin et je suis en ce moment tout à fait indigne de l'honneur que vous me faites en me proposant de jouer dans la philarmonie. Néanmoins, j'espère que le désir de vous être agréable me tiendra lieu de savoir-faire si toutefois le peu de jours que je puis passer à Rome me permettent de prendre part à la bonne musique qu'on fait sous vos auspices.[c] Ivanoff me charge de vous exprimer ses remercimens sincères pour l'attention dont vous voulez bien honorer son talent naissant.[d] Il travaille toujours sous Nozzari et profite en même tems des conseils de la bonne madame Fodor. Je trouve la réputation qu'a ce premier d'être mauvais maître tout à fait dénuée de fondement. A mon arrivée à Rome je me ferai un devoir de vous communiquer mes idées à son égard.[e] Je prendrai la liberté en même tems de faire quelques observations sur l'opinion que M. Donizetti a énoncée au sujet d'Ivanoff.[f] D'après l'avis de tous ses amis et des personnes qui connaissent le métier, il ne doit pas perdre de tems et commencer sa carrière aussitôt que cela se pourra.

Veuillez bien Madame la Princesse, fair nos remercimens à Madame Vlasov[g], au Conte Ricci,[h] M—rs Bruni,[i] Rogealine [j] et tous nos amis pour s'être rappelé de nous. Je vous supplie de dire mille choses de ma parte à mademoiselle Marietta[k] que je remercie infiniment de son aimable attention.

Agréez l'assurance du profond respect avec lequel j'ai l'honneur d'être

Madame la Princesse
votre très humble serviteur
Michel Glinka

a) Glinka was waiting for news from his childhood friend Nikolay F. Remer, who was at that time attached to the Russian embassy in Naples. A few days after writing this letter to Volkonskaya, Glinka joined Remer, with whom he then travelled from Naples to Rome.[25]

b) Glinka arrived in Rome on February 29. As he stated in his letter to the Princess, he stopped there for just a few days, intending to proceed north through Bologna, Parma, Modena, Piacenza, and to arrive in Milan by the middle of March.

c) Although for the first few months abroad he enjoyed relatively good health, during the winter in Naples Glinka was again plagued by a chronic nervous disorder and an unpleasant dermatological condition. By the time he left Naples he was in such poor state that he had to refuse the Princess' invitation to appear at the Philharmonic Society of Rome, of which Volkonskaya had been a member since 1822. Assuring her of his desire to participate in the making of "good music" at her home, Glinka refers to the frequent gatherings at Volkonskaya's where instrumental, chamber, and vocal music was performed on a high professional level.[26]

d) *Nikolay Kuzmich Ivanov* (1815-1880), a member of the Imperial Chapel Choir, made such an impression on Glinka with his voice that the composer invited him to accompany him abroad. For over a year Glinka was Ivanov's sponser, guide, accompanist, and musical mentor, contributing immensely to his artistic development. As is seen from this letter, he also tried to promote Ivanov's career. After Milan, Glinka took him to Rome and Naples. Forgetting what he owed the composer, Ivanov was carried away with his success and became impudent and ungrateful. In summing up their relationship, Glinka observed: "On the whole, Ivanov was a difficult person, hardhearted and dimwitted. His only merit was his lovely voice and an instinctive ability to imitate other singers. We never quarreled, nor could we claim that we were good friends. When we parted in Naples, our relations ended."[27]

e) *Andrea Nozzari* (1775-1832) was a celebrated tenor, for whom Rossini had written several parts. By the time Ivanov studied with him, Nozzari's voice had already started to weaken. Limiting his opera appearances, Nozzari devoted more time to teaching. Glinka later wrote that "In Naples Nozzari and Fodor were for me representatives of an art reaching *nec plus ultra* perfection.[28] *Josephine Fodor-Mainvielle* (1793-1879) was acclaimed by Stendhal as a great soprano of the time. Born in Paris, she was brought by her musician parents to Petersburg, where from her very debut she enjoyed tremendous success. In 1808, after marrying the French actor Mainvielle, she returned to France. While still an impressive performer, she decided to retire from the stage and to devote herself to teaching.

f) Gaetano D. Donizetti (1797-1848), a leading figure in the Italian opera, is assigned a place between Rossini and Verdi. his most representative compositions for comic opera are *Don Pasquale* and *La Fille du Régiment*. His dramatic operas include *Lucia di Lammermore, Anna Bolena, La Favorita,* and *Faust.* Glinka became acquainted with Donizetti's works when still in Russia, and later attended performances of his operas all over Europe. In Naples he met Donizetti personally. In 1832, Glinka wrote variations on themes from Donizetti's opera *Anna Bolena,* which were published the same year in Milan. A theme from Donizetti's opera *Elisir d'Amore* provided the inspiration for Glinka's *Impromptu en Galop.* The musicologist and music publisher Riccordi placed Glinka in the same category with Bellini and Donizetti but noted that he is "more learned as regards counterpoint."[29]

g) Maria (alias Magdalena, Madlena) Alexandrovna Vlasova, née Beloselskaya-Belozerskaya (1787-1857) — the older sister of Princess Zinaida Volkonskaya, different from her in every respect. Unlike the beautiful and talented Zinaida, Vlasova was unattractive, rather naive and utterly unsophisticated. In 1805, she married chamberlain A. S. Vlasov, a noted art connoisseur and bibliophil. Widowed in 1825, Vlasova moved to her sister's.[30] Together with Zinaida, she left Russia in 1829 for Italy, converted to Roman Catholicism, and spent the rest of her life in Rome. Vlasova overtook all the responsibilities of their complex Roman household, and the albums of the thirties show that the hospitality of the kind-hearted Vlasova was appreciated by her sister's famous guests.[31] Maria Alexandrovna was totally devoted to Zinaida, "Sorella dolcissima," to whom, as she said, she was obliged for " . . . all my life, happiness, and tranquility."[32]

h) Count Miniato Ricci (1792-1860) born in Florence, was known in Italy and Russia as a talented amateur singer, poet, and translator. When in Rome, he met the daughter of the Russian general Pyotr M. Lunin, Ekaterina, (1787-1886), who, after having graduated from the Bologna Philharmonic Academy, continued to live in Italy. She married the handsome but impoverished Count in 1817, and in 1819 they left Italy for Russia. In Moscow, they settled in the imposing Lunins home, which soon became a center of the capitol's music life. After Zinaida Volkonskaya moved to Moscow in 1824, she often appeared with both Riccis in operas and recitals.[33] Count Ricci translated into Italian the poems of Derzhavin, Zhukovsky, and Pushkin, and himself wrote poetry in Italian. In the fall of 1828, Ricci, who was already separated from his wife, left Russia for his native Italy. It was common knowledge that he was having a serious romance with Zinaida Volkonskaya, who also moved to Rome in 1829. For many years they maintained a close relationship, and the Princess' friends always inquired about Ricci in their letters to her.

i) Fyodor Antonovich Bruni (1799-1875) — representative of the Russian academic school. Born in Milan of Swiss parentage, he was brought to Russia at the age of eight. He studied in the Petersburg Academy of Fine Arts from 1809 till 1818. In 1819, he went to Italy to continue his studies. The memoirs of the sculptor Galberg indicate that Volkonskaya brought Bruni to Rome and that he stayed in her house. At that time he made two portraits of Zinaida, one in the costume of Tancrede — the part she was then performing in the Rossini opera. In 1835, he went again to Rome, where he resumed close contact with Volkonskaya. Back in Russia in 1841, Bruni continued to make portraits as well as to work on commissions to decorate the halls of the Hermitage, the palace of Baron Shtiglits and the recently built St. Isaak Cathedral. In 1855, Bruni became chancellor of the Academy of Fine Arts.

j) "Mr. Rogealine" — *Nikolay Matveevich Rozhalin* (1805-1839): philosopher, essayist, translator. At the age of nineteen, he graduated from Moscow University, where he majored in classical and German philology. In 1825, he became a member of the philosophical society "The Lovers of Wisdom." Rozhalin published several essays, reviews, and translation, and was best known for his Russian translation of Goethe's novel *The Sorrows of Young Werther.*[34] Often called "The Moscow Werther," he was influenced by Schelling and Goethe. Rozhalin met frequently with Princess Volkonskaya before 1828, when he left Moscow for Germany as a preceptor for the children of General Kaysarov. In 1829, together with Volkonskaya and Shevryev, he visited Goethe in Weimar.[35] Shevyrev persuaded Rozhalin to take his place as tutor for the young Prince Volkonsky. Rozhalin went to Rome and stayed with the Volkonskys from 1831 till 1834. He used these years most productively, studying antiquity in Rome. Already suffering from tuberculosis, he nevertheless decided to return to Moscow, where he died the day after his arrival. The manuscripts of Rozhalin's works also came to a sad fate: they were destroyed in a fire while being transported to Russia.

k) Mademoiselle Mariette — is most likely Marietta Capalti, one of the Capalti sisters mentioned in the diary of V. A. Zhukovsky on January 18/30, 1839.[36] A frequent guest of Volkonskaya's salon, she was remembered and liked by her hostess' Russian friends. Glinka said in his letter to S. P. Shevyrev, sending his regards to Princess Zinaida and her family, "Don't forget also the darling harmonizer." Actually, Glinka coins the word "sozvučnica" which we translated not entirely satisfactorily as "harmonizer") from "sozvučie" and now obsolete "sozvučit'," which implies both harmony and the second voice in duet. This shows that he knew and valued her as a singer.[37] In Vlasova's album of the same period, there are two compositions in prose written by the sisters Capalti, both dated March 26, 1832, a month after Glinka's visit.[38] In the fifties, Marietta Capalti, married into the Ricci family, lived in Rome, and continued to sing occasionally.[39]

LETTER FROM ALEXANDER IVANOVICH TURGENEV
TO PRINCESS Z. A. VOLKONSKAYA

This letter, written in French, bearing no place name, and signed with almost indecipherable initials, seemed quite enigmatic at first reading. We attempted, however, to extract some information about its author from the text. Was he a Frenchman or a French-speaking Russian? What was his relationship to Princess Volkonskaya, his social standing, his occupation? The first clue is the reference to *Les Fleurs du Nord*, which is the French translation of the title of the Russian almanac *The Northern Flowers*. This indicates that the letter was written by a person who read Russian. The central part of this letter, in which the author comments on Volkonskaya's travel notes, shows that he was indeed a Russian who was close to literary circles. Following this is a request that the Princess contribute her Russian essay "The Tyrol" for publication and a proposal to her sister to write a description of their famous Roman villa. All this suggests that the author of the letter was connected with some Russian literary publication.

We turned out attention next to those issues of *The Northern Flowers* which followed Vol. VI, No. 6, 1830 containing Volkonskaya's travel notes mentioned in the letter. The almanac was founded in 1825 by Anton Delvig, and ceased publication after his sudden death on January 14, 1831. It was Pushkin who decided to prepare its final issue in order to donate the proceeds to the late Delvig's younger brothers. Having himself contributed several works, Pushkin asked his friends to help him attract more authors.[1] In light of these facts, we took a closer look at the handwriting of the letter and its confusing signature. The entangled initials, the second of which looks like a stylized "P," are strikingly similar to Pushkin's sometimes inconsistent French script. We had to dismiss at once, however, the assumption that Pushkin could have been the author of the letter, since he never left Russia, whereas the letter speaks of personal visits both to Volkonskaya, who had been in Rome since the spring of 1829, and to St. Aulaire (the French ambassador to Rome, 1831-1833). It also mentions Rozhalin, who was in Rome from 1831 until the spring of 1834.

With the locus established as Rome and the time span reduced to the period between 1830 and 1833, we continued our search for the author among the Russians in Volkonskaya's Roman circle. The familiar form of address, "Chère Corinne," places him within the group of her close friends. His expression of gratitude "Merci pour Joukoffsky" hints at some favor extended by Volkonskaya to the Russian poet, who was apparently a friend of the addresser. Bearing in mind our earlier assumption that the author of this letter was probably connected with a Russian literary journal, we finally singled out Volkonskaya's old friend Alexander Ivanovich Turgenev.

A former statesman and now a tireless traveler, *littérateur*, and intellectual cosmopolite, Turgenev had arrived in Rome on December 5, 1832, and had taken up residence at the Hotel Damon on the Via della Croce. He was there until June 1833, when he rushed to his brother's wedding in Switzerland. On December 14, 1833 he was already back in Rome, and remained there until March 6, 1834, when he began his return trip to Russia.[2] Turgenev was perfectly at home in all the European capitals and knew what and whom to see in Rome. His friend Henri Beyle (Stendhal) prepared him an itinerary supplied with his own notes, and himself often served as guide.[3] The brilliant and amusing Turgenev, a dilettante *par excellence* who impressed even Chateaubriand with his erudition, enjoyed great success in Roman international society, often overshadowing his more famous friends.[4] In addition to his active participation in social and literary functions, Turgenev devoted considerable time to serious study in the Roman archives. As a result of this work, ten years later he published two impressive volumes of historical manuscripts covering the period between 1075 and 1719.[5] Turgenev had a passion for writing letters and, as Vyazemsky joked, "Grimm-Pilgrim Turgenev" corresponded with all kinds of people, both known and unknown to him. Vyazemsky praised him highly for these letters, calling them "a strong broth" much needed in Russian literature, and remarked that if they were collected, many novels could be composed from them.[6] We too are indebted to Turgenev for his correspondence: it helped us to follow his path in Rome and to establish the authorship of this letter, which had been so puzzling at first.

What place can be assigned to Volkonskaya during Turgenev's busy days in Rome? His letters and diary show that from the first week in Rome he frequently met with the Princess, now in society, now at her villa in Lateran, now at the studios of Russian artists. Volkonskaya showed him around Rome, Naples, and Pompeii.[7] She also arranged many practical matters for the notoriously lazy Turgenev, and when his close friend, the poet Zhukovsky, arrived in Rome exhausted after a long illness, Volkonskaya surrounded him with her care and attention.[8]

Having made these preliminary observations, we reexamined the handwriting of the letter, comparing it with Turgenev's French script. Now it appears obvious that the first initial of the signature, "A," was followed by "T," which we first took for "P." This confirmed that Alexander Ivanovich Turgenev was indeed the author. The following commentary will offer further proof of our conclusion.

One sheet of yellowed paper, 12.5 x 20cm, written on both sides with pale black, now faded ink. Instead of the signature, two entangled initials. Unpublished.

[n.p., n.d.,]*a*
[Rome, Saturday, December 10/22, 1832]

Hélas! Demain, dimanche, il m'est impossible de venir dîner avec vous. J'ai promis ailleurs et j'ai dû refuser M. St. Aulaire,*b* mais après demain, *lundi*, je suis à votre service.*c* J'ai voulu passer chez vous et vous remercier des deux petits volumes que j'ai parcourus avec le plus grand plaisir. Je connaissais déjà le portrait et j'ai reconnu le pays aux beautés agrestes au portrait que vous en avez tracé dans les *Fleurs du Nord.*d* L'idée de la perle, qui doit vous rappeler une larme est mieux qu'une pensée; c'est un sentiment et qui plus est: celui d'une femme. L'observation sur la manière de louer les artistes en s'extasiant sur les paysages est d'une hardiesse rare. Il y a de la vérité et de la poésie dans votre prose, chère Corinne,*e* et si je ne craignais pas de ne pas recevoir de Madame Votre Soeur la description de votre villa, je vous aurai demandé un extrait de votre journal de voyage sur le Tyrol.*f*
Merci pour Joukoffsky. Je lui écris à l'instant même et je lui parle de vous.*g*
Hier on ne m'a remis que les deux almanachs, mais point de *Chronique.*h* Qu'est-elle devenue? J'espère vous voir avant lundi.
Rappelez à Mr. Rog[eal]ine la matinée que nous avons passée ensemble. Les 4 pag[es] ne sont point encore remplies.*i*
Mes hommages à votre soeur.

a) The place of writing can be established as Rome (see above). The date of this letter can also be defined precisely. The references to the cancelled visit to Volkonskaya on Sunday, the request to postpone the visit until Monday, and the mention of St. Aulaire, Rozhalin, and her sister's description of the villa serve as helpful clues. Going through Turgenev's correspondence, we came upon a letter to Vyazemsky dated

December 12/24, 1832 (which fell on a Monday), in which Turgenev describes his visit to Volkonskaya and comments on the same subjects that are mentioned in the letter in question.[9] There is good reason to assume that the visit announced in Turgenev's letter to the Princess for the "day after tomorrow" is the one he describes in his communication to Vyazemsky of December 12/24, 1832. Thus the date of Turgenev's letter to Volkonskaya can be determined as Saturday, December 10/22, 1832.

b) Louis Clair de Beaupoil, Count de St. Aulaire (1788-1854) was a politician, the author of several historical studies, and a member of the French Academy. In addition to holding other diplomatic posts, he had served as the French ambassador to Rome (1831-1833), Austria (1833-1841), and England (1841-1848). Turgenev admired his intelligence and erudition; he was also quite taken by his beautiful wife.[10] The postponed visit to St. Aulaire, of which he writes here, finally took place on December 16/28, 1832.[11]

c) Before dining at the villa on Monday, December 12/24, Turgenev spent some hours with the Princess: "I went with her to several galleries, and today I am dining at her villa."[12]

d) One of the two volumes of the almanac *The Northern Flowers* contains a fragment from Volkonskaya's "Travel Notes. Weimar — Bavaria — Tirol." (1830, No 6). Describing the Bavarian town of Berneck, she writes of a river called "Pearl River," and uses a rather tired image comparing pearls with women's tears: "It is named after the pearls that are formed there. Notice the similarity between a woman's most precious adornment and teardrops. Are not pearls created to remind our sex, even when we are festively attired, of our fate?"[13] Tears as a symbol of grief, or the "sweet tears" of love, were recurrent images in Romantic poetry. In that same issue of *The Northern Flowers* (No 6), together with Volkonskaya's travel notes, there appeared three poems developing the image of tears: Vyazemsky's "Tears," Delvig's "The Tear of Love," and Delaryu's "A Tear of Love."

e) Turgenev often called Volkonskaya "Corinne," "Korinna," "Korinna Alexandrovna," or "Korinna-Zeneida," after the heroine of Mme. de Staël's famous novel.

f) Volkonskaya's sister, *Maria (Magdalena) Alexandrovna Vlasova,* née Princess Beloselskaya (see note "g" to Glinka's letter) moved with her to Rome in 1829 and spent the rest of her life there. Turgenev asked Vlasova to write a description of Volkonskaya's recently built and already famous villa, with its antiquities and busts commemorating the Princess' friends and relatives. In his letter to Vyazemsky of December

12/14, Turgenev writes: "Zeneida enlivened the emptiness of her villa with memories of the living and the dead. I asked M. A. Vlasova to copy all the inscriptions for you, and to describe the antiquities of their villa. I intend to use this in an article for Pushkin's journal."[15] The article, which was never written, was intended for the final issue of *The Northern Flowers*, for which Pushkin had asked Turgenev to seek additional contributions. Volkonskaya's travel notes, part of which appeared in issue No 6 (1830) and No 7 (1831), remained unfinished. Turgenev praises them lavishly in the hope of receiving from her the next installment for Pushkin's issue. However, for the final issue of *The Northern Flowers* prepared by Pushkin (No 8), Volkonskaya contributed not the "Travel Notes," but two of her Russian poems: "To my Star," and "The Funeral Song of the Slavic psaltery player."

g) Zhukovsky was in Switzerland at that time, convalescing in Vevey, and Turgenev tried to persuade him to come to Rome. His expression of thanks to Volkonskaya most likely refers to the encouraging words she added to his letter urging Zhukovsky to come to Italy.[16] In March, after several months of postponement, Zhukovsky finally decided to go to Italy. He arrived in Civitavecchia on May 16, 1833, and then, together with Turgenev, went to Naples and Rome.[17]

h) "Chronique" is most likely Turgenev's own work, *The Chronicle of a Russian Abroad*, which had been published in installments since 1827 in various Russian periodicals. Here he apparently refers to "A Letter from Paris," which appeared in Ivan Kireevsky's journal *The European* in 1832.

i) "Mr. Rog." is the young philosopher, classical philologist, and translator, *Nikolay Mikhaylovich Rozhalin* (see note 'j' to the letter of M. I. Glinka). Rozhalin was in Rome at the time of Turgenev's letter to Princess Volkonskaya and tutored her son Alexander. Turgenev had a very high opinion of ". . . this learned and intelligent Rozhalin" who often guided him in his Roman walks. He found him extremely knowledgeable, ". . . no less then Henri Beyle (Stendhal), but approaching antiquity in a different way." He reproved Rozhalin, however, for his excessive modesty and lack of scholarly drive, trying to persuade him to write and publish.[19] This is the meaning behind the reference to Rozhalin in this letter. It is most likely that the four pages which Turgenev mentions to the Princess were also intended for Pushkin's volume of *The Northern Flowers*.

TWO LETTERS
FROM PRINCE PYOTR ANDREEVICH VYAZEMSKY
TO PRINCESS Z. A. VOLKONSKAYA

Prince Pyotr Andreevich Vyazemsky was one of Zinaida Volkonska-ya's closest friends. It is difficult, however, to determine when they first met. Being almost the same age, moving in the same social circles, and having parents who were well acquainted, they probably crossed each other's paths more than once during their childhood and adolescence. The young Vyazemsky knew Zinaida's father well and considered him one of the most courteous and enlightened men of his time.[1] We shall not attempt to discuss all the numerous references to Princess Volkon-skaya in Vyazemsky's letters and notebooks, but will offer only a brief outline of their relationship.

In the fall of 1819, when the Prince was living in Warsaw, he met frequently with Volkonskaya, who had stopped there on her way to Italy. Perhaps it was then that he heard Zinaida sing for the first time. The Prince was so impressed that he compared her voice and style to those of the famous Borgondio.[2] Volkonskaya's early literary efforts, however, left Vyazemsky, a discriminating critic, rather indifferent.[3] But when she moved to Moscow in 1824 he became a faithful visitor at her salon, enriching it with the spirit and wit of his conversation. Vyazemsky introduced the Princess to several important literary figures, and through him she maintained contact with Pushkin, who, whenever in Moscow, was a frequent guest at her salon.[4] In 1827, while still the head of the literary journal *Moscow Telegraph*, Vyazemsky published some of Volkonskaya's works.[5]

Princess Zinaida was a loyal and generous friend. She tried to help Vyazemsky out of the difficult situation he found himself in after his forced resignation in 1821: he had fallen into disgrace with the government on account of the liberal views he had expressed while serving under Governor General Novosiltsev in Warsaw. Since Vyazemsky was suspected of having close ties with the Polish and Russian opposition, Volkonskaya's intercession with Tsar Alexander I was particularly important.[6] Four years after the Princess' departure from Russia, Vyazemsky observed that her absence was still felt in Moscow's cultural life.[7] On another occasion he wrote: "In Moscow, Zinaida Volkonska-ya's house was an artistic gathering point that attracted all the truly remarkable personalities of contemporary society ... Everything in the house bore the imprint of devotion to art and ideas."[8]

After Volkonskaya settled in Rome in 1829, she continued to communicate with Prince Vyazemsky. In her letters from Italy the Princess showed a lively interest in Russian literary life and in their common friends. She was particularly concerned about Pushkin's new publishing venture, his *Literary Gazette*, and asked Vyazemsky to take out a subscription for her.[9] In 1833, in addition to their direct correspondence, Vyazemsky often included messages to Volkonskaya in his letters to Alexander Turgenev, then in Rome. One of these letters indicates that Vyazemsky was trying to clear her library through Russian customs for shipment to Rome. This was not so easy, as he complains to Turgenev: "The spiritual aspects of customs, i.e., censorship, is not in our hands."[10]

In July 1834, after the Vyazemskys learned that their daughter Praskovia ("Pashenka") was suffering from tuberculosis, they began planning a trip to Italy in the hope that the change of climate would help her.[11] This would be the Prince's first travel outside Russia. For years he had intended to go abroad, first with Alexander Turgenev, then with Griboedov, and later with Pushkin, but none of these plans had materialized.[12] And now the anticipation of the long-awaited trip was clouded by his complete absorption in Pashenka's illness: "Everything for me is in some kind of fog and overshadowed by one thought . . . Why did I have to go abroad for the first time in such a state of mind?"[13]

Prince Vyazemsky, his wife Vera Fyodorovna and their three daughters went first to the small German city of Hanau to consult there the well-known physician Dr. Kopp, who had been enthusiastically recommended by Zhukovsky. But Italy was their ultimate destination, and Vyazemsky started to prepare for the trip soon after arriving in Hanau. On September 27 he wrote to his friend "Princess Zeneida," asking her to suggest the most economical route to Rome and to help them get settled there (see Letter I). She answered promptly, but the journey to Rome, complicated by bad weather and Pashenka's illness, took about six weeks. The Prince was again conscious of the indifference he felt even when his "poetic dream," his visit to Rome, was about to be realized.[14]

The Vyazemskys arrived in Rome on December 12, 1834. Everything had been prepared for them by Volkonskaya: "Like a caring sister or a gentle mother, Zeneida made arrangements for us and prepared everything so comfortably that from the first step, from the first minute, we felt perfectly at home there."[15]

Rome did finally conquer Vyazemsky. His letters were still full of sadness and concern, but he knew that nothing more could be done for

Pashenka and so allowed himself to get acquainted with Rome, meet old friends and make some new ones. On the very day of his arrival, late in the evening, he dashed to the Coliseum to see it by moonlight. Whether alone, together with friends, or accompanied by the ill-reputed but knowledgeable "wall-guide" ("stenovod," as he jokingly called him) Visconti, he familiarized himself with the city. In the evening, Vyazemsky frequently visited the residence of the Russian ambassador, Guryev, and many of the famous Roman salons. He also found time for long conversations with such enlightened statesmen as the ambassadors Bunsen and Lützov, as well as with the famous linguist Cardinal Mezzofanti to whom he had been introduced by Volkonskaya. He even paid a visit to Madame Letizia, "la maman de Napoléon," and became so fascinated with the old woman that he decided to call on her again. Surprised that she spoke such poor French, he quipped that she probably hadn't taken the trouble to learn it, feeling that it would not serve her for long.[16] As for Roman artistic circles, Vyazemsky often visited "one of the most pleasant houses in Rome," that of the French painter Horace Vernet. He also frequented the colony of Russian artists, which included Bruni, Bryulov, and Kiprensky. An ardent music lover, Vyazemsky attended many concerts and operas.[17]

Of particular importance for Vyazemsky was his acquaintance with Henri Beyle, the French consul in Civitavecchia, famous under the name of Stendhal. The Prince had already read and admired *The Red and the Black*, "a remarkable creation of our time,"[18] and he was delighted to learn that "next door to me lives the famous Stendhal, who looks like a fat salesman . . . I have not met him yet, but intend to sharpen a French madrigal to hook him on," he wrote on December 16. After their first encounter, around December 15, they continued to see each other whenever Beyle came to Rome.[19]

In spite of the many impressions Vyazemsky absorbed in Rome, he felt that he had not yet captured its spirit. "Ich kenne noch nicht das Land," he complained, paraphrasing Goethe.[20] But if he did not feel a real affinity for Rome the city, he was perfectly at home in the palazzo where the Princess had lodged his family and where she herself occupied a large apartment at the time. During the five months in Rome, when a slight improvement in Pashenka's condition was followed by a hopeless decline, Volkonskaya surrounded the Vyazemskys with affection and care. She often dropped in on them informally; on March 5, together with Maria Pototskaya, she came to sing for the bedridden Pashenka. The Princess asked the Vyazemskys to her recently built villa in Lateran. On January 3, 1835, she gave a reception in honor of Vyazemsky, at which he met two Italian poets, G. C. Belli and J. Ferreti.[21] On January 13, the Princess invited the Vyazemskys to a New Year's celebration, but they decided to stay home "because of the superstitious fear of leaving poor Pauline alone on New Year's Day." Concerned as he was over his daughter's illness, Vyazemsky still cherished illusions about the final outcome. The last flash of hope encouraged the Prince to make a short trip to Naples: he left Rome on February 10 and returned on February 12 to learn that Pashenka's condition had worsened. The last month in Rome passed in silence. Only once did Vyazemsky overcome his anguish and write to his son Pavel. His letter, which reads like a literary essay, contains a detailed description of the Roman carnival.[22]

Pahsenka died on March 23, 1835 and was buried in Rome on March 26. Again the Vyazemskys were assisted and comforted by Volkonskaya. When the family went to Naples on April 7, their younger daughter remained in Rome with the Princess. In contrast to Vyazemsky's usually detailed and witty notes, his diary entries for this period were laconic: a mere twenty lines to cover almost five months in Rome.[23] After eight days Vyazemsky returned to Rome, leaving his wife and daughter in Naples. A week later, on April 22, 1835, he set out on the long return trip to Russia to resume his duties. The last lines of the Prince's Roman diary show his exhaustion and despair: "I am turning over my thoughts like stones, piling them one on the other — a Sisyphean labor."[24]

After Princess Vyazemsky and her daughters left Rome, it was Volkonskaya who took care of Pashenka's grave. She expressed her sympathy to the grieving father in the Russian poem "To Prince P. A. Vyazemsky. On his Daughter's Death." Here the Princess assures him that he is not abandoning the lonely grave, but is entrusting it to her: "Ty edeš' ... no eja mogilu / Ostaviš' mne ne sirotoj: / Tak solnca zamenjaet silu / Luč mesjaca v noči svjatoj." ("You are going, but you leave her grave to me: it is not orphaned. Thus in the holy night the moonlight replaces the power of the sun.")[25]

Vyazemsky arrived in Petersburg on May 29, 1835. A month later, on June 30, he reflected on his experience of the past year in a letter to Alexander Turgenev: "It is strange: in Rome I valued all the impressions which had an immediate influence on my wound — I looked for them. But here I am afraid of them, my heart shuns them, although I am constantly preoccupied with my grief. For me the whole trip is like a horrible dream which came over my soul."[26]

Letter I

Four pages of excessively brittle yellow paper, 12.5 x 21.8 cm, partly damaged, written in faded black ink. On the reverse side postmarked "Hanau, 27 Sept. 1834," with the address "à Madame / Madame la Princesse Zenaida Wolkonski / née Mlle Bieloselski / recommandée aux soins obligeans / de la légation de S. M. l'Empereur de toutes les Russes à Rome." *Published.*[27]

Hanau 15/27 Septembre 1834

Savez-vous, chère [*et bonne*] Princesse, que nous avons quitté la Russie, que nous sommes en Allemagne et que nous nous acheminons vers vous, c'est-à-dire vers Rome? C'est la mauvaise santé de ma seconde fille qui a motivé notre voyage. Nous sommes venus tout droit à Hanau pour consulter le docteur Kopp qui nous avoit été fortement recommandé par Joukoffski et par les médecins de Pétersbourg. Dieu merci, nous avons jusqu'à présent tout lieu de nous féliciter d'avoir suivi cette indication.[a] Comme la saison était trop avancée pour aller aux eaux (vu que nous n'avons quitté Pétersbourg que le 11/(23) août, [*les craintes*] pour l'état de la poitrine de Pauline ne s'étant prononcées qu'en Juillet), Mr Kopp nous a retenus ici pour étudier la maladie et pour baser le traitement qu'il y auroit à suivre.[b] Nous sommes ici depuis près de trois semaines et nos craintes pour la poitrine se sont dissipées. La santé de Pauline s'améliore lentement, mais cependant d'une manière assez satisfaisante et si Dieu le donne nous pourrons nous remettre en route dans le courant du mois prochain.[c] C'est à Rome que l'on nous conseille de passer l'hiver et je m'y prends d'avance pour venir me placer avec tous les miens sous votre protection tutélaire. Donnez-vous, je vous prie, la peine d'éclairer mon inexpérience et de me guider dans les mesures que j'aurai à prendre. C'est à cette fin que je prends la liberté de vous poser quelques questions en vous priant de m'y faire répondre par quelqu'un des vôtres et surtout par le Comte Ricci, si il se trouvoit à Rome pour le moment. Je compte trop sur son amitié pour douter de la bonne volonté qu'il mettra à me rendre service et pour me faire scrupule de m'appeler tout franchement à son obligeance.[d] Voici de quoi il s'agit:

Nous aurons besoin d'un appartement de quatre chambres exposées au soleil: ceci est une condition indispensable pour la santé de ma fille, et comme de raison dans le quartier le plus salubre de la ville.^*e* Comme condition de second ordre, et dans l'intérêt économique, nous désirerions être logés à bon compte, car vous savez [*bien*] que nous n'avons pas d'argent de trop et que notre voyage a dû déjà nous imposer des sacrifices assez pénibles.^*f* Pour arriver à ce double but, c'est-à-dire pour être logés confortablement et économiquement devons-nous prendre (ou [*faire*] arrêter d'avance) un appartement dans un hôtel garni, ou bien en chercher un dans une maison privée et [*par consequent*] nous monter tant soit peu en ménage, avoir une cuisinière etc. A combien pourroit monter le mois d'une manière ou de l'autre? J'entends bien sans aucune recherche, [*ni fantaisie*], que le nécéssaire et une honnête aisance. Notre ménage est composé de ma femme, de nos trois filles et de deux femmes de chambres.^*g* Quant à moi, je ne fais que les accompagner, une fois que la santé de Pauline sera remise ou du moins en bon train, que je les aurai établies, que j'aurai salué vous et mon patron, je me presserai de retourner dans mes [*foyers*] et dans mes douanes, car je n'ai obtenu qu'un congé de quatre mois et craindrai de passer pour de le contrebande si je me présentais plus tard.^*h* Ma famille fera probablement un séjour de quatre à cinq mois à Rome, de novembre jusqu'en avril. Quelle serait la meilleure route, c'est-à-dire la plus commode et la moins coûteuse à prendre pour se rendre directement à Rome, de Francfort par exemple?^*i* Vous qui connaissez les grandes routes de l'Europe en tous [*leur*] sens, comme je connais la route de Moscou à Ostafiewo, vous avez certainement parcouru bien des fois cette distance et par terre et par eau, et par poste et *sur des longues* (comme on dit dans notre bon Moscou *na dolgix*) ou avec un *vetturino*, et nul mieux que vous ne sauroit me dire l'exacte vérité.^*j* Je me'en remets donc à vous en plaine et franche confiance et ne vous adresse pas même les formalités de rigueur, pour vous demander pardon de l'ennui que je vous cause et de la peine que je vous donne.

Je juge d'après moi et comme l'absence n'a porté aucune atteinte aux sentiments que je vous avois [*voués*] à l'époque d'heureuse mémoire de votre séjour à Moscou, j'aime à croire que la bienveillance [*que*] vous m'avez témoignée est aussi du petit nombre des choses de ce monde, que les révolutions physiques, sociales, romantiques et fantastiques de nos jours ont laissé *in statu quo*. Je n'ai aucune nouvelle à vous donner de la Russie et encore moins de Hanau, qui est une très bonne ville, mais hermétiquement fermée. Je viendrai respirer librement et chaudement auprès de vous et me *dégermaniser* ou me *dépomme-de-terriser* dans le pays *wo die Zitronen blühn*.^*k* Toute ma famille se joint à moi pour vous dire combien nous serons heureux de vous revoir et pour vous présenter nos hommages bien sincères et bien dévoués. J'attends avec impatience et reconnaissance préalable votre supplément bénévole au guide du voyageur, car j'ai plus de foi en vous qu'en le conseiller de guerre de S. A. le duc de Saxe-Gothe.[1] Adressez-moi, je vous prie, vos renseignements à *Hanau* (près de Francfort sur le Main) *poste restante*. Mes hommages à Madame votre soeur et mes amitiés au cher Comte Ricci."

Wiazemski

a) *Dr. J. H. Kopp* (1777-1858), German physician, author of several medical books, popular with the Russians who came to him in Hanau for treatment. Among his patients were Zhukovsky, Alexander Turgenev, Yazykov, and Elagina. Zhukovsky had such great faith in him that he advised Elagina: "First admire your squint-eyed Kopp, then the Rhein."[28]

b) Having left Petersburg on August 23, 1834, the Vyazemskys sailed from Kronstadt to Travemünde. Exhausted after the rough crossing, they rested for two days in Lübeck, and then went directly to Hanau, where they arrived on September 8, 1834.

c) The early fall in Hanau, with the initial success of Pashenka's treatment, brought them new hope: "Doctor Kopp is pleased with Pashenka, hence we are pleased with Doctor Kopp — and I am pleased with Hanau, too."[29] Vyazemsky was so encouraged that he took three short trips with his elder daughter Maria. They visited Frankfurt, Wiesbaden, Cologne, and a large part of the picturesque Rhine area.

d) Instead of modest rooms in a pensione, Volkonskaya found a large and beautiful apartment for them in the Palazzo Conti on the Piazza della Minerva, which met the requirements set out in the Prince's letter.

e) Vyazemsky emphasized his limited means by underlining: "Vous savez bien." Volkonskaya, who had earlier interceded on his behalf, was already well aware of Vyazemsky's constrained financial resources. The eight years he spent without employment (1821-1829) had shaken his financial stability. In a remarkable document intended for Tsar Nicholas I, "A Declaration about Prince Vyazemsky, written by himself," he depicts with his usual penetration and with utmost honesty the broad spectrum of social and cultural events of the decade 1819-1829, placing himself within this complex context. He concludes this amazing confession with a request for an official position, justifying it by reference to his proven abilities and the necessity of supporting a large family.[30]

f) The Vyazemskys traveled in a group of seven: Prince Pyotr Andreevich, his wife *Vera Fyodorovna* (1790-1866), their three daughters, *Maria* (1813-1849), *Praskovia* ("Pashenka") (1817-1835), *Nadezhda* (1822-1840), and two Russian maids who accompanied them.

g) Having first received a four-month leave of absence from his new office in the Ministry of Finance, Vyazemsky soon became aware that it would be necessary to ask for an extension. On November 8, 1834, he wrote from Munich to his Petersburg friends that it would take three weeks to reach Rome and at least two weeks to help his family get settled there.[31] The Prince needed his new position so much that he expressed anxiety about the impression his request might make. He begged his friends to approach the Minister of Finance, Count Kankrin, with caution. Zhukovsky again succeeded in arranging for an extension of Vyazemsky's leave abroad with the Tsar.

h) Volkonskaya responded without delay. On October 26, Vyazemsky was already writing to Petersburg: "According to the information gathered here and received from Princess Zinaida in Rome, we will go to Italy by way of Munich, which means through the Tyrol."[32] Poor weather and Pashenka's condition detained them in Munich until the middle of November. Then they followed the planned itinerary: the Tyrol, Trento, Verona, Bologna, Florence, and Rome.

i) From here on Vyazemsky switches to the lighter tone more characteristic of his usually elegant and witty letters. He compares Volkonskaya's wide experience of travelling throughout Europe with his own knowledge of only the forty-one verst route from Moscow to his estate Ostafievo, and he uses a colloquial expression, *na dolgix*, translated into the amusing French *sur les longes*. The Russian idiom, denoting a slow coach trip, substitutes synecdochically the result (a slow trip) for its agent (poor horses). Using the Italian *vetturino* instead of the Russian *kučer* (coachman), Vyazemsky makes another switch, which brings about a humorous mixture of three languages and three stylistic levels.

j) In expressing his friendship and affection for the Princess, Vyazemsky again plays with words coined after the model of the French *déraciner* (to unroot). The first, *dégermaniser* (to un-Germanize) is a calque following the morphological pattern of the French *dé-racin-er*. The second, *dé-pomme-de-terr-iser*, is another type of coinage following the same morphological pattern, based on the contiguity of *racines* (roots) with *terre* (earth), and resulting in the pun: *dé-pomme-de-terr-iser* (*pomme de terre*: potato). This playful passage ends with a contrasting coda — a quotation from Goethe's "Mignon." Vyazemsky's preoccupation with "Mignon" is evident in two poems he later wrote in Italy: "Florencija. Ty znaeš kraj" (1834), and "Kennst du das Land" (1835).

k) We assume that the selection of the Duke of Saxony (in French, Saxe-Gotha), whose able counselor of war Vyazemsky compares with Volkonskaya and her strategic genius, is motivated merely by the paronomastic similarity of the French *Gotha* (here, "*Gothe*") with the name Goethe, suggested by the quotation from "Mignon." Thus this solemn letter with its many requests, which certainly was not easy for Vyazemsky to write, ends on an unexpectedly positive note. Although the author's mood is still sad, the letter nevertheless indicates a joyful attitude toward literary craftsmanship and word play.

Letter II

One sheet of paper, 13 x 21.8 cm, folded in four and sealed in the center with Vyazemsky's signet. On the reverse side, the following address written in the Prince's hand: "Eja Sijatel'stvu / Knegine Zenaide Aleksandrovne Volkonskoj." The letter is not dated and the place where it was written is not indicated. It was only marked on the bottom: "ce dimanche." On the top of the blank page, there is a note, possibly in the handwriting of Alexander Nikitich Volkonsky: "Léttres intimes." *Unpublished.*

[n.p., n.d.]
[Florence, April, 12/24, 1835]*a*

On vient de me remettre, Princesse, votre billet au moment où j'avois déjà fait ma toilette de voyage. Je suis très peiné de ne pouvoir me render à vos ordres et de n'avoir pas pris définitivement congé de vous. J'ai été toute la journée en l'air à cause de la noce de [Timiriazeff] et je ne suis rentré chez moi que pour me mettre en route.*b* Voici la lettre pour Joukoffski que je vous prie de remettre au Comte Ricci en lui faisant agréer mes adieux et l'assurance des sentimens distingués que je lui porte.*c* Quant au portefeuille, ayez la bonté de me le faire envoyer par la poste ou de le faire remettre à mon homme d'affaire.*d* Je prends aussi la liberté de vous prier de dire mes regrets aux demoiselles Ocouloff*e*; je comptais les voir encore avant mon départ, mais vraiment je n'ai pas eu la tête à moi, ni ne l'ai maintenant. Vous devez vous en apercevoir au décousu et au désordre de mon billet.*f* Lisez-le avec indulgence et agréez avec bonté l'hommage de mes tendres respects et de mon dévouement inaltérable.

Wiazemski

ce dimanche

a) The dating of this letter is based on its content and the note "ce dimanche" ("this Sunday") inserted at the bottom to the left of the signature. Vyazemsky apologizes here for not coming to take formal leave of Volkonskaya before his departure, referring to his fatigue and depression. We know that the Prince left Rome on April 22 and arrived in Florence on April 24. Neither date fell on a Sunday. Apparently the exhausted and confused Vyazemsky failed to follow his habit of double-dating letters and diary entries and here automatically used only the old Julian style of dating, according to which Friday, April 24 (N.S.) corresponded to April 12 (O.S.), which indeed in 1835 fell on a Sunday. Hence, this short letter to Volkonskaya was written on Friday, April 24, 1835, the day of the Prince's arrival in Florence.[33]

b) As already mentioned in the introduction, two weeks after Pashenka's death, the Vyazemskys went to Naples with Alexander Turgenev, whom the Prince called "our nanny-tutor-guardian." After a week of rest and sightseeing, Vyazemsky and Turgenev returned to Rome, leaving the family behind. They arrived on April 15, and Vyazemsky had one week to prepare for the long return journey to Russia. During these last days in Rome he definitely visited Volkonskaya several times, since his younger daughter, Nadezhda, was staying with the Princess. Vyazemsky may have avoided a final visit with Volkonskaya in order to spare himself and his daughter, whose health was causing him great concern, the pain of parting.

c) Vyazemsky knew that his close friend Zhukovsky was expected in Italy shortly. In this letter to Volkonskaya he enclosed a message which he asked Count Ricci to give to the poet when he arrived in Rome.

d) Apparently Vyazemsky had left his *portefeuille* at Volkonskaya's. "Mon homme d'affaires," the banker Valentini, recommended to him by Turgenev, managed financial transactions for many of the Russians in Rome.[34]

e) At the time, the *Okulov sisters*, Anna (1794-1861) and Daria (1811-1865), were visiting in Rome. They were Vyazemsky's neighbors at Ostafievo, and he had known them since childhood. Anna (by marriage Diakova) was considered one of the foremost amateur singers in Moscow. She studied voice with Count Ricci and Volkonskaya, to whom Vyazemsky had introduced her in 1825. To Daria (by marriage Shipova), Vyazemsky dedicated one of his best poems. He also wrote for the sisters the text of a song to be performed at one of the Okulov family celebrations.[35]

f) In a letter of the same date written from Florence to his wife, Vyazemsky also complains of depression, confessing that he is fighting the desire "to leave the battlefield and to return" to Rome. He writes of his concern for Nadezhda's health, and asks Vera Fyodorovna to consult Dr. Kopp in Hanau.[33] This confirms our assumption concerning the reason for the Prince's failure to bid farewell to Volkonskaya and his daughter.

Three months later, summing up his experience of the past year, Vyazemsky wrote to Alexander Turgenev: "The whole trip seems to me now as a terrible dream which engulfed me, or rather everything else appeared as if it was a dream, which from then on took possession of my soul."[36]

In several instances we had to reconstruct Vyazemsky's texts — of the manuscripts in the Volkonskaya Archive, his are among the least legible. The Prince himself was often apologetic about his handwriting: "From my awkward scribbling which is even more clumsy and ugly now than before, you must see that I am writing with effort, because you, too, are probably reading my letters not without effort."[37]

As for Vyazemsky's French writing, it is better than could be expected even from an educated Russian of his time. It is idiomatic with a distinctively individual style. Some of the grammatical flaws and inconsistencies can be explained by the changing French grammar at that time as presented in the French Academy Dictionary (editions of 1740, 1762, 1798, and 1835). The same mistakes could have been made by an educated native Frenchman as well.[38]

THREE NOTES
FROM VASILY ANDREEVICH ZHUKOVSKY
TO PRINCESS Z.A. VOLKONSKAYA

There are three signed, unpublished notes in the Volkonskaya Archive from the renowned Russian poet Vasily Andreevich Zhukovsky to Priness Zinaida which do not indicate when or where they were written. The text, however, contains several clues which reveal that they were written in Rome. The most obvious is Zhukovsky's mention of the Corso festivities and of a visit to the Pope. His reference to a meeting with the Russian writer Gogol, who arrived in Rome for the first time in March 1837, confirms that these lines could have been written only during Zhukovsky's second visit to Rome, which took place between December 4/16, 1838, and February 1/13, 1839. A closer look at these eight weeks, as they are reflected in his diary and correspondence, permits a more precise dating of each note. Short as they are, these letters are of undeniable interest: they shed light on the neglected issue of Zhukovsky's relationship with Volkonskaya, and also offer an additional glimpse of his visit to Rome in 1838-1839.

After several months of traveling in Germany, Austria, and northern Italy, Zhukovsky arrived in Italy on December 4/16, 1837, in the cortege of the Crown Prince Alexander (the future Tsar Alexander II), for whom he had been appointed a tutor in 1826. Before leaving Russia, Zhukovsky devised a well-planned curriculum of art history for his royal pupil, in which Rome and its treasures occupied an important place.[1] When in Rome, however, Zhukovsky became so entranced with the city, which had already captivated him during his first visit in 1833, that many of his educational plans remained unfulfilled. He plunged himself into the whirlwind of Roman life. His diary and letters show that he frequented the diplomatic and social circles which he had known from the past.[2] He was, however, more attracted to the art galleries and artists' studios. An accomplished artist himself, Zhukovsky spent hours sketching Roman landscapes. Gogol, often observing him working on his drawings in Volkonskaya's garden, remarked: "He makes very good sketches a dozen a minute."[3] Zhukovsky spent hardly a day without visiting the Russian painters then studying in Rome, such as A. A. Ivanov, P. A. Bruni, O. A. Kiprensky, and their already established Western confrères — D. A. Ingres, H. Vernet, V. Camuccini, and Henry Williams. His evaluations of these artists and their schools were often quite original and revealed a true understanding of art.[4]

But it was the city itself which occupied most of Zhukovsky's time and attention. He studied the city seriously, every evening making detailed notes in his diary to register his impressions. Zhukovsky became fascinated with Gogol, whom he came to know well: "Gogol is like a flash of lightning. He lives and breathes Italy; he is always an artist and often amusing."[5] They walked and rode through the city for hours, and spent days discussing Gogol's new works.[6] Twice Zhukovsky arranged for Gogol to read his works before the Crown Prince. According to his diary, the poet met Gogol twenty-three times during his stay in Rome. Zhukovsky did not accompany the Crown Prince on a sixteen-day trip to Naples, but preferred to stay in Rome meeting with Gogol almost every day. As A. Turgenev said, "he fell in love with Rome . . . and started to neglect his duties."[7] The entire Italian experience was of great importance for Zhukovsky's inner development. Soon after leaving Italy, he wrote to the poet Ivan Kozlov: "I am healthy in body but sick with longing for Italy, which we have abandoned as a lover abandons his bride whom he loves passionately, but from whom fate has torn him prematurely."[8]

What place did Princess Volkonskaya occupy in Zhukovsky's Roman visit? While in Russia, they had been acquainted but had not established a close relationship. In 1825, the poet complained to Alexander Turgenev that he had not yet heard Volkonskaya sing.[9] They developed friendly relations in 1833 during Zhukovsky's first visit to Italy, when he and Turgenev met with the Princess either in Naples or Rome almost every other day.[10] According to his diary, when Zhukovsky returned to Rome in 1838, he at first called on Volkonskaya quite often. Then their relationship seemed to be more remote, and his visits to the hospitable villa in Lateran became less and less frequent.[11] The references to Volkonskaya in Zhukovsky's diary were now brief and cool. He does not comment on her new image as a totally devout Catholic, and does not refer to people or conversations in her house. All his allusions to her are now contained in short, matter-of-fact statements: "Visit to Volkonskaya . . . dined . . . had supper at the villa . . . " On one occasion, the bare entry "lunch at the villa" is followed by a note: "Her wonderful verses to me."[12] This scanty information about the relationship between Z. A. Volokonskaya and V. A. Zhukovsky makes his short letters to her worthy of closer attention.

I.

A folded page of yellowed paper, 7½ x 9½ cm. On the reverse side: à Madame la Princesse Volkonsky Z. *Published.*[26]

[n.p., n.d.][a]
[Rome, Wednesday, January 18/30, 1839]

La colère a raison, mais l'amitié a tort. Protiv družby k Vam ja ni čem ne provinilsja. A dannogo slova byt' u Vas tret'ego dnja ne sderžal bez sobstvennogo vedoma: prospal čas.[b] Mne samomu i dosadno i smešno. V čas postarajus' byt' k Vam vmeste s Gogolem.[c] Do svidanija.

Žukovskij.

La colère a raison, mais l'amitié a tort. I have not in any way failed in my friendship for you. And I did not intentionally break my promise to visit you the day before yesterday: I overslept. I am myself both annoyed and amused by this. At one o'clock I will try to visit you together with Gogol. Good-bye.

Zhukovsky.

a) The date of this note can be established by examining Zhukovsky's schedule as recorded in his diary. It can be seen that during the first two weeks he called on Volkonskaya quite frequently (December 7/19, 9/21, 10/22, and 11/23). Later, however, his visits became much less regular, with lapses of eight, nine, and even fourteen days. After not having seen the Princess for almost two weeks, Zhukovsky failed to come "day before yesterday" ("tret'ego dnja"), as promised. In this undated note which was written in response to a letter from the apparently disappointed Volkonskaya, he offers an explanation and announced that he will call on her the same day with Gogol. In Zhukovsky's diary there is an entry for January 18/30 confirming this visit.[13] Thus we were able to establish January 18/30, 1839 as the date of this note. Further consideration will support this conclusion.

b) Zhukovsky had a habit of taking an afternoon nap. His diary for January 16/28 shows that although complaining of cold weather he visited the studios of four painters and spent the whole afternoon in the

Vatican Museum and the Cathedral of Saint Peter.[14] This makes the explanation in his letter plausible: exhausted and chilled, he probably fell asleep and missed the evening at Volkonskaya's.

c) Zhukovsky indeed visited Volkonskaya together with Gogol, as he promised in his note. As arranged, they came for dinner, served according to Italian custom around one o'clock. In his diary Zhukovsky noted: "Gogol's birthday ... at Volkonskaya's. Music. Marcello's psalms. Ricci, Corsini, Capaldi sang."[15] It should be noted, however, that the day given here as Gogol's birthday does not correspond to the generally accepted date: March 20/April 1. Since Zhukovsky left Rome almost two months before Gogol's actual birthday, this may refer to his name-day, Saint Nicholas' day (January 23/ February 4), which was being celebrated at this gathering a few days early.

In Volkonskaya's Roman library there was a copy of Zhukovsky's poem *Undina.* The dedication, in the poet's handwriting, reads: "To the Princess Zeneida Alexandrovna Volkonskaya in memory of our friendship. January 18/30, 1839. Rome. V. Zhukovsky."[16] Evidently Zhukovsky presented this book to the Princess on the same day that he wrote the note announcing his visit.

II.

A small page of faded paper, 7¼ x 4¾ cm. *Published.*[26]

[n.p., n.d.][a]
[Thursday. January 26 / February 7, 1839]

My ostaemsja zdes' ešče do buduščej sredy.[b] Nynče ne mogu s vami exat' po toj pričine, čto teper' edu k Pape, a v tri časa na Korso.[c] Nel'zja li ustroit', čtoby u vas otobedat' v Voskresen'e? ili v Subbotu? Uvedom'te kogda.[d] V Voskresen'e udobnee ibo posle Corso.[e]

Ž(ukovsky)

We will be staying here until next Wednesday. I am unable to go with you today because I am going to see the Pope, and then at three o'clock — to the Corso. Would it be possible to arrange to have dinner with you on Sunday? Or on Saturday? Let me know when. It would be more convenient on Sunday, since this will be after Corso.

Zh(ukovsky)

a) Zhukovsky's diary shows that he and the Crown Prince were received by the Pope on January 26/February 7, 1839, and that immediately thereafter they went to the Corso. This information helped to establish that his second note to Volkonskaya was written on the same day, January 26/February 7, 1839.[17]

b) The visit to Rome by the Crown Prince and his suite was curtailed by order of the Tsar. Zhukovsky comments on this change of plan in his diary entry for December 24/January 5: "Italija dlja nas lopnula" ("Italy is out for us"). A month later, on January 25/February 6, a decision was made to extend their stay in Rome until the end of the carnival, and Zhukovsky informed Volkonskaya about this postponement the next day.[18]

c) The trip to Palacordo with Volkonskaya which Zhukovsky was obliged to postpone eventually took place on Sunday, January 29 / February 10, 1839.[19]

d) Zhukovsky went to Villa Volkonskaya on Saturday, January 28 / February 9, 1839, again together with Gogol. The Princess read him her poem, which he praised: "wonderful verses."[20]

e) Both the Crown Prince's entourage and Zhukovsky himself were enthusiastic over the Corso, attending the carnival six out of the eight days it lasted. The vivid description in his diary of the last day of the festival is surprisingly similar to Gogol's and Vyazemsky's carnival scenes.[21]

III.

A sheet of blue paper, apparently cut from a larger page. 3¾ x 4¾ cm. *Published.*[26]

[n.p., n.d.]^a
[Rome, Monday, January 30/February 11, 1839]

Vaša popravka prekrasnaja. Posylaju vam spisok (tak že s nekotorymi popravkami) vašix Angelov, oni stojat svoego imeni.[b] Marco Visconti ja kupil, i tak ne presylajte.[c] Do svidanija, nadejus' zdes' ešče, a ne v storone angelov.[d]

Žukovskij.

Your correction is excellent. I am sending you your Angels (also with some corrections). They deserve their name. I have bought Marco Visconti, so don't send it. Good-bye. I hope to see you again here, and not in the land of the angels.

Zhukovsky.

a) This note was most likely written on January 30/February 11, 1839, the day after Zhukovsky went with Volkonskaya to Palacordo. It is possible that he wrote it at the home of her close friend, Count Ricci, whom he visited two days before his departure.[22] This may explain why he used paper of a different type than usual. The reference to Volkonskaya's offer to send him Grossi's novel *Marco Visconti* also confirms our dating: she would have had time to do this on January 31/February 12, which was Zhukovsky's last day in Rome.

b) Here Zhukovsky speaks of Volkonskaya's poem "Four Angels," which he returned to her with his corrections and compliments. The poem was published in 1836 in the *Moscow Observer*.[23]

c) In October 1838, Zhukovsky purchased a copy of the novel *Marco Visconti* by Tomaso Grossi, published in 1834, and read it with great interest during his Italian trip. Viewing the landscapes of Lombardy, he compared them with Grossi's descriptions.[24]

d) This parting formula is typical of Zhukovsky's romantic motif of "this world" as opposed to "the other world." It also appears in his letter to Alexander Turgenev, in which he writes that he is desolate at not having heard Volkonskaya sing: "It seems that I am destined to die before having heard Zeneida here; maybe there, in purgatory, I will listen to her sing before the throne of the Almighty."[25]

FIFTEEN LETTERS FROM TSAR ALEXANDER I
TO PRINCESS Z. A. VOLKONSKAYA

In the archive of Z. A. Volkonskaya there are fifteen letters written to the Princess by the Russian Tsar Alexander I. These letters, covering a period of thirteen years (1813-1825), reveal the different stages of their relationship, which is still puzzling in many ways. Six of these letters were published in 1868 by the Princess' son, A. N. Volkonsky. But his scrupulous censorship, aimed at guarding the honor of his recently deceased mother, resulted in substantial cuts, which distorted the real nature of her involvement with the Tsar.[1] The other nine letters, some longer and more significant, have remained unpublished until now.

We are aware that the *amitié amoureuse* cultivated at that time, an attitude finding its expression in an affected style, full of suggestive allusions and exaggerated revelations, did not necessarily indicate an actual romantic involvement. The Tsar's letters to Volkonskaya, however, offer evidence of a close and complex relationship going far beyond the usual court flirtation.

Unlike the other numerous affairs in Alexander's life, his intimacy with Princess Volkonskaya was not a subject of open discussion. Now and then observations were made that "the Tsar found pleasure in Princess Volkonskaya's conversation" and that he "liked to relax from his military and political duties in her company."[2] There were also occasional echoes of muted gossip. On the whole, however, their relations were treated by contemporaries with the utmost discretion. It must be noted that the official documentation we have for this period is scarce. Most of Alexander's personal papers in the Imperial Archives were destroyed. Materials on the Tsar's personal life which are not in private archives, if not destroyed or lost, are meager and not of much help.[3]

Much later, in studies devoted to Volkonskaya, her relations with Alexander once more became the subject of attention and more open speculation.[4] But again, whatever was reported was based on assumption and is not reliable historical material. Therefore we must conclude that the only valid sources which can elucidate the long overlooked question of Princess Zinaida's involvement with Alexander I are the Tsar's letters to her in our archive. Revealing as they are, however, these letters represent only fragmentary glimpses of Alexander's intimacy with Volkonskaya. In order to gain a clearer picture of this elusive relationship we must see it in its broader perspective.

It is not easy to determine when Alexander started to distinguish the young Zinaida from the other beauties at his court. We know that at the age of eighteen Princess Zinaida Beloselskaya was introduced to the Russian court and appointed maid of honor to the Dowager Empress Maria Fyodorovna. In December 1808, as lady in waiting to Queen Louise of Prussia, she participated in the whirl of receptions and galas given in honor of the visit of the Prussian royal couple. In January 1809, there were more festivities, this time on the occasion of the betrothal and wedding of Grand Duchess Ekaterina Pavlovna. Princess Zinaida had many opportunities to meet the "irresistible Tsar and to breathe the atmosphere of adoration which surrounded him. Most likely it was during this period that Alexander noticed the beautiful, spirited and talented Zinaida.

It would be appropriate to take a closer look at Tsar Alexander's relations with women. Around 1811-1812 he was ready for a new romance. His passionate liaison with Maria Antonovna Naryshkina, which had begun in 1802, was on the point of breaking off. He was hurt by her poorly concealed infidelities, but did not return to his estranged wife, Empress Elizaveta, whom he had married at the age of sixteen. Instead, he consoled himself with a series of brief affairs.[5] Court gossip singles out several ladies who attracted the attention of the Tsar. But perhaps the most stable relationship in Alexander's life was with his sister, Grand Duchess Ekaterina Pavlovna. The publication of the Tsar's letters to her by Grand Duke Nikolai Mikhailovich in 1910 shed a new light on their mutual affection. Alexander's letters to his favorite sister, "la folle délicieuse" ("the delicious fool"), reveal the possibility of an unexpected aspect to their intimacy, which gradually was loosing its fraternal character.[6]

Alexander loved women and knew how to captivate them. While personally remaining detached, he was able to make every one of them feel that at the moment only she was important to him.[7] It is difficult to evaluate the depth and duration of these involvements, and it is also not clear which of them were merely platonic. But apparently some were, since several of his contemporaries referred to the Tsar as "Don Juan Platonique."[8]

On February 22, 1811, Zinaida Beloselskaya married Prince Nikita Volkonsky. This was a marriage of convenience which had been arranged for Zinaida by her stepmother. On November 18 of the same year, her son Alexander was born. The Tsar offered to be his godfather, and on November 25 attended the christening in a chapel at the Winter Palace.[9] From the very beginning this marriage brought Zinaida no happiness. Early in 1812, after the birth of her son, she suffered a severe mental breakdown, which her contemporaries termed a "temporary madness." Her recovery was slow. Only toward September 1812 did she gradually start to improve.[10]

The war was then at a critical point. The French advanced into Russian territory and soon occupied Moscow. However, five weeks later the French troops began their unexpected retreat, and the whole country was galvanized by a general upswing of patriotism. There could be no better therapy for Princess Zinaida, and she was caught up in the popular enthusiasm, acquiring an entirely new attitude toward life and becoming receptive to new experiences.

By the beginning of 1813 Alexander, too, had become a changed man. He was no longer insecure and hesitant in his decisions. Determined to bring about the final downfall of the French army, he refused to make any concession to Napoleon: "He or I, I or he, but we cannot rule together. I have learned to understand him, and I will not be betrayed by him again."[11] These were the Tsar's finest hours. He proved that Napoleon was not wrong in evaluating him as more intelligent than was commonly assumed, and as more capable than all his ministers.[12]

A close personal contact of Tsar Alexander with Zinaida Volkonskaya preceded the first of his letters to her which are preserved in the Princess' Archive. An attentive reading of these first letters makes it evident that during this period Alexander was romantically involved with the Princess.

In January 1813, when the military situation became stabilized, the Tsar suddenly decided to invite the wives of three of his generals to join his military suite. Although he did not want the Empress Elizabeth to accompany him, he was now delighted to be surrounded by "a small feminine court." The first to arrive was Princess Zinaida, who came with her two year old son and her sister-in-law Sofia Volkonskaya. They were followed by Kutuzov's granddaughter, who was married to General Sadan.[13] From a letter of Field Marshal Prince M. I. Kutuzov we learn that on February 28, 1813, Princess Zinaida was already in Kalish: "Zénèide Volhonsky, whose manner I like very much, is here."[14] Four weeks later, the German General H. V. Boyer, describing a dinner he had attended at Kutuzov's, noted that Princess Volkonskaya was seated next to his host.[15]

In the informal atmosphere of the military suite the rapprochement between Princess Zinaida and the Tsar rapidly developed. His frequent visits were noticed and recorded.[16] The first letters to Volkonskaya indicate that Alexander's feelings for her were more serious than those for many of the other ladies he had previously courted.

On the whole, the letters themselves offer many clues about the real nature of this puzzling relationship. It is first necessary, however, to sift through the numerous gallantries which Alexander used with such mastery. When he speaks of Zinaida's "angelic kindness" or tells of his impatience to throw himself at her feet and assures her of "his devotion for life," he may be paying tribute to the style of his epoch. But, aside from this, there are many instances where the real voice of Alexander can be heard.

The letters make evident that the Tsar and the Princess met frequently. Some of his visits were informally announced in letters and notes, written just a few hours before his arrival (III, VII, IX, XIII, XIV, XV). Although Volkonskaya often stayed with her sister-in-law, it can be assumed that she received the Tsar alone. We find in the letters references to these visits, which Alexander anticipated with great impatience (I, V, XII). Several times he thanked Zinaida for the indulgence with which she treated him, assuring her that "these moments will never be effaced from (my) memory" (V). The letter of May 14, 1813 (I), initiated a dialogue about a reward ("une récompense"), which Alexander expected to receive from Volkonskaya. This suggestive discourse was continued in some of the following letters, from which we learn of the Princess' response (II, VI). In an unpublished six-page letter written to Zinaida from Peterswaldau on May 28, 1813 (II), the Tsar made a long declaration of the feeling for the Princess which had overpowered him at the very moment he first met her, and which had become even stronger after she allowed him to approach her more closely. The date and the extent of this closeness, however, is not made clear. Intimacy is merely suggested by subtle hints and allusions.

Alexander occasionally mentioned Zinaida's husband, Prince Nikita Volkonsky, who at that time served as his aide-de-camp. Although he claimed to have a friendly attitude towards him, it is evident that the Tsar disliked the Prince. Often in writing Zinaida, Alexander ironically referred to him as "your man" (II, VI). He frequently used him as his messenger ("courrier ordinaire"), and Prince Volkonsky had to carry the Tsar's amorous epistles to his own wife. An element of jealousy was probably also present: in one of the letters (V), Alexander explained his absence by not wanting to impose on the Princess during a short visit from her husband. Elsewhere he sarcastically remarks that Prince Volkonsky was holding on to her skirts (VII). The Tsar realized that he could not completely ignore Zinaida's husband. At the same time he claimed that he would not hesitate to confess his feelings for the Princess "before the whole universe, as well as before your husband himself" (II).

The Princess became more drawn to Alexander as the correspondence progressed. We see from the Tsar's letters that she sometimes complained of being neglected. During this early stage of their romance, Alexander answered her reproaches with impassioned denials (VI).

Perhaps even more important than the texts of the letters are the conditions under which the Tsar took time to write them, always in his own hand and often at great length. May-October 1813 were decisive months on the battlefield as well as in diplomatic negotiations. The Tsar was present at the front and was personally involved in planning military and diplomatic strategy. During these days Alexander could not find the time to read the dispatches of his chancellor, N. P. Rumyantsev, and for weeks failed to respond to his most urgent inquiries. On June 12, 1813, when he finally answered Rumyantsev from Peterswaldau he stated: "I can truly say that I have had at my disposal not one day, or even a night. Add to this that only once have I spent two days in a row in one place and now we are in continuous motion."[17] Even Grand Duchess Ekaterina Pavlovna accepted the fact that Alexander had no time for correspondence. On May 17, 1813, she thanked him for not forgetting her birthday at a time "when the destiny of the universe is in your hands."[18] Preoccupied and exhausted as he was, the Tsar managed to write long letters to Princess Volkonskaya and to visit her whenever possible. In his letters he gave detailed descriptions of the battles, with the exact figures concerning the gains and losses of the participating armies. In several instances he chivalrously chose to represent these victories as a tribute to the Princess, and he rejoiced that they gave him an opportunity to meet her afterwards (I, II, IV).

The first period in the relationship between Zinaida Volkonskaya and Tsar Alexander suddenly came to an end with his letter written from Schaffhausen in December 1813 (VII). Their romance was obviously finished: three and a half years passed between this letter and the next one from Petersburg of May 12/24, 1816. It is difficult to say what caused the rupture between Alexander and the Princess. Since we have at our disposal only a limited knowledge of the facts, all we can do is offer some speculations. We can deduce from the Tsar's letters that Zinaida was not always easy to deal with. Although we do not know her part in this dialogue, we can assume that she needed constant avowals of devotion and respect. Besides this, Zinaida's husband was not as accommodating as had been the spouse of the Tsar's previous mistress,

Naryshkina.[19] We have already seen from several references to Zinaida's husband and also to her brother-in-law, Prince P. M. Volkonsky, that their attitude may have been irritating to the Tsar. It should also be noted that Volkonskaya, unlike Naryshkina, frequently asked Alexander for favors. From his letters it is evident that the Princess not only interceded on behalf of her husband, relatives and friends, but also tried to influence the Tsar in his political decisions (Letters II, VII, VIII, X, XI, XII, XV).[20] Alexander's attitude toward this is predictable from his earlier statement about the non-interference which he had made a condition of his ten-year liaison with Naryshkina: "... otherwise everything would have been finished."[21] Toward the end of 1813, the whole relationship with Volkonskaya may have become a burden for Alexander, particularly at the time when he was at the zenith of his newly acquired glory as the "saviour of Europe."

Another factor leading to their estrangement may have been the Tsar's renewed closeness with his sister, Grand Duchess Ekaterina Pavlovna. Recently widowed, she now clung to her brother, being impressed by his new stature. After having been separated for more than a year, they spent much time together in Prague in the early fall of 1813. Alexander's rather cool letter to Princess Zinaida from Schaffhausen (VII) was written two days after he arrived there to visit his sister, who probably knew about this disturbing relationship and made an effort to put an end to it. Six months later, the Grand Duchess would try to lure him to London, promising to recreate the happy days spent in Schaffhausen: "We will have a second Schafhouse!" Whatever the reasons may have been, this was the end of the romance between Tsar Alexander and Princess Zinaida Volkonskaya.[22]

The second period of their relationship is represented by two letters: one written in Petersburg on May 12/24, 1816, and a shorter note of October 8/20, 1817. The Princess had almost completely disappeared from Alexander's life. These were turbulent years, and the Tsar's behavior during this period justified Chateaubriand's evaluation of his personality: "The Emperor of Russia has a strong soul and a weak character."[23] This dichotomy consistently manifested itself in Alexander's conduct at this time. In Paris, where he was enthusiastically greeted by the people, his behavior to the newly installed king, Louis XVIII, and to the ladies of the Napoleonic clan, was impeccable, even at the expense of Russia's national interests. He was justly acclaimed "the king of hearts of the Parisian salons." However, the statesmen assembled in Vienna preferred to see in the Russian Tsar the superficial man mocked by Byron as the "autocrat of waltzes and of war."[24]

Volkonskaya was with the court in Paris, London, and Vienna, but her name was never linked to the Tsar's because she no longer belonged to his inner circle. In December of 1814, at the peak of the Vienna Congress' festivities, Zinaida delivered a child, a son who died soon after birth.[25] This loss, as well as the experience of the war and her relationship with Alexander, had changed the Princess. Hurt and disillusioned, she adopted a new attitude toward life. The years 1814-1819 turned out to be a prolonged journey from one European capital to another. This provided her with more than mere amusement: eager for new experiences and new knowledge, she developed tremendously during these years. The new way of life, the image of the new Zinaida, was the cause of a reproof in the Tsar's letter to her of May 1816, which she received in Paris (VIII). The next, shorter letter of October 8, 1817, was more neutral, and does not offer much new information about the state of their relationship (IX).

The last period of the Tsar's communication with Princess Volkonskaya opened with the letter of February 3, 1821, from Laybach. There are six letters written within the next five years, which turned out to be the most trying in Alexander's life. Everything went wrong for him. After a decade of victorious wars, he, "the blessed," "the Agamemnon of our time," found himself in a position of defeat. His cherished idea of the Holy Alliance had failed. New congresses in Troppau, Laybach, and Verona were, as Metternich stated, controlled by the Austrians.[26] His earlier tendency to suspiciousness, nourished by treason and betrayal, was now becoming an obsession. Insurrections in Spain, Northern Italy, Naples, and Greece confirmed his belief that the revolutionary spirit was not confined to France alone. Then came the mutiny of his favorite Semyonovsky regiment. Unable to accept or to crush the spirit of liberalism,[27] which he himself had supported in his earlier days, the Tsar chose to let Arakcheev take an active part in state affairs. He moved away from his closest friends, such as P. M. Volkonsky and A. N. Golitsyn, replacing them with people of Arakcheev's mold.[28] Alexander's long illness in 1824 and the sudden death of his illegitimate daughter Sofia Naryshkina contributed to his growing mysticism and the remote, unresponsive state of mind which he reached during the last two years of his life.

The final six letters to Princess Volkonskaya have none of the dry, detached tone evident in the Tsar's earlier reprimands to her. Again, there are assurances of sincere friendship and expressions of gratitude for the Princess' constant devotion (X, XI, XII, XV). Now he is willing to help Volkonskaya to arrange her own personal affairs and to intercede on the behalf of others (X, XII, XV). Alexander also began to complain about the pressures of his duties, "the enormous burden which weighs upon me, absorbing all of my time" (XV). The dominant tone of these last letters was one of friendship and sincere affection "which had never ceased to exist."

In this Alexander was right: in spite of the vicissitudes of their relationship, Volkonskaya's devotion to the Tsar never wavered, and his death was a great personal loss for her.

When, seven months after the Tsar's last letter to her, he died unexpectedly in Taganrog, Princess Volkonskaya lamented his death in her first poem in Russian "To Alexander I," and wrote a long article describing his last days.[29]

The correspondence and relationship between Alexander and Zinaida Volkonskaya began when the Tsar was at the height of his achievements, and ended during the twilight of his reign.

Letter I

A light gray, well-preserved sheet of paper, folded, each side 11.1. x 18.1 cm. Watermarked with light stripes. A heavy envelope, 10 x 12 cm. The address, in Alexander's hand: A/la Princesse Zénèide Wolchonsky. Under the last line, Alexander's characteristic long flourish. *Published, with some inaccuracies, by A. N. Volkonsky.*

Jauer, le 14 mai 1813

Si une bonne intention devait jamais mériter une récompense, certainement j'ai obtenu celle qui pouvait me faire le plus de plaisir dans l'éloignement où je me trouve de vous Princesse, par la charmante lettre que cela m'a value de votre part. Je ne puis assez vous exprimer combien j'ai été touché de tout ce que vous avez bien voulu me dire. Croyez que j'en sais sentir le prix.[a] Le porteur de celle-ci vous rendra compte de la manière dont nos troupes se sont encore illustrées et si l'entier succès n'est pas tel que nous aurions pu le désirer, les événemens qui si sont passés n'en sont pas moins glorieux pour notre brave armée. Ce n'est qu'avec la persévérance qu'on vient à bout des choses difficiles.[b] Espérons que la Providence Divine bénira nos efforts. Nous sommes tous dans les meilleures dispositions possibles.[c] — A tous les vœux que je forme pour le succès de nos armes s'y joint aussi celui bien sincère qu'ils puissent me valoir le bonheur de vous revoir au plus tôt. — Veuillez en attendant me conserver une place dans votre souvenir au quel je tiens tant, et rappelez moi je vous prie à celui de la Princesse Sophie.[d] Agréez aussi l'homage d'un attachement aussi respectueux que sincère.

A.

a) This letter is apparently an answer to an earlier communication from the Princess. We know that on May 20 she went to a court reception in Toeplitz, and on May 12 she visited Goethe at his residence.[30] Thus the letter was sent to Toeplitz, which was further from the front than Jauer. It seems that Zinaida had already assumed a friendly and affectionate tone with the Tsar, since he expressed delight at her "charming letter" which "touched (him) so much."

b) The military situation to which the Tsar was referring was quite complex. After Napoleon occupied Dresden on April 26/May 8, the armies of the coalition retreated, preparing for a major battle in Bautzen. Napoleon's forces at Dresden outnumbered those of the coalition by fifty percent. The battle of Bautzen took place on May 8/20 and lasted for thirty-six hours. Both Alexander and Napoleon were present on the field. When the situation became critical, the Tsar ordered an organized retreat towards Reichenbach and Goerlitz. The future course of events proved this to be a wise decision. But Alexander did not want to witness the withdrawl of his troops, and left the battlefield.[31] The coalition forces lost not less than 12,000 men. Nevertheless, this was not a defeat for them: the French, even in their victory, were left in a dangerous position, and Napoleon understood it very well: "The armistice saved us, for the days of Jena and Austerlitz had passed."[32] When Alexander was writing this letter to Volkonskaya, he already knew that on the following day, May 15/27, Austria would deliver an ultimatum to Napoleon, threatening to declare war.[33] All this confirms that the Russian Tsar had reason to be optimistic in his letter to the Princess, stating: "We are now in the best possible situation."

c) We have in this letter a reference to "la Providence divine," which Alexander saw as guiding his efforts. This statement reappears in almost all his letters to the Princess. Religion at this point was becoming more and more important for Alexander, and even during the most difficult days he found time to read the Scriptures. Two days after this letter to

Volkonskaya, he communicated to his friend, Prince Golitsyn, that this reading was becoming increasingly significant for him.[34]

d) Princess Sofia G. Volkonskaya (see note 'h' in the chapter on Kozlov). Her husband, *Prince Pyotr Mikhailovich Volkonsky* (1776-1852), was one of the central figures during the Alexander years, and the closest person to the Tsar himself. The Prince was in Alexander's immediate circle of friends before the latter became Tsar. During the campaign of 1812-1814, Volkonsky was first his adjutant, then chief of headquarter. For his participation in battles, he was awarded many military honors. When the Tsar fell under the influence of Arakcheev, the Prince nevertheless remained faithful to him until the end. In 1826, the new Tsar Nicholas appointed Volkonsky court minister, and in 1834 bestowed upon him the highest title "Highness" ("Svetlejšij").

Letter II

Heavy, pale yellow paper, folded in two, 19 x 22.5 cm. Besides these four pages, a single page of the same size, one side of which is used. The paper has an English watermark, "Horn-on-Shield," topped with a crown, made before 1794. The envelope, 13.6 x 11.4 cm. with the seal of Alexander I. The address, written in Alexander's hand: A / Madame la Princesse / Zénèide Wolchonsky, née / Beloselsky. *Unpublished.*

Peterswaldau le 28 May [1813]

Vous avez paru être etonée Princesse, de ce que je me suis servi du mot de *récompense* en parlant de votre avant dernière lettre. Mais coment dois-je rendre la sensation qu'elles ont produit sur moi, et surtout la dernière? En la comparant à l'effet que cause une récompense me paroit encore l'exprimer bien faiblement. — En effet que pouvais-je lire en même tems de plus aimable, de plus spirituel, comme aussi de plus flatteur pour moi? — Vous n'avez pas pu ne pas vous convaincre, combien depuis le moment que je vous ai connu, j'ai mis toujours de prix à tout ce qui venait de vous. — Ce prix n'a pu qu'augmenter encore depuis que vous m'avez permis de vous approcher. Je n'ai ambitionné qu'un peu de bienveillance de votre part, et sous ce rapport votre délicieuse lettre comble tous mes vœux.[a]

Vous le dirai-je plus d'une fois, j'ai craint que vous ne vous effarouch-
iez du sentiment que je vous ai voué, et si la pureté de ce sentiment me
rassuroit au fond de mon cœur, je tenais beaucoup à l'être par vous
même et à voir la preuve que vous ne le méconaissiez pas. — Sous ce
rapport encore, votre lettre en calmant mes inquiétudes m'a causé la plus
douce jouissance. — L'affabilité avec la quelle vous me traitez, a rem-
pli l'unique désir, que je me suis cru en droit de former. — Vous me
dites que ma lettre s'adressait à votre cœur et qu'elle y a été reçue . . .
Permetez-moi de mettre celle-ci à la même adresse. Elle m'est si chère.
C'est le mien qui me la dicte et qui en avouant l'intérêt le plus vif, l'affection la plus sincère pour vous, croit n'avoir rien à se reprocher: bien
loin de là, [je] confesse hautement ces sentiments devant l'univers entier
comme devant votre mari même. — C'est votre *homme* (sic) qui sera le
porteur de ces lignes et je n'ai pas le moindre scrupule qu'elles passacent à sa censure s'il le faut.[b]

Maintenent pardonez-moi cet élan qui s'est placé sous ma plume involontairement. J'avais besoin de vous exprimer ma manière de sentir. Je
ne la crois pas indigne de vous être offerte.

Que de grâces j'ai à vous rendre pour l'intérêt si chaud que vous
témoignez à nos armes. — Vous savez déjà que la *promise* aux *cent
mille bayonettes* achève de préparer sa dot; il est sûr qu'elle est d'une
lenteur assomante. Elle nous à engagé d'attendre quelques semaines
encore et de conduire une suspension d'armes à cet effet. Voilà pourquoi
nous nous reposons, tout en nous préparant à revenir encore plus
vigoureusement au combat[c]

Vous ordres ont été exactement remplis et le *Courier fièvreux* a avalé
tout ce qu'on lui a prescrit; le voilà en état de venir vous rejoindre, sa
fièvre l'ayant quitté depuis plusieurs jours.[d] Quand à *l'amoureux* c'est
grâce à la négligeance impardonable du C. Tolstoy qu'il est resté sans
réponse ayant dit de lui écrire, que je le recevais très volontiers à mon
service où il peut devenir *Courtisan diplomate* si cela lui convient avec
les émolumens habituels de ces places. Si vous le jugez à propos Princesse, Vous pouvez lui répéter la même chose. Je vais soigner aussi l'affaire du petit Gérambe dès que j'aurai la note que votre mari ne m'a pas
encore remise.[e]

Veuillez présenter mes respectueux homages à la Princesse Sophie, en
la remerciant pour son aimable souvenir.

Il faudrait enfin, que du moins pour la forme, je vous fasse des
excuses sur la longueur de cet épître, mais j'aime mieux m'en remettre
à votre angélique bonté et indulgence et vous supplie de croire que le

moment de vous revoir est attendu avec la plus vive impatiance sans
cependant malheureusement pouvoir me dire quand je puis en avoir
l'espoir.[g]

Veuillez en attendand ne pas m'effacer entièrement de votre souvenir
et me croire à tout jamais tout à vous de cœur et d'âme.

A.

Peterswaldau
28 mai 1813

a) The idea of a "reward" ("récompense"), which appeared at the
beginning of Alexander's letter of May 14, 1813 (I), recurs three times
in his correspondence with Volkonskaya: this indicates its significance
in their relationship. We can reconstruct the attitude of the Princess from
the text of the Tsar's letter. Apparently she showed a certain reserve and
uneasiness when faced with this suggestive question, but at the same
time she confessed that Alexander's letter had "reached (my) heart."
We find here one of the most direct expressions of Alexander's feeling
for Volkonskaya: he is explicit in stating without reservation the importance he attached to their relationship. This unrestrained expression of
emotions and a rather unrespectful reference to the Princess' husband
explains why her son Alexander did not publish this letter.

b) "Votre homme" ("Your man") — thus the Tsar frequently
referred to Zinaida's husband, Prince Nikita Volkonsky, to whom he
gave the awkward task of delivering these billets-doux to his own wife.

c) After the retreat from Bautzen (I), the armies of the coalition began
to regroup and accumulate fresh forces. It was finally decided to accept
the offer of the French to conclude an armistice, which had been signed
five days earlier. But soon Napoleon, who was the initiator of this truce
began to be doubtful about its outcome. His suspicions were justified:
during the six weeks of suspension of military action, the coalition army
significantly enlarged its forces.[35]

For several weeks the Tsar stayed not far from Reichenbach, in the
castle Peterswaldau, which belonged to the brother of the well-known
poet, Count Stollberg. It was there that he succeeded in persuading Austria to declare war on Napoleon, and in concluding an important agreement with England, which would give Russia a generous subsidy for
maintaining 150,000 men in the field. These achievements were crucial
for the further course of military action, and explain Alexander's satisfaction with his period of rest in Peterswaldau where, on the very day of
the armistice, this letter to Princess Zinaida was written.[36]

d) Alexander ironically refers to Zinaida's husband as "a messager with fever."[37] Volkonskaya asked the Tsar to give her husband a promotion and an appropriate civilian post in the diplomatic service. This request was further discussed in letters V, VIII, and IX.

e) *Edouard de Gérambe* (1795-1847) was the eldest son of Ferdinand de Gérambe (1772-1848), a prominent figure of his time: an Austrian general who enlisted in the Spanish army to fight against Napoleon. After the Treaty of Tilsit, de Gérambe was sent to organize a foreign legion to England. In February 1813 he was arrested by Napoleon's men and returned to France. In 1817 he became a Trappist monk. Volkonskaya had apparently reminded the Tsar of the imprisoned general Gérambe and asked him to help his son Edouard. The Princess succeeded in her intercession, and the "young Gérambe" entered the Russian army, where he served for thirty-four years. He was killed in the Caucasian war in 1847.

f) On the same day that Alexander wrote this long epistle to Volkonskaya, he sent a short note to the Grand Duchess Catherine. It is one of his most impersonal and reserved letters to her: he avoids here his usual intimate tone and addressed himself to "mes chéres amies," thus including his younger sister Marie.[38] It seems that Alexander's involvement with Princess Volkonskaya had now overshadowed all his other relationships. In this letter he promises to meet his sisters in Neustadt. We know that on June 4/16 the Tsar left Peterswaldau. He probably stopped in Toeplitz where Volkonskaya was then staying (see note 30).

Letter III

One page, folded 11 x 18.5 cm, written on one side. Small envelope, 10.4 x 12 cm, with the address in Alexander's hand: A / la Princesse Zénèide / Wolchonsky. On the reverse side of the envelope, added by Princess Zinaida: "1813". *Published.*

[n.p., n.d.]*ᵃ*
[n.b. June 4/16 n.a. the begin. of August 1813]

Je suis impatient Princesse, de pouvoir me mettre à vos pieds; hier déjà j'ai aspiré à ce bonheur, mais le ciel, ou plus tôt le Prince Schwarzenberg avec le general Radetzky*ᵇ* en ont voulu autrement en restant jusqu'à 11 heures chez moi. Puis-je me présenter chez Vous entre 7 et 8 heures? — En attendant veuillez recevoir mes homages respectueux.

A.

a) Although this brief note was placed by Prince Alexander N. Volkonsky as the first of the six letters which he published in 1868, we assume that it had been written after the letter of May 28/June 9, 1813 (II) and before the one of August 21, 1813 (IV). Our assumption is supported by several facts. One of them is that the Tsar entered into close collaboration with the Austrian Field Marshals Schwarzenberg and Radetzky after the armistice of June 18, 1813. We can attempt to narrow this dating. On June 4/16, after having left Peterswaldau, Alexander wrote an affectionate letter to the Grand Duchess Catherine asking her to meet him in Neuestadt, a small town close to Toeplitz.[39] We believe that during the following eight weeks, while in Toeplitz and its area, the Tsar wrote this note to Volkonskaya, who was still there, before moving further to Prague. In the next letter from Toeplitz of August 21, 1813 (IV), the Tsar was writing to the Princess, who was already in Prague, about the happy hours he had spent with her, possibly referring to the meeting announced in the note in question.

All this permits us to offer a tentative dating of this note, which limits it to eight weeks, between June 4/16, and the beginning of August, when Volkonskaya left Toeplitz for Prague.

b) *Prince K. P. Schwarzenberg* (1771-1820), Field Marshal, commander of the Austrian armed forces after Austria declared war on Napoleon. Schwarzenberg played an important part in the victories in Dresden and Leipzig. He was, however, known to be initially in opposition to the Tsar's strategy of attacking Leipzig with the whole of the allied forces — the plan which later proved to be so successful. *Joseph Wentzel Radetzky* (1766-1858), Austrian general, later Field Marshal. He took an active part in the military action against Napoleon after Austria entered the war. The Tsar had frequent strategic meetings with both Schwarzenberg and Radetzky. Later, in 1821, Radetzky participated in the negotiations in Laybach.

Letter IV

Four pages of thin, ivory colored paper, 18.5 x 22 cm, water-marked with narrow lines. A heavy envelope, 10.5 x 12.2 cm, with the Tsar's seal, addressed in his hand: "A la Princesse Zénèide Wolchonsky." On the reverse side, marked by the Princess: "Toeplitz 21 août 1813." *Published.*

Toeplitz, 21 août [1813]

Il m'est impossible Princesse, d'attendre le départ de *Courrier ordinaire*[a] pour vous exprimer toute ma gratitude pour votre charmante lettre et pour tout ce que vous voulez bien dire de si aimable. Je ne désire qu'une chose: c'est de ressembler, ne fusse que de loin à l'être que vous avez décrit et que vous avez bien voulu nommer de mon nom, et dont cependant je suis encore trés loin. — C'est à vous seule qu'appartient ce rare talent de rendre aimables ceux, avec qui vous vous trouvez, étant douée vous même de cette amabilité naturelle et indulgente envers les autres, qui met chaqu'un à l'aise devant vous. — Aussi passer des heures près de vous est une jouissance véritable.[b]

Vos vœux été exaucés et les journées du 17/29 et du 18/30 ont couvert notre Armée, et surtout la Garde, d'une gloire immortelle. — Tout le Corp de Vandamme a été détruit, les Généraux, l'État Major, 12,000 prisoniers, 81 canons et tous les bagages ont été pris. En même tems l'armée de Silésie a fait des prodiges de valeur et a enlevé à l'ennemi déjà 103 pièces d'artillerie et plus de 18,000 prisoniers. Le Prince Royal de Suède a eu pour sa part 42 canons et 6,000 à 7,000 prisoniers. — Comme vous voyez, grâce au Tout-Puissant, les choses ne vont pas mal.[c]

— Continuez, je vous supplie, à vous intéresser un peu à nous autres guerriers et soyez sûre d'avance du tribut de reconnaissance, que nous vous en portons. — A la première occasion possible, j'expédierai *le Courrier Ordinaire* pour Vienne et il passera par conséquent par Prague en allant et en revenant. — Veuillez recevoir je vous prie mes remerciemens pour le thé. Comme il me vient de vous, je ne puis me résoudre à l'envoyer en Cadeau et j'aime infiniment mieux le garder pour moi.[d]

Croyez Princesse à l'attachement bien vray que je vous ai voué pour la vie. Mille homages à la Princesse Sophie.

A.

a) As Alexander notes here, he did not send this letter to Prague, where Princess Zinaida was staying, through his "regular messenger," but by official courier. We have already observed that the issue of the delivery of the Tsar's letters to the Princess by her husband ("le courier ordinaire") comes up in several of Alexander's letters (II, VI). The identity of this "courier ordinaire" was confirmed by a footnote in A. N. Volkonsky's publication of six letters from Alexander to his mother.[40]

b) This passage in which Alexander describes the Princess' charms is interesting mainly because of its reference to his lengthy meetings with her: "The hours (sic) spent with you are a true happiness for me."

c) After the expiration of the armistice, the troops of the coalition were prepared for a new confrontation with the French. But at this point Napoleon was much less confident of victory, because Austria had now entered the war on the side of the Russians, and two of his outstanding generals, Jomini and Moreau, had defected to the enemy. On August 11/23 the armies of the coalition began to move towards Dresden. The Tsar urged an immediate attack, but was opposed by Schwarzenberg and Moreau. The postponement of the offensive later proved to be a mistake: Napoleon thus gained time to move his army to Dresden, where he was later supported by Marshal Vandamme. Two days of fighting, August 14/26 and 15/27, brought the French victory.[41] But, as Caulaincourt observed, "The victory at Dresden was the last ray of the star which lit the fortune of Napoleon." Only two days later, the exhausted French troops had to face the attack launched by the allies in Kulm, where on August 18/30 they suffered a disastrous defeat.

The list of casualties which Alexander gave to Princess Volkonskaya in this letter corresponds to the official statistics established later. The Tsar's behavior on the battlefield is noted in many sources: Alexander spent forty-eight hours in the most dangerous position, taking no rest, and being completely drenched by the continuous rain.[42] The victory at Kulm was a turning point in the war. The optimism expressed by the Tsar in the letter to Princess Volkonskaya written three days after the victory was perfectly justified. It is noteworthy that Alexander presents this victory as a tribute to the Princess' patriotism: "all your wishes have been realized."

d) A sentimental note enters even Alexander's thanks for the tea which the Princess had sent to him, apparently with the suggestion that he forward it to his family in Russia (tea was an object of luxury at that time).

Letter V

One page, folded, 18.7 x 22.4 cm. A section (4.7 x 4.9) of the second page has been cut away, thus removing from the letter the Tsar's signature and possible postscript. The envelope, 11 x 18.5 cm., addressed in Alexander's hand: "A la Princesse / Zénèide Wolchonsky." On the reverse side, in Princess Volkonskaya's hand, is added: "1813." *Unpublished.*

[n.d., n.p.]*ᵃ*
[between the end of Sept. and Oct. 4, 1813]

Le billet que je viens de recevoir de votre part Princesse, m'a bien vivement touché: la discrétion seule m'a empêché de venir prendre congé de vous hier soir et troubler le peu de moments que vous aviez à passer encore avec votre mari. Mais c'est avec empressement que je profite de ce moyen de vous exprimer combien je suis reconnaissant pour toute l'indulgence avec la quelle j'ai été reçu chez vous.

Ces moments ne s'effaceront jamais de mon souvenir.*ᵇ* Puissent vos vœux, Princesse, s'accomplir: rendre une paix stable à l'univers est mon unique ambition. Tous vos ordres seront exactement accomplis.*ᶜ* Quand à votre mari, l'amitié que je lui porte se joint encore à tout le soin que je mettrais à exécuter vos désirs.*ᵈ*

Veuillez être l'interprète de mes sentimens auprès de la Princesse Sophie. Avec quelle impatience j'attendrai le moment qui me procurera de nouveau le bonheur de vous revoir et de vous exprimer de bouche ce que ma plume rend si imparfaitement. Conservez-moi toujours un peu d'intérêt et croyez à l'assurance du dévouement respectueux que je vous porte à tout jamais.

(no signature)

a) This undated letter was mentioned in Alexander's long epistle from Leipzig of October 10, 1813 (VI). The Tsar wrote there that his preceding letter had not been sent because he had missed the courier (again — "votre homme," referring to Zinaida's husband, who had left for Prague earlier than expected.) At first he did not want to add this letter to the one he was mailing from Leipzig, since he found its mood too gloomy: "maudasse pour son contenu" (V-f). But he enclosed it nevertheless, since it contained an answer to the request made by the Princess (V-d). This enables us to establish the date of this letter as the end of September or the first days of October, certainly not later than October 4, when the battle for Leipzig had started. Most likely, it had been written by the Tsar earlier in Toeplitz, and was intended to be sent to Prague, where Princess Volkonskaya was staying at that time.[43]

b) Apparently the romance between the Tsar and Princess Zinaida was still at its peak, and their reunion, after a few weeks of separation, was entirely to Alexander's satisfaction: "Those moments will never be erased from my memory."

c) The Tsar again refers to a subject frequently mentioned in his letters to Princess Volkonskaya: her vivid interest in the course of military events. Here Alexander touches on an important issue: his determination to achieve the total defeat of Napoleon. This resolution was not, however, unanimously accepted by the Russians.[44] Since Russia itself had been freed from the invaders, many considered that the continuation of the war in Europe was not in the interest of the Russian people.

d) The Princess' husband, Nikita Volkonsky, is mentioned twice in this letter: first, as an obstacle preventing the Tsar from seeing Zinaida as often as he would like; then, in Alexander's answer to a request from the Princess, probably concerning her husband's promotion. N. G. Volkonsky, a colonel and the Tsar's aide-de-camp, was later promoted to general. After the end of the war, he was also assigned some diplomatic tasks which were neither demanding nor flattering to his ego.

Letter VI

One page, folded in two, each side 22.2 x 18.5 cm, all of them
fully used, and a single page of the same size, written only on one
side: a total of five pages, signed by Alexander. A sealed envelope,
10 x 11.7 cm, with the address: "A / Madame la / Princesse Zénèide
/ née Belosielsky / à / Rome." The envelope is slightly torn, having
probably been eagerly opened. On the reverse side, marked by the
Princess: "Leipzig, 10 October, 1813." *Published with some substantial cuts.*

Leipzig le 10 Oct[obre] 1813

C'est au milieu de nos grands mouvemens stratégiques que j'ai reçu
Princesse, votre délicieuse lettre sans datte, que votre homme m'a
apporté de Prague, mais qui ayant été remise au beau frère, selon sa
noble habitude, a trainé, au moins deux jours, dans les poches de sa
nombreuse garderobe, avant que j'aye pu l'obtenir prétextant chaque fois
que c'est dans un troisième habit qu'il l'avait fourrée, quoiqu'il en avait
déjà deux sur le corp à la fois.[a]

Avant d'aller plus loin, permetez-moi de vous faire homage d'un récit
abrégé des résultats immenses que la Providence Divine nous a fait
obtenir dans les mémorables journées de 4, 5, 6, et 7 où Napoléon en
personne après avoir réuni toutes ses forces a été complètement battu
devant Leipzig. 300 canons, 23 généraux et 37,000 prisoniers sont les
fruits des exploits immortels de nos braves Armées.[b] C'est l'Etre
Suprême *seul* qui a tout guidé et au quel nous devons ces succès écla-
tans.[c] Je ne doute pas de la part que vous y prendrez, Princesse, et je
m'empresse de vous envoyer le courier ordinaire pour Vous rassurer sur
sa bonne santé et pour lui faire obtenir *sa récompense*, car j'en ai été très
content.[d]

Venons à votre chère lettre — Elle seroit complètement délicieuse
comme je vous l'ai déjà dit, si elle n'avoit fini par un blasphème:
"*M'avez vous oublié*" dittes vous! — Une idée pareille peut-elle seulement se présenter à votre pensée, et n'est-ce pas une injustice de votre
part dont j'avais quelque droit d'être à l'abrit?[e] Mais je conviens au reste
avoir eu une apparence de tort vis à vis de vous, et voici le fait. —
Quand l'autre fois j'ai envoyé ma lettre à votre homme, il étoit déjà parti
pour aller l'équiper à Prague, de manière qu'elle m'est restée. La trou-

vant maussade pour son contenu, je n'ai pas été empressé à vous l'envoyer et je l'aurais détruite si elle ne contenait une réponse à ce que vous m'aviez demandé; je la joins ici.*f*

Recevez toute ma gratitude pour tout ce que l'ordre de la Jaretière m'a valu de si aimable, de si enchanteur de votre part. Sans m'en croire complètement digne, je partage absolument votre manière de penser sur la chevalerie et j'ai toujours préféré ces principes; si sentir avec feu tout ce qui vient de la part d'une femme belle et aimable est un des titres à cet ordre, j'ose prétendre avoir du moin celui-là. Plus que jamais veuillez me croire pour la vie tout à vous de cœur et d'âme et je dirais aussi: *Hony soit qui mal y pense.* Mille respects à la Princesse Sophie.

A.

a) This letter, too, begins with a reference to the way it was delivered. Brought from Prague by the Princess' husband ("votre homme"), Prince N. G. Volkonsky, it had later been given to his brother-in-law, General P. M. Volkonsky, a person close to the Tsar. But the two-day delay annoyed Alexander and caused his long tirade about Volkonsky's forgetfulness. The first paragraph, up to the words "permetez-moi de vous faire homage," was completely omitted in the edition by the Princess' son, A. N. Volkonsky. The reason for this does not require comment.

b) After the defeat in Kulm, Napoleon became convinced that it was not in his power to change the course of events: "There are no scientific combinations which can compensate at this point for the depletion of our ranks . . . 125,000 against 350,000!" He was justly convinced that the fate of France was to be decided on the field of Leipzig. As for the coalition, disagreements about strategy continued in Leipzig, too, but Alexander insisted this time on a unified attack. He himself was constantly in the field at the head of the army, overseeing the most dangerous positions. The battle continued for four days, October 4-7, and turned into a blood-bath. It cost both sides enormous sacrifices. The figures given in this letter by the Tsar to the Princess were not exaggerated. Metternich's statistics were even higher. The famous "Battle of the Nations" in Leipzig accomplished the final destruction of the French army. Napoleon's next step was his retreat across the Rhein.[45]

c) The Tsar's letters to Volkonskaya (Ic), like his other communications of this period, reveal his deep belief in "Divine Providence." Already in 1812, Alexander spoke of himself as "a happy accident," and instrument in the power of the Supreme Being. Now, discussing such important events as the defection of General Moreau, he said that "only God can bring us a happy outcome, not all the Moreaus in the world."[46]

d) Here is another variation on the theme of a "reward" (IIA), this time directed toward the "ordinary courier," the husband of Princess Volkonskaya. The persistence of the Tsar's references to the Princess' husband may be indicative of Alexander's jealousy. This section is, understandably, also omitted from A. N. Volkonsky's edition.

e) This emotional passage is omitted from A. N. Volkonsky's publication as well.

f) The Tsar refers to one of his preceding letters (V*a*) which was, indeed, written in a gloomy ("maudasse") mood. There, again, one can find traces of his resentment towards the unavoidable husband, N. G. Volkonsky, whose promotion the Tsar had just approved (see our note IV*d*). This part is exluded from edition of 1868.

g) On July 27, 1813, the London chapter of the Knights of the Garter awarded the Tsar its decoration. The traditional ceremony was performed about the middle of September in Toeplitz, where Sir Thomas Tyrwhitt had finally located the Tsar. This explains Alexander's reference to the order, its principles, and its motto, which had become a proverbial expression, and was actually quite suitable for the present situation.[47]

Letter VII

Two folded pages, 18.5 x 22 cm, written on six sides. The first page is marked with the number "1"; the first side of the second folded page with the number "2." The envelope is addressed in Alexander's hand: "A / la Princesse Zénèide / Wolchonsky." On the reverse side is noted in the Princess' hand: "Schafhouse, 1813." *Unpublished*.

[n.d.]
[December 30, 1813 / January 11, 1814]
Schaffhouse*a*

Depuis quelque tems Princesse, la fatalité me poursuit pour les moments où je reçois vos lettres. Cette fois-ci encore ne faut-it pas que la dernière m'arrive l'avant-veille de mon départ quand je me trouvais plus surchargé d'occupations que de coutume et où véritablement je ne pouvais disposer d'une minute.[b]

Quoique j'espère pouvoir vous présenter mes homages en personne aujourd'hui, je ne veux pas me priver cependand du plaisir de vous exprimer ma reconnaissance par ces lignes, pour votre lettre et pour les félicitations qu'elle contient. Agréez de même je vous prie, tous les vœux bien sincères que je forme pour votre constant bonheur, je pourais ajouter, que *je ne cesse de former*, car persuadez-vous, que je n'attends pas le renouvellement des années pour vous souhaiter toutes les prospérités possibles. J'espère que vous connaissez de longue date l'attachement vray et respectueux que je vous ai voué.[c]

Je suis bien enchanté d'avoir empêché que dans la chute du Rhin il ne s'en fasse deux nouvelles: celles des deux Princesses Wolkonsky que menaçoient de s'y jetter à ce que vous me dittes si leurs maris n'arriveroient. L'un est déjà là pour vous retenir par votre robe, et l'autre doutant aparement que la résolution de la Sienne soit aussi précipitée, tardera peut-être encore un jour d'arriver.[d]

Veuillez recevoir tous mes remerciemens pour la belle estampe que vous m'avez envoyée, je la conserverais comme un souvenir de vos bontés pour moi. — J'ai admiré la beauté de la gravure moins que celle du dessin et j'ai trouvé votre réflexion sur le Diable très juste. Mais je vous avouerais que j'ai été choqué du *flegme* du Père Adam dans un moment comme celui que représente le tableau. — Si au réel les choses se sont passées d'une manière aussi calme, convenez que le Papa Adam est encore plus inexcusable d'avoir enfreint la défense qui lui a été imposée.[e]

C'est à Dieu que vous avez demandé pardon de votre réflexion Princesse et c'est à vous que je demande grâce pour la mienne. — Vous me citez d'une manière charmante une fable de la Fontaine, mais en même tems vous m'avez donné la peur que mes promesses ne soyent rangées au nombre de fables.[f] Aussi vais-je faire mon possible pour vous prouver qu'elles sont des réalités et je comencerais par faire une mercuriale à Galitzin et Gourief, car c'étoit à eux à soigner l'expédition de l'oukase pour Spada. Tous s'écrivent à Pétersbourg et s'envoyent chez moi pour être signé, car ici on n'a ni le tems, ne les employés nécessaires pour les écrire.[g]

Quand à Madame Aufresne, je vais réécrire au Duc sur son compte; il faut que les premiers ordres ayent été perdus en chemin ou noyés dans le vinaigre des purifications du Prince Kourakin pour la Peste.[h] Le compte Tolstoy a reçu et expédié les ordres pour Kimmel et pour

Kamensky, dès que j'aurais reçu les éclaircissements que j'ai demandé sur sa manière de servir, si ils sont favorables, je ne tarderais pas un moment à le nommer.*[i]*

Me permetrez-vous à 6 heures après dîner de me présenter chez vous? J'attendrai avec impatience ce moment et vous présente mes homages respectueux.

A.
Schafhouse Le Dimanche matin.

a) This unpublished letter, marked only "Schafhouse. This Sunday morning," was written on Sunday, December 30, 1813/January 11, 1814, in Schaffhausen, where the Tsar had arrived from Freiburg on December 26, 1813/January 7, 1814.

b) The opening sentences of this letter introduce a tone which is completely new in Alexander's correspondence with Princess Volkonskaya: he politely attempts to excuse himself for not having answered her letters by referring to the pressing obligations which were taking up all of his time. This new attitude is in striking contrast to that of the trying days of Dresden and Leipzig when the Tsar had always found time to write long letters to the Princess. (Letters II, III, IV, VI).

c) The last of Princess Volkonskaya's letters to the Tsar apparently contained her felicitations on the approaching new year. In replying to this, Alexander assured her of his sincere and respectful (sic!) attachment, and added that he hoped she would achieve a "lasting happiness," which he had *not ceased wishing her*. In spite of this flattering tone and emphatic underlining, the whole passage reveals an obvious change in attitude. We have already observed that this letter occupies a transitional place in the correspondence between the Tsar and the Princess: it closes the first group of letters, and can be regarded as a sad coda to their romantic relationship. This, however, needs further elaboration.

Alexander's frequent meetings in Prague with Grand Duchess Ekaterina Pavlovna had apparently revived all aspects of their intimacy. The Tsar's arrival in Schaffhausen was preceded by his letters to her, in which he expressed his impatience for their next meeting ("... j'attends Schafhouse avec impatience"). Although Alexander spent only four days there, this encounter seemed to be mutually satisfying since, a few months later, the Grand Duchess used the memory of Schaffhausen to coax the Tsar to come to London: "Come! My house is waiting for you! We will have then a second Schafhouse (sic). You will find much happiness here."[48] Thus, Alexander had apparently enjoyed himself thoroughly in Schaffhausen, where he had again fallen completely under the spell of his sister, who succeeded in putting to an end his romance with Volkonskaya.

d) This letter, which seems impersonal and empty when compared to the preceding ones, contains a few pleasantries, by which Alexander tried to compensate for his embarrassment at the unspoken decision to end his relationship with Princess Volkonskaya. Referring to the crossing of the Rhein by the allied forces, the Tsar could not help reverting to his habitual ironic attitude towards the Princess' husband, this time extending it to his brother-in-law, P. M. Volkonsky. The crossing of the lower Rhein was a sore subject for the Tsar: he was outraged that the Austrians had entered Switzerland, thus breaking its neutrality and violating an agreement signed in Frankfurt.[49]

e) Influenced by her father, a knowledgable collector, Princess Volkonskaya had assembled an impressive collection of original engravings and, on occasion, generously offered them to her friends (Mme de Staël, among others). The one she had sent to Alexander for the new year was engraved in Leipzig by M. Schreyer. It represented the temptation of Adam and prompted a long and rather banal commentary from the Tsar.

f) The Princess' mention of a fable by La Fontaine was probably intended as an allusion, which the Tsar correctly perceived, to his delay in carrying out her requests. The fable in question is, most likely, ''The Fox and the Raven.''

g) One of the Princess' requests regarded *Antoine Spada* (1779-1843), a French emigrant of Portuguese origin and a former Capuchine monk who left the order after the Revolution. Spada spent several years in the services of Zinaida's father, Prince Beloselsky, as tutor, secretary, and librarian. In 1812, by that time a Russian subject, he was appointed honorary librarian of the Petersburg Public Library. In 1819, Spada moved to Odessa, where he first taught French in the Lyceum, then worked in the local library, and finally became director of the Odessa Museum of Antiquities. Among Spada's rather insignificant writings was an historical study in four volumes dedicated to Alexander I. Spada was not liked in Russia, but Princess Zinaida, who had known him since childhood, was attached to him.[50] She had asked the Tsar to have Spada appointed to the position of censor, an office which he received in 1814. However, Alexander's response to this request displays irritation which was a new note in their relationship.

h) *Madame Aufresne* — the widow of the famous Swiss-French actor whose stage name was Jean Rival (1720-1806). Acclaimed by Voltaire

("He gives my plays more ésprit than I have ever put into them.") and Goethe ("He declared war on everything that was not natural"), Aufresne was nevertheless not duly appreciated at the Comedie Française. For this reason, in 1785 he decided to accept the invitation of the Empress Catherine II and went to Russia. While in Petersburg before her marriage, Princess Zinaida had the opportunity to see Aufresne on the stage. It is possible that she took acting lessons from him or from his daughter: later in life, the Princess was admired not only as a remarkable singer, but also a good actress. Here, in this letter to the Tsar, Volkonskaya supports the request of Aufresne's widow to promote her son, who was already a state servant.

i) Prince Alexander Kurakin — (1752-1818) Vice Chancellor of the Empire. Before holding this position, he was assigned important diplomatic missions to Napoleon. Although the Tsar entrusted Kurakin with demanding assignments, he often displayed a rather ironic attitude toward him. Here he mocks the precautions Kurakin had taken ("purifying vinegar") against the plague.

j) Count Nikolay Alexandrovich Tolstoy (1761-1816) — general, *Ober Hofmeister.* Starting in 1802, when he escorted the young Tsar to Memel, Tolstoy accompanied him in all his travels. He was with Alexander during the campaign of 1812 and 1813. Toward the end of 1813, Tolstoy was forced by illness to return to Petersburg, from where he conducted his official duties.

k) Having left Schaffhausen on the morning of December 30, 1813/ January 11, 1814, Alexander probably visited Princess Volkonskaya as planned that same evening. The Tsar stayed in Basel for four days, until January 4/16, 1814, but it is not known if this was their final meeting before they parted, their romantic relationship not to be resumed.

Letter VIII

One page, folded in two, each side 11 x 18.5 cm. On the bottom of the left side, marked "Pétersbourg, le 12/24 Mai 1816." This is the only letter signed with the Tsar's full signature: "Alexandre." The paper has a watermark: "1815." The envelope, 10 x 11.5 cm, is addressed in the Tsar's hand: "A la Princesse / Zénèide Wolchonsky." On the reverse side, the same date is marked by the Princess. *Published with cuts.*

Vous êtes bien dans l'erreur de croire Princesse, que jamais je vous en aye voulu pour votre intérêt dans l'affaire de Labédoyère. — Si vous aviez peut-être tort d'y mettre cette insistance, je n'ai certainement jamais méconu le motif, et j'ai sais très bien y reconaître la sensibilité de ce cœur angélique, qui vous distingue.[a] — Aussi la manière dont je vous en ai parlé chez la Duchesse de Courlande, aurait dû vous dissuader complettement de l'idée, que je voulais vous *gronder*, comme vous l'appelez dans votre lettre.[b]

Le fait est, que si je vous en ai voulu, ce n'étoit sûrement pas pour Labédoyère, mais je vous l'avouerais sans déguisement, pour la prédilection que vous sembliez éprouver pour ce Paris avec toutes ces futilités et sa *dépravation*.[c] Une âme aussi élevée, aussi supérieure que la vôtre, me paraissait peu faite pour toutes ces frivolités, et je les croyais une chétive nouriture pour elle. L'attachement sincère que je suis accoutumé à vous vouer depuis si longtems, me fesait regretter le tems que vous perdiez ces occupations trop peu dignes à mon avis de vous intéresser. Voilà l'exposé bien franc Princesse, de mes griefs.[c]

Encore une fois, ce n'est que le sentiment d'attachement que je vous porte, qui peut les autoriser et il viendra un tems où vous sentirez, que vous aimant comme je le fais, je n'avais pas si tort peut-être, de regretter ces momens perdus pour votre bonheur réel.

Vos désirs au sujet de vos effets, seront exactement remplis et j'ai donné des ordres nécessaires à cet égard.[d] C'est avec véritable plaisir, que je verrai arriver le moment, qui vous ramènera chez nous et me donnera la possibilité de vous réitérer de vive voix, les expressions de tous les sentimens que je vous porte. Recevez en attendant mes homages respectueux.[e]

Alexander
Pétersbourg, le 12/14 mai, 1816

a) The Tsar wrote this letter to Princess Volkonskaya, then in Paris, from Petersburg, where he had returned after having spent thirty-five of the preceding thirty-eight months abroad (from October 1812 to December 1815). During the two and a half years which had elapsed since his last letter (VII), Alexander had not resumed communication with the Princess, who had remained in Europe all this time. She lived mostly in Paris, where she felt perfectly at home and had established close connections in society as well as in artistic circles.[51]

In this letter, which the Princess' son published with cuts, Alexander refers to the Princess' plea to save the life of Count Charles La Bédoyère (1786-1815). A French colonel who had served under Napoleon, La Bédoyère marched with his regiment to Grenoble to meet the Emperor when he reached the French shore after having escaped from Elba. During the "Hundred Days," La Bédoyère was promoted to the rank of general. He was the last to leave the battlefield of Waterloo. After the defeat of Napoleon, La Bédoyère was tried for treason and condemned to death. He and his young wife belonged to the French aristocracy, and many members of the old regime tried to save his life. Both the Volkonsky Princesses appealed to the Tsar, asking him to spare La Bédoyère. Alexander was obviously annoyed with the incident itself and with those who tried to intervene: he even accused Prince S. G. Volkonsky of inciting his sisters to actions which he regarded as interference in France's internal affairs.[52] But now, six months later, the Tsar showed a much more lenient attitude.

b) Alexander refers to a conversation with Volkonskaya at the Paris residence of "la Duchesse de Courlande." This meeting took place in Paris in the salon of the Duchess some time between July 21/August 2, 1815, when La Bédoyère was arrested, and September 15/27, when the Tsar left Paris for Brussels after having signed the Charter of the Holy Alliance.

Catherine Willhelmine Sagan, Duchess of Courland (1781-1839), was married first to the Russian Prince Trubetskoy, and then to the French Prince Louis Rohan. At the time of the Vienna Congress, she was preoccupied with "political amusements." It was said that Metternich was interested in having his mistress close to the Tsar, since first Princess Bagration and then the Duchess of Courland shared notoriety as Alexander's paramours. A Viennese police report quotes the Tsar as saying that he was literally "offered Duchess Sagan."[53]

c) The main idea of this letter is Alexander's disapproval of the life that Princess Zinaida was now leading abroad. It was not the social contacts of the Princess to which the Tsar objected: he considered perfectly acceptable her circle in Paris, which included Queen Hortense, Countess de Boigne, Mlle. Cochelet, and Viscount Sosthène de La Rochefoucauld. Alexander reprimanded Volkonskaya for what she valued most: her artistic contacts and especially her own appearances in private theaters.[54]

d) During her four years of travelling, Volkonskaya accumulated a large amount of luggage, including many items aquired abroad. The Tsar had apparently given orders concerning its transportation to Russia.

e) This letter did not have the desired effect. The Princess continued postponing her return to Russia. From Paris she went to Rome, then back to Paris, and returned to Russia only a year later, in April 1817.

f) In the 1868 edition, the third and fourth paragraphs, in which, after a rather harsh reprimand, the Tsar speaks of his affection for Volkonskaya and also mentions her requests, are omitted. The Princess' son also cut from the second paragraph the words: "et sa dépravation" and "je suis accoutumé."

Letter IX

One folded page, 22.5 x 19 cm, written on one and a half sides. No envelope: part of the second page is used for the address, written, as usual, in Alexander's hand: "A / Madame / la Princesse Zénèide Wolchonsky." Marked on the reverse side by Volkonskaya: "8 Octobre 1817." *Unpublished.*

Je profite du premier moment de libre que j'ai Princesse, pour vous accuser la réception de votre billet. Je serais venu tout de suite chez vous si mes occupations ne m'en eussent empêché.*[b]*

Ce soir je me trouve libre, mais je crains bien, n'en ayant pu vous prévenir plus tôt, que vous n'ayez pris quelque engagement et que vous ne puissiez plus me recevoir. Si par contre rien ne vous empêche, je suis prêt à venir chez vous aussi tôt votre réponse reçue.*[c]* Agréez en attendant mes homages respectueux.

> A
> [n.p.]*[a]* [Moscow]
> Lundi Soir
> le 8 Oct[obre] 1817

a) This brief letter, which contains no indication of the place from which it was sent, was written in Moscow. Having left Petersburg on August 25 / September 6, the Tsar arrived there after his travels in the western part of Russia at the beginning of October. We know that he reached Moscow ahead of the imperial family and the court, which joined him on October 10/22, 1817.[55]

b) The "occupations" to which Alexander was referring were connected with the festivities marking the founding of the Church of Christ the Saviour, scheduled for October 12/24, 1817. The church was to be a monument to the sacrifices and ultimate victory of the Russian people in the war of 1812. The Tsar himself supervised the design of the building, which was executed by the architect K. L. Vitberg, and also took part in planning the celebration. The whole court and diplomatic corps came to Moscow for this occasion.

c) Princess Volkonskaya also came to Moscow for this major social event. She stayed at the Beloselsky's palatial residence on the Tverskaya, where, as we see from this letter, she was expected to receive the Tsar. Apparently amicable communication was again established between them after an interruption of four years.

Letter X

Four pages of heavy paper, (22 x 18.5 cm), different from that used in previous letters, watermarked "1815." A large sheet, 22 x 18.5, folded in two. The envelope, 9.8 x 11.5 cm, addressed in the Tsar's hand: "A la Princesse / Zénèide Wolchonsky." On the reverse side, in the Princess' hand, marked "Laybach 22 Jan./3 Février 1821." *Unpublished.*

Une occasion sûre se présantant pour Rome, je la saisis avec empressement Princesse, pour vous offrir mes remerciements les plus empressés pour votre lettre du 20 Décembre.[a]

Doutter que non seulement *"quelque fois je me rappelle de vous,"* mais que je pense à vous bien souvent, serait une injustice véritable de votre part. J'ose dire que vous avez eu trop de preuves de sincère attachement que je vous porte, pour n'en pas avoir la conviction. Ainsi si cette assurance là peut ajouter le moins du monde à votre contentement, j'éprouve un plaisir réel à vous le répéter.

Comme vous le dittes, nous voilà bien près, et sans cependant que je puisse me livrer à l'espoir de vous revoir. — S'il ne tenoit qu'à moi, les Conférences de Laybach seroient transportées à Rome; mais il y a tant de choses dans ce monde, qu'on ne peut pas toujours arranger comme on les voudraient![b]

Venons à madame d'Alopéus. — Veuillez lui présenter mille respects de ma part. Combien je suis peiné de la sçavoir souffrante. — Il faut absolument qu'elle se donne tout le tems nécessaire pour soigner sa crise dans un climat chaud, et de mon côté, vous me trouverez bien empressé comme de raison, de lui en faciliter les moyens. — Celui, le plus aisé, le plus commode à mon avis serait de lui envoyer une somme d'argent évaluée, d'aprés ses besoins pour deux ans, de manière à ce qu'elle puisse écrire à son mari, qu'elle n'a plus besoin de ses secours, et qu'il peut se dispenser de lui rien envoyer, parce qu'elle se trouve pourvue du necessaire, à condition qu'il la laisse en Italie. Il me parait que c'est la manière la plus simple d'arranger la chose. — Toute autre et que exigerait des Oukases, paraîtrait extraordinaire, surtout pour une beauté comme Madame d'Alopéus. — Veuillez donc m'informer quelle est la somme dont elle aurait besoin pour ses frais pendant deux ans, et j'aurais un vray plaisir à la lui faire passer.[c]

Pour la pension de Squance, c'est une affaire plus difficile à arranger. Les règles établies s'y opposent, car pour accorder une pension, ou pour en augmenter une qui est fixée dèja, il faut nécessairement quelques services rendus. Or dans ce cas il n'y en a aucun à citer. — La friponerie de l'Oncle est un obstacle qui s'y joint, d'autant plus que dans les pièces de son procès, il y en a qui déposent, qu'il faisoit payer les sommes qu'il escamotait au Lombard, à ses parens en Italie.[d]

En finissant ces lignes, laissez-moi vous répéter encore une fois que les sentimens d'attachement respectueux que je vous ai voués, ne peuvent jamais varier. Recevez-en l'assurance bien sincère.

Alexandre
Laybach
le 3 Février / 22 Janvier 1821

a) This was the first time Princess Volkonskaya made a long stay in Rome. She came to Italy early in 1820 and remained there, with short interruptions, for almost three years, until July 1823.

b) The Congress of Laybach (January-May 1821) was a continuation of the Congress of Troppau, which had failed to resolve the urgent problems menacing the European alliance. When the Tsar arrived in Laybach he was faced at once with a wide range of disturbing events. The political situation in Spain, Italy, and Greece was far from settled, and the revolutionary movement continued to spread throughout Europe. The Tsar was still deeply affected by the October mutiny of his favorite Semyonovsky regiment, and he began to perceive the insurrections in Europe as a manifestation of the same political radicalism which had caused the French Revolution. All these events troubled Alexander greatly. No one understood the Tsar's new frame of mind better than Metternich, who also knew how to take advantage of it. "If any man ever changed directly from black to white, it is he," wrote the Austrian statesman. The Tsar "distrusts his army, his ministers, his nobility, and his people. And in such a state of mind, a man cannot lead."[56]

This is the situation which Alexander envisioned when he told Princess Volkonskaya that it would be impossible for him to come to Rome. It is significant that at this time Pope Pius VII invited Alexander to Rome. The papal Secretary of State, Cardinal Consalvi, a close friend of Princess Zinaida, considered this visit to be of great importance. However, the Tsar, who had at first accepted this invitation, later refused to come. It has been suggested that his mother, Dowager Empress Maria Fyodorovna, alarmed by his mystical tendencies and sympathetic attitude toward the Catholic Church, pleaded with him not to go to Rome.[57]

c) Madame Alopeus: *Jannette Alopeus, née Wenckstern* (?-1869) was the wife of David Maksimovich Alopeus (1769-1831). Alopeus was a noted Russian diplomat with a German military background whose positions included ambassadorships in Sweden, Berlin, Naples, and Wuertemberg. His young wife, a celebrated beauty, had a great many admirers, ranging from Tsar Alexander to his political adversary Nikolay Turgenev.[58] Court gossip hinted that the Tsar was at one time not indifferent to Countess Alopeus' charms; some sources indicated that their relations were even closer. There was also a rumor that Madame Alopeus played a role in Alexander's rupture with Naryshkina.[59] Perhaps for this reason the Tsar was reluctant to grant her an official pension. In 1835, Madame Alopeus, widowed for three years, married Pavel P. Lopukhin (1790-1878).

d) *Squancy* (sometimes spelled by the Russians as Scassi or Sassi) — an Italian married to a Russian. Squancy lived and served for many years in Petersburg reaching the rank of court counsellor. His financial situation was, however, unstable, and he was affected by some shady dealings to which the Tsar referred. In 1818-1819, Squancy went with his family to Florence where the society treated him as a "russified Italian." When he returned to Russia, Volkonskaya tried to use her influence with the Tsar to secure a better pension for Squancy. In 1824, while serving in the Caucasus, Squancy got involved in some financial fraud for which General Ermolov called him an Italian charlatan. This indicates that the Tsar was right in his evaluation of Zinaida's protegé.[60]

Letter XI

One piece of yellowed paper, folded in two, each side 19 x 22.5 cm. The envelope with the address in Alexander's hand: A la princesse Zénèide / Wolchonsky.'' On the reverse side, marked by the Princess: ''Brixen 13/25 Dec. 1822.'' *Unpublished.*

Vous m'avez envoyé tant de papiers avec votre dernière lettre, qu'il est juste qu'à mon tour, j'use du même droit.[a] Voici donc une incluse, que je vous prie de remettre à Madame Narishkin en réponse à sa lettre, en lui disant mille choses de ma part.[b]

Pour vos papiers Madame, souffrez que je vous en parle, par une autre occasion n'ayant pas une minute à moi.[c]

Recevez l'assurance de l'attachement sincère que je vous porte.[d] Mille respects à la Princesse Sophie et à Aline.

Brixen 13/25, Décembre 1822

a) Evidently the Princess had sent the Tsar several papers needed as documentation for the cases she was presenting to his attention. It is difficult to state with certainty the exact nature of her requests. We know, however, of several examples of Volkonskaya's intercession on behalf of friends and acquaintances. One such instance involved the dismissal of her close friend, Prince P. A. Vyazemsky, who had been accused of both unacceptable political views and frivolous personal behavior.[61] Another request may have been made on the behalf of her step-mother, Princess A. G. Beloselskaya, who was involved in litigation concerning her property, Krestovy Ostrov. It is also known that Volkonskaya asked the Tsar to rectify the injustice suffered by the cook Silik, a Crimean Tatar, and to return him from Siberian exile.[62]

b) Alexander's complete break with his mistress, M. A. Naryshkina, had long been a well-known fact. Hence, he did not hesitate to ask Volkonskaya to deliver some papers to Naryshkina, whom he occasionally contacted with regard to the arrangement of the estate of their daughter, Sofia. As early as 1818 Alexander said that he could now only remain a complete stranger ''to this person, after all that she had done to me.'' Four years later, his attitude towards his former mistress became so hostile that he avoided all personal contact with her.[63]

c) As for Princess Volkonskaya, she obviously annoyed the Tsar by sending "so many papers." This is seen from the above sentence, containing the formal "Madame" which Alexander used whenever irritated. That Alexander was busy and had no time at his disposal was true. After the end of the Congress in Verona, which he later referred to as "those fatal days in Verona," the Tsar was both unhappy and disappointed. There again Metternich and Wellington had appeared as the central figures. Chateaubriand later quoted Alexander's solemn words aimed at justifying his policy in general and his actions towards Greece in particular: "Providence has not put 800,000 soldiers at my disposal to satisfy my ambitions, but to protect religion, morality, and justice."[64]

d) The Tsar became increasingly distrustful of people and more unstable in his behavior, allowing himself to be discourteous and to show anger.[65] At the same time he spent hours kneeling in prayer. We see that this emotional state comes through in his short letter to Princess Volkonskaya from Brixen, where he arrived from Venice on December 11/23, 1822. The present letter was written on the day after the celebration of Alexander's forty-fifth birthday. On the following day, December 14/26, he left Brixen for Bavaria, and then continued on to Russia, arriving on January 20/February 1, 1823. Thus ended his final trip to Western Europe.

Letter XII

Two sheets of yellowed paper, 18.5 x 22 cm., folded in half; written on six of eight pages. No envelope: the letter is placed in a folded sheet of paper, sealed. The address is written in the Tsar's hand: A / Madame la Princesse / Zénèide Wolchonsky. *Unpublished*

C'est le Prince Pièrre que je charge de ces lignes pour vous, Madame.[a] Je vous dois depuis bien longtems une réponse, et si vous m'imputez mon silence comme un tort vis à vis de vous, je viens vous demander de l'indulgence, ou plutôt mon absolution. Les circonstances sont plus coupables que moi.[b] Votre première lettre où vous me parliez de vos désirs, pour que votre mari fût attaché à la Cour, n'a plus trouvé le Prince Pièrre ici et m'est parvenue au moment où je me mettais en route pour faire mon dernier voyage.[c] Le tems me manquait pour vous répondre. Une seconde, m'est parvenue pendant mon voyage et la troisième pendant ma maladie qui m'a fait passer une grande partie de l'hyver couché.*d* Plus tard, je vous croyais en route pour revenir en Russie.*e* Enfin, voici une bonne occasion pour vous adresser quelques lignes et vous dire, que j'ai été bien sensible à tout ce que vos lettres contiennent d'amical pour moi. Croyez que je vous le rends bien par une affection sincère et qui n'a jamais varié. Ainsi, les appréhensions que vous avez paru avoir un moment, que j'avais quelque chose contre vous, sont plus qu'injustes et vous pouvez compter à tout jamais sur les sentimens que je vous ai voué.*f* Aussi c'est avec une véritable impatiance, que j'attends le moment où je pourais vous revoir.

Quand à votre demande pour votre mari, de la manière dont vous l'entendiez, elle n'étoit pas éxécutable et se trouvoit en opposition des usages reçus ici. Nous en parlerons au reste, quand nous nous retrouverons ensemble.*h* En attendant, veuillez me concerver Souvenir et bons sentimens et recevez l'assurance réitérée de tout l'attachement que je vous porte.

A
Zarscoye Celo [Carskoye Selo]
8 Juin
1824

a) The Tsar had asked Prince P. M. Volkonsky, Zinaida's brother-in-law, to deliver this letter to her as soon as she returned to Russia. Since the exact date of the Princess' arrival in Petersburg is not known, we are giving its tentative date as the beginning of July, 1824. It became known in Petersburg's inner circles that a letter from the Tsar was waiting for Volkonskaya there.[66]

b) The circumstances which the Tsar mentions here were grave, indeed, to occupy his time and attention. In early 1824, Alexander had become completely dominated by Arakcheev. Impressed by his success in the bloodless creation of military colonies, he began to follow Arakcheev's advice almost blindly. This soon resulted in a dramatic reshuffling of the government. The spring of 1824 brought the dismissal of two of Alexander's close friends who had occupied the highest positions in the Russian bureaucracy. Prince A. N. Golitsyn was degraded to the office of head of the postal ministry. As for Prince P. M. Volkonsky, the Tsar's decision was even more unexpected and arbitrary. While the Prince was abroad, Alexander had the weakness to accept Arakcheev's request to appoint General Dibich as chief of state. Then, when Volkonsky returned, he found his position taken and the Russian Tsar completely under the influence of Arakcheev. However, Alexander did not remain indifferent to the rupture with his closest friends and to the dismissal of many deserving and faithful state servants. He became even more withdrawn, and was overcome by deep depression.

It is hard to say what concerned Prince P. M. Volkonsky more: the injustice he himself had suffered, or the pitiful condition of the Tsar, whom he had served for twenty-seven years. For whatever reason, he forgot his pride and accepted "le portefeuille de la court," a humiliating position which put him in charge of the court staff, kitchen, stable, etc.[67]

c) Alexander refers here to his last trip, which had taken place in 1823, from August 16 to November 3. During these ten weeks, the Tsar attended maneuvers and inspected military units of the Russian army from Brest to Orel. He also had meetings with the Austrian Emperor Franz and the German Prince Wilhelm. "Prince Pierre" is P. M. Volkonsky (see above).

d) In the very beginning of 1824 the Tsar fell dangerously ill. Struck down by a horse, he suffered from complications from an injury to his leg. Moreover, on January 6 he caught a severe cold, which developed into a bad case of pneumonia. This, combined with a state of depression and a general lassitude, made his condition serious. Confined to bed for two months, he gradually began to recover only toward the middle of March.

e) The Princess kept postponing her return to Russia, which she had left in September 1819. Three weeks after this letter to her from the Tsar, who was expecting her to arrive soon, she was reported still to be in Europe.

f) The estrangement to which Volkonskaya was obviously referring in her letter is undeniable, although Alexander tried to convince the Princess of his unfailing devotion. A gradual rapprochement began after 1819, when the Tsar's letters became warmer and more personal.

g) Prince Nikita G. Volkonsky, Zinaida's husband, had not received a civilian appointment after the war. He was given occasional commissions, some of which were beneath his rank and position in society. Although the Princess knew that Alexander, for whatever reason, disliked her husband, she requested that he arrange a suitable position for him. We know that the Tsar kept his promise: one and a half years later, the widowed Empress Elizabeth wrote to her mother in Baden that among those who followed the Tsar to Taganrog was Prince Nikita Volkonsky, whose present rank was "not an aide-de-camp, but a general of the suite."[68]

Letter XIII

One folded page, 19 x 22 cm. No envelope: on the reverse side of the folded page is written: "A / Madame la Prin[cesse] Zénèide Wolchons[ky]." The letter is sealed with the Tsar's seal. In different hand, noted "sans date.' *Unpublished.*

[n.p., n.d.]*a*
[Moscow, between July and August 16, 1824]

Me permetrez-vous de venir vous offrir Madame, mes félicitations et mes meilleurs remerciemens pour votre envoy de hier, cet aprés díner à 5 heures?*b* Recevez en attendant mes homages respectueux.

A
Mercredi, matin

a) This note, containing neither the date nor the place from which it was sent, offers no clues for a precise dating. We accept Prince A. N. Volkonsky's placing it after the letter written in Brixen on December 13/15, 1822 (XI). Knowing that Princess Volkonskaya returned to Russia only at the beginning of July 1824 (and the Tsar did not go abroad after January 1823), we can assert that the note was written after this date. We also know, however, that Alexander's letter of June 8, 1824 was his first communication with the Princess upon her return to Russia (Letter XII). This allows us to determine that this note had been written in Petersburg and to narrow its dating to the time between July and November 1824, when Volkonskaya moved from Petersburg to Moscow. But since the Tsar left Petersburg on August 16 for a long trip to the central and eastern parts of Russia, from which he returned only on October 24, we can further narrow the dating of this letter to a period of six weeks: four weeks in July and two in August.

b) Alexander's congratulations most probably refer to the publication of Volkonskaya's prose work which appeared in Paris in May 1824 under the title *Tableau slave*, in Russian translation. We can assume that he was thanking her for sending him a copy of this book.[69]

Letter XIV

One folded page, 22 x 18.5 cm. Written on both sides. On the envelope: "A la / Princess Zénèide Wolchonsky." On the reverse side, noted in the Princess' hand: "Sans date." *Unpublished.*

[n.d.]*[a]*
[St. Petersburg, between July and August 16, 1824]

Je suis à vos pieds Princesse, pour le si aimable billet que je viens de recevoir à l'instant. Le bonheur de vous revoir est trop grand pour qu'aucun autre sentiment puisse être écouté et j'implore le permission dans le courant de la soirée de me présenter chez vous. Je m'en fais une vraye fête. Je garde le silence sur tout le reste de votre billet non que vous m'ayez convaincu, il s'en faut de beaucoup, mais pour terminer un sujet qui vous donne occasion, de me traiter beaucoup trop favorablement.*[b]*

Les beaux fruits que je tiens de votre inapréciable bonté, ont été reçus avec la plus vive reconnaissance. — Recevez je vous prie l'homage de mon respectueux attachement.

(no signature)

a) This undated letter follows the preceding note (XIII). We believe that it was also written in Petersburg in the same period as the previous two letters (XII, XIII).

b) The letter is written in a warm, affectionate tone, reminiscent of Alexander's earlier epistles. At this time, the Tsar was becoming increasingly isolated from his surroundings and estranged from even his closest friends. Free of any romantic attachments, and, apparently, of any desire to have them, he appreciated his relationship with the Princess, whom he valued as a faithful and trustworthy friend. It can also be assumed that he was now impressed with the new maturity of Volkonskaya, who had developed into a striking personality during the last ten years.

c) After the illness he suffered in the winter of 1824, the Tsar continued to follow a strict diet, which consisted mainly of fruit. This explains why Princess Volkonskaya had sent him the fruit for which he thanked her in this letter.

Letter XV

One page, 22 x 19 cm., folded in two; written on four sides. *Published*, with cuts.

Il faut l'inépuisable indulgence que vous m'avez toujours témoignée pour me traiter comme vous avez la bonté de le faire, car vous auriez droit de me croire et ingrat et insensible; et cependant je suis ni l'un ni l'autre. L'imense besogne qui pèse sur moi et qui absorbe tous mes momens, me fait paraître tel. [a] Mais il faut que je vous dise avant tout que la joye de vous voir si près, de vous savoir dans quelques heures est extrême. C'est entre quatre et cinq que je me présenterais à votre porte avec l'impatience la plus vive de vous exprimer combien je suis touché de la manière amicale dont vous me traitez malgré mes torts.[b] Ayant si peu des momens à moi, je ne voulais prendre la plume que pour vous annoncer en même tems que j'ai réussi à arranger ce que vous m'aviez demandé. Cela a trainé parce qu'il y a plus d'une difficulté à vaincre pour y parvenir.[c]

Au revoir donc et recevez en même tems l'assurance du sincère et respectueux attachement que je vous porte à tout jamais.

A.
Zarskoye Célo [Carskoe Selo]
le 2 Avril
1825

a) With every year the "enormous burden" of which he complains in this letter, weighed more heavily on the Tsar's shoulders. The year 1825 did not bring any relief from the pressure of the complex issues with which Alexander was now unable to cope. In the Near East, Turkey's behavior was calling for more resolute action. In Russia itself, the new order established by Arakcheev was evoking a strong opposition. Alexander was aware of the discontent in his country. He knew of the plot which involved many of his trusted officers who had taken part in the victorious war, but he refused to crush the movement, which was aimed at putting an end to his reign.[70]

His personal life was far from happy. The death of his illegitimate daughter, Sofia Naryshkina, in July 1824, still affected him deeply. As his former mistress, M. A. Naryshkina, observed, his last years were poisoned by dark moods and suspicion. He trusted no one and even began to fear for his personal safety. This may suggest why Alexander came to cherish the few people, among them Princess Volkonskaya, whose devotion and sincerity were beyond doubt.

b) This letter was written on Easter. Two days later, on April 4, the Tsar left Petersburg for his last trip to Poland. The timing of this letter is revealing: that Alexander managed to visit the Princess amidst preparations for a long journey, and especially on a holiday, as important for both family and state celebrations, is indicative of his attitude to Volkonskaya.

The three words "malgré mes torts" were omitted from the text published by the Princess' son.

c) Here the Tsar writes that he was finally able to fulfill the Princess' request, most likely the promotion of Prince N. G. Volkonsky to the rank of General.

This was Princess Volkonskaya's first visit to Petersburg since she had moved to Moscow in the fall of 1824. As always, she stayed at the palatial residence of her stepmother, Princess A. G. Beloselskaya. It was there that she received Tsar Alexander on April 2, 1825. This was to be their last meeting. The affectionate tone of Alexander's letter shows a new warmth in this old friendship. With the infatuation and intimacy of the early years over, the Tsar established a relaxed, friendly relationship with Princess Zinaida. He was aware of his part in the rupture of their early relations and of his indifferent attitude of recent years.

This letter marks the end of the correspondence between Princess Zinaida Volkonskaya and Tsar Alexander I. The thirteen years covered by these letters represent an extremely important period of political and cultural change in both Russia and Europe. Many significant events of this era are reflected here. Many historical figures are discussed. The participants of this dialogue, only one voice of which has been presented, were fascinating figures who have not lost their interest to the present day.

NOTES ABOUT ALEXANDER'S FRENCH WRITING

In publishing the letters of Alexander I, we follow our principle of presenting the manuscripts in their original form without any editing. However, the Tsar's written French requires at least a brief commentary. A pupil of La Harpe, he followed rather inconsistently the rules of French grammar, which were undergoing substantial changes introduced by the Academy (1740, 1762, 1798) and by the grammarians of the Enlightenment Age. Although Alexander spoke correct and elegant French, his writing was characterized by inconsistant usage of both old and new grammatical rules.

a) An almost obsolete for that time -oit ending for the past: *avoit, paroit, rassuroit,* etc.

b) Deletion in the plural of consonants which are not pronounced (accepted by the Academy after 1740, but opposed by the language reformers): *tems, longtems, parens, sentimens, momens,* etc.

c) Omission of the second intervocalic consonant in accordance with the rules accepted earlier (Duclos, Girard): *comencer, coment, prisonier, homage, courier, aparement, friponerie,* etc. There occur, however, some vacillations: *dites/dittes, jeter/jetter, complètement/complèttement.* Some words, such as *homme, approcher, affabilité,* among others, are spelled as required with double consonants.

d) There is an occasional substitution of the final -t by -d: *cependend, attendand, quand,* etc.

e) A tendency to use -a- with the nasal -n- as recommended by Wailly, but not generally accepted: *conférance, impatiance,* etc.

f) Etymologically motivated usage of two words which later will be contracted into one unit: *aussi tôt, plus tôt, la quelle, chaque un, de hier,* etc.

g) Certain spelling principles were at that time accepted by some grammarians but rejected by others, thus creating confusion, like *concerver, passacent* (accepted by Wailly), *abrit* (accepted by Beauzée) and the obsolete forms such as *sçavoir, vray, j'aye, hyver.*

h) There are cases of simplification of vowel combinations as in *malheuresement, remerciment* which the Tsar uses along with the forms *malheureusement, remerciement.*

i) There is a tendency to interchange the future tense and conditional mood: *verrai-verrais; j'aurai-j'aurais; commencerai-commencerais,* etc.

j) The inconsistent capitalization of the days of the week and the names of the months.

Although the letters were neatly written (the Tsar never used the same pen twice), the sentences are not always well constructed. Here, however, the haste in which Alexander wrote his long epistles has to be considered.

We will conclude our observations by noting how Alexander's mentor, La Harpe, evaluated his pupil's written French in 1789: "The Grand Duc Alexander," he wrote, "can take a dictation rather fast and write it with ease. The mistakes he makes occur because French words are not spelled as pronounced."

As we see, this manifested itself twenty-five years later in the Tsar's letters to Princess Volkonskaya.

SEVEN LETTERS FROM CARDINAL ERCOLE CONSALVI
TO PRINCESS Z. A. VOLKONSKAYA

"It was a moral power that had to be taken under consideration in Europe."[1]

"The siren of Rome." (Napoleon)[2]

The Volkonskaya Archive contains seven previously unpublished letters written by Cardinal Ercole Consalvi to the Princess between 1815-1823. What did the Vatican's Secretary of State, who excercised such an important influence on the course of events in his time, have in common with the Russian Princess Zinaida Volkonskaya? What prompted the Cardinal to write long letters to her in which he expressed admiration and devotion? When and where did they first meet? Before turning to these letters one must take a broad look at the background of their relationship.

Cardinal Consalvi's and Princess Volkonskaya's paths did not cross until 1814, when they were both in London. On his way to England, Consalvi stopped in Paris on June 2, one day after the Princess had left for London. Hence, they could not possibly have met there. On June 4, the Cardinal proceeded to England where he stayed for twenty-six days promoting the interests of the Papal state.[3] From his first day in London, he sought an audience with the Russian Tsar Alexander, to whom he was to deliver a message from Pope Pius VII. This was not an easy task, however, since at that time all the European rulers were assembled in London, discussing and celebrating the recent victory over Napoleon. Consalvi was finally received by Alexander just before the Tsar's departure from England. Meanwhile, true to his usual strategy, the Cardinal immersed himself in London's social life, knowing that this would help him establish the needed political connections. As the first cardinal to visit England in two hundred years, Consalvi succeeded in overcoming the traditionally hostile English attitude towards the Vatican. Thus, the Prince-Regent of Great Britain had every reason to call him "the cardinal-seducer." London society was taken not only by his charm and intelligence, but also by the dramatic appearance of the handsome Cardinal attired in black silk and red stockings.[4]

Although we do not have direct documentation, we believe that Consalvi met Volkonskaya in London. In pursuit of an audience with the Tsar, the Cardinal was obliged to approach Prince Pyotr Volkonsky, and was most likely invited to his residence where the Prince's sister-in-law

Zinaida was also staying. It is understandable that Consalvi would seek contact with Prince Volkonsky and his sister-in-law, as both were close to the Tsar. Still another link between them was Madame de Boigne, a good friend of the Cardinal and the Volkonskys.[5] This leads us to the near certainty that Cardinal Consalvi became acquainted with Princess Zinaida Volkonskaya in London. They resumed this relationship six months later in Austria during the Vienna congress.

Consalvi was one of the first to arrive in Vienne, on September 2nd, 1814. He wanted to prepare the groundwork for the difficult task of restoring the Vatican as a state, as well as for several other, more marginal, but still important issues. To resolve these questions the Cardinal had to face the four leading powers: Russia, Austria, Prussia, and England. The agreement that was finally reached was discussed in detail in his long letter of June 12, 1815, to Cardinal Pacca.[6] The ten months in Vienna were filled by a well-planned strategy intended to establish closer political ties. This ranged from offical negotiations to attendance of dinners, receptions, balls, concerts and theaters. To secure his position with the Russians, the Cardinal tried to win over the Tsar's inner circle. His meetings with Razumovsky, Nesselrode, Stackelberg and Italinsky were followed since the agents of Vienna's secret police were assigned to record the Cardinal's comings and goings. Because he was opposed by Metternich, however, Consalvi was not invited to attend the regular meetings of the Congress.[7]

On November 3, 1814, Consalvi was received by the Tsar. The Cardinal repeated his invitation to Rome, first extended in London, which was this time accepted by Alexander. Nothing had been resolved, however; the eleven-point program of Russia's demands still had to be answered.[8]

On September 3, 1814, Consalvi attended a reception at Count Razumovsky's, at which Princess Volkonskaya was singing. The Cardinal, himself an amateur musician, could not have remained indifferent to the performance of the Princess, who was an accomplished singer. We find a record of this evening in the diary of the ambassador from Piedmont, Marchese di San Mazzano: "Cardinal Consalvi came to see me, Castelafar dined with us ... After dinner, we went to Rasumowsky; Princess Wolkonki (sic!) was singing."[9]

During this time Consalvi had also visited Prince de Ligne, whose modest house in Moelkerbastei attracted people of intellect and wit. Princess Volkonskaya, who was close to Prince de Ligne, an old friend of her late father, was a frequent guest at his home. We can assume that besides the recorded meeting at the Razumovskys' and probably numerous unrecorded encounters at social events, Zinaida would meet Consalvi in Prince de Ligne's salon as well.[10]

The Cardinal left Vienna on June 18, 1815, after having spent more than ten months there — too long to sustain his glory, as one Austrian diplomat commented, but he accomplished many tasks while there.[11] Back in Rome, the Cardinal immersed himself in state affairs, and Russia continued to occupy an important place in his busy schedule. Now he had to confront the Tsar on the fundamental issue of authority to appoint Catholic clergy: the system used in Russia and its provinces "contradicted the very principles of the Catholic church." The Cardinal was assigned a key role in the long unresolved dialogue between Pius VII and the Tsar, since the Pope "saw everything through the eyes of Consalvi."[12]

The Cardinal's diplomacy at this time was as skillful as ever. He established close ties with Russian diplomatic and social circles in Rome, and continued to attempt to influence Alexander's attitude towards the Vatican. In 1822, he nearly succeeded in receiving the Tsar in Rome: Alexander first accepted the invitation of the Pope, but later declined it. There were rumors that Dowager Queen Maria Fyodorovna, afraid that her mystically-inclined son would be attracted by the Catholic Church, insisted that he stay away from Rome.[13] The Tsar's letter to Zinaida Volkonskaya of February 3, 1821, in our archive, indicated that she, in her turn, had attempted to convince him to visit Rome.

The issue of Roman Catholicism in Russia continued to be of constant concern for Consalvi, even during the last year of his life when the new Pope removed him from the position of Secretary of State. Among the last recommendations, he left to Pope Leon XII, was the suggestion that he follow a firm policy toward Russia, a policy built on circumspection which does not flag for a single day.[14]

All seven letters from Cardinal Consalvi were written during the Princess' stay abroad, covering exactly the three-year period from October 10, 1820 to October 10, 1823. We have already suggested that Consalvi's interest in Volkonskaya was influenced, at least initially, by the importance of Russia and its leaders to the Vatican. The Cardinal's biographer, Crétineau-Joly, gave enlightening commentary on Consalvi's attitude toward the important foreigners. The Cardinal offered truly royal hospitality in his splendid villas ". . . to diplomats, writers, foreigners who could be useful to the Papal state with their official as well as private relations . . . They found in him a tireless guide, an advisor, a courtisan who knew well how to charm them . . . His presence induced an atmosphere of a perpetual festivity and embellished all monuments and ruins . . . ''[15]

Princess Volkonskaya, with all her political and social connections, including the Russian Tsar, was certainly worthy of his attention. Her beauty, talents, and intelligence should also be taken into consideration. Were one to search for another motive, the financial interests of the Papal state could be ascribed a certain role as well. A contemporary of the Cardinal, Massimo D'Azeglio, speaks of his tactic of "attracting foreigners, or rather their money."[16] We know that Volkonskaya later gave her large fortune to the Vatican, but we are reluctant to accept this motive as the decisive factor. Undoubtedly, one of Consalvi's primary goals was the conversion of the Russian Orthodox to Roman Catholicism. Although this issue never arises in his letters to the Princess, it must have been important to the Cardinal: the influential Princess was a most desirable subject for conversion. During the last two decades many Russians had been converted to the Catholic faith, and fifteen years later, so was Zinaida Volkonskaya. The affairs and inspirations of the Russian Catholics were discussed in unpublished correspondence between Consalvi and Italinsky, the Russian ambassador to the Papal state, with whom the Cardinal was on friendly terms.[17]

It is interesting to note how other contemporaries of the Cardinal evaluated him as a man. Some saw in him "a person who was half clergyman and half man of society." This opinion was contradicted, however, by no less a figure than Napoleon, who observed: "He is a person who does not like to be taken for a clergyman, but he is indeed one, and more so than all the others."[18] Apparently this complexity was everpresent and had created the whole man: Consalvi the Cardinal and Consalvi the Secretary of State. That Consalvi was an aristocrat brought up in the best traditions of eighteenth-century Italy may account for his characteristic ease in relationships with beautiful, intelligent, and socially prominent women. The closest to him was Duchess Devonshire, who, having "all of Rome" at her disposal, preferred to them all Consalvi, her faithful friend of twenty-four years.[19] Countess Albany, Madame de Boigne, and Zinaida Volkonskaya were among his close friends. It is only his relationship with the Russian princess, however, that has passed unobserved. To fill this gap, the seven letters which Consalvi wrote to Volkonskaya prove particularly important.

The question arises of how Consalvi's personality came through in his letters to Volkonskaya. Although he discusses the important events of the time, his letters are far from either sparkling with wit or being distinguished by profound ideas. It has to be taken into account that Consalvi was writing not in his native Italian, but in French, which he knew only fairly well. His written French speaks for itself: it has occasional misspellings, awkward syntax, and an unexacting style. As for his spoken French, which he had plenty of opportunity to use, it was of rather modest quality as well. One of his frequent interlocutors, Lulu von Thürnheim, observes that the intelligent ("geistreich") Cardinal was hindered in expresseing his ideas by his imprecise, clumsy, and sometimes stuttering French.[20] In contradiction to this opinion, Madame de Boigne praised the lucidity of Consalvi's discourses, which she believed were unimpaired by his French.[21] Cardinal Consalvi's intelligence and achievements were admired by many, though there were some critical voices as well. The most prominent of them was that of Stendhal.[22] One of Consalvi's contemporaries, the afore-mentioned D'Azeglio, may have been right in saying: "Though Consalvi had great talents, his was not one of those splendid intellects that can embrace the past and the present at a glance, and link the future harmoniously with them."[23] Whether or not Cardinal Consalvi was a person of broad vision and original thought, he was indisputably one of the important men of his time and he still fascinates those studying Roman Catholicism.

At this point there arises the question of what attraction Princess Volkonskaya found in her contact and later friendship with Cardinal Consalvi.

The years 1814-1823 had not been easy ones for the Princess. Although she had developed intellectually and artistically during this period, her personal life had been far from happy. It suffices to outline some of the events. The beginning of 1814 brought an end to her romance with the Tsar. In 1814, while in Vienna, she lost a newborn child. The following few years only deepened the estrangement from her insignificant husband, Prince Nikita. To compensate for the unfulfilled expectations of her inner life, she chose to travel from one European capital to another, immersing herself in their social life and occasionally appearing on private stages as a singer and sometimes as an actress.[24] Having returned to Russia in 1817, she preoccupied herself for a while with the education of her son Alexander. At the same time, she became romantically involved with her secretary, a handsome Italian, Signor Barbieri, who, in 1819, accompanied the Princess on her trip abroad. While in Rome for three years (1820-1823), she became active in local musical life, participating in the concerts of the Roman Philharmonic Society.[25] On the surface, the Princess' life was quite exciting, but it can be seen in retrospect how unhappy she actually was during that time. This became particularly evident from the letters of Archimandrite

Pavsky written a few years later in Moscow. His response to a letter of Zinaida's makes it clear that she had been in a state of depression, overcome by a fear of death and punishment for her sins.[26] Volkonskaya did not find in Russian Orthodoxy the answers to the questions which tormented her. And when we read the stern, ponderous reprimand of the Russian priest, we can easily understand how comforting the spiritual support of Cardinal Consalvi was and how congenial his love and understanding of art and music must have been for the Princess. Yet another attraction was the beauty of the Roman Catholic Church as the focal point for all the arts: music, painting, and architecture.

Cardinal Consalvi had brought the Catholic Church close to Volkonskaya, he made it comforting and accessible. His letters show how well the Cardinal knew both the art of making himself needed and ways of attracting those whom he wanted to charm. In 1823, concerned with state affairs and bed-ridden, the Cardinal writes to Volkonskaya about the sorrow caused by her departure. In a lengthy passage he asked her to regard him as her representative in Rome: "This would be a remedy for me during your absence, which is so painful for me." Two months later, after the death of the Pope, Consalvi, still ill and grieving, removed from his post as Secretary of State, writes a long and affectionate letter to the Princess, assuring her:

Always count me among your most faithful, most devoted friends; I am now, and always will be one. Dispose of me as you would of a thing which you possess totally.[27]

Consalvi, "the seducer," thus certainly played a decisive role in putting Volkonskaya on the road to conversion. As in many other instances, the letters of Princess Volkonskaya could not be located in the archive of Cardinal Ercole Consalvi.[28]

Letter I

One sheet of yellowed paper, 18.5 x 24.5 cm. *Unpublished.*
All seven letters of cardinal Consalvi are written on paper with the watermark 'Briglia.' No envelopes are preserved. The letters are signed and dated at the end.

Madame la Princesse,

Ayant attendu en vain qu'on vienne chercher de la part de Votre Excellence le billet pour la libre extraction de la douhana (sic) des effets lui appartenant, je prends le parti de la lui transmettre.*a* Je prie Votre Excellence de croire que je m'estimerai heureux dans toutes les occasions où je pourrai m'employer à la servir et je la prie aussi d'agréer que je lui souhaite l'assurance de ma considération la plus distinguée, avec laquelle j'ai l'honneur d'être.*b*

> De Votre Excellence
> Le très devoué et très obèissant serviteur
> Card[inal] Consalvi
> Rome, ce 10 Octobre, 1820

a) Cardinal Consalvi speaks here of the arrangement he made to clear Volkonskaya's luggage from customs. Since she had been in Italy already for more than nine months, having left Russia in the fall of 1819, it is most likely that this concerns the heavy baggage which was sent to her from Russia. From the letter of Stendhal, we know that Volkonskaya left Milan for Naples on March 3, 1820.[29] After approximately two months in Naples, the Princess moved to Rome where she stayed for almost three years, until July 1823.

b) The parting formula in this first letter from Consalvi to Princess Zinaida, exemplifying the epistolary style of the time, is much more formal and distant compared with those of his later communications.

Letter II

Four pages, 19.5 x 26 cm., written on one side. *Unpublished.*

Madame la Princesse,

Je ne manquerai pas Mardi de profiter de votre gracieuse invitation pour entendre chanter et voir jouer l'incomparable [Curioni] qui devrait bien être le vainqueur pour ne pas nous priver de le voir et de l'entendre jusqu'à la dernière scène de la pièce.*a* Je ne sais pas si Mardi l'Ambass[adeur] d'Autriche reçoit. Si cela était, il me faudrait seulement retrouver à la fin de [la soirée] une petite heure pour y paraître.[b]

Je n'ai pas bien compris ce que vous m'avez dit de M. Gentz,[c] mais M. le Comte Barberi[d] me l'expliquera demain s'il vient avec M. Priest[e] ainsi que vous me l'annonciez.

Agréez, Mad[ame] la Princesse, l'assurance des sentiments que vous connaissez au plus dévoué de vos serviteurs et admirateurs.

> Le Card[inal] Consalvi
> ce 19 Janvier [1821][f]

a) Alberico Curioni (1785-1875) — a famous Italian tenor reputed to be a good actor as well. Curioni was a soloist in the San Carlo Opera in Naples, but also appeared in all the major opera houses of Europe. Stendhal remarked that Curioni was the most handsome singer of the Italian stage, and "this never comes amiss in a singer."[30] The opera in question was probably Beethoven's *Fidelio*, first produced in Vienna in 1805, then staged in its final form in 1815, and performed in 1820 as a tribute to the Austrians then in Rome. Consalvi refers to Florestan's victory over his enemy: saved from execution, he sings in the last scene of the opera.

b) The Austrian military and political presence in Rome was strongly felt at this time. The memoires of this period record frequent receptions, galas, and balls held at the Austrian embassy.[31] On October 1820, at the Congress in Troppau, the Emperors of Russia and Austria, together with the Prince Royal of Prussia, had discussed the situation in Naples, and Austria was given a key position in the area. This explains the importance Cardinal Consalvi puts to his appearance at the reception of the Austrian ambassador, Count Apponyi.

c) Friedrich von Gentz (1764-1832) — an important statesman and political writer.[32] Von Gentz was Metternich's right hand and participated actively in the Vienna Congress, of which he was the secretary general. His contemporaries called him "Secretary of Europe," since he took part in all the important congresses of his time. When Rome became a center of political activity for Austria, von Gentz appeared there and played an important role in the complex handling of the revolution in Naples, and the reinstatement of King Ferdinand. Count von Gentz knew both Consalvi and Princess Volkonskaya from the time of the Vienna congress.

d) Count Giovanni Barberi (1748-1821) — a prominent lawyer and prosecutor who distinguished himself in serving the Vatican since 1780, when Pope Pius VI appointed him head treasurer ("fiscale generale") and made him a "monsignore" — a rare title for a layman. Barberi became known widely as prosecutor in the famous 1790 Cagliostro trial which he later described in four well-documented volumes. After the French Revolution, Barberi maintained a low profile, but after 1814 resumed a position in the Vatican. Princess Volkonskaya remained close to the Barberi family; they are mentioned in Consalvi's letters VI and VII.

e) Alexis Guignard St. Priest (1805-1851) — diplomat, historian, member of the French Academy, peer of France. Born in St. Petersburg to a French emigré, Count Armand St. Priest, later governor of Odessa, and a Russian Princess, Sofia Golitsyna, he was educated at a French college in Odessa headed by the Jesuit Abbé Nicole. It was in Odessa that Princess Volkonskaya met the young Alexis and his parents. Alexis St. Priest left Odessa early in 1821 for Paris, and on the way there stopped in Rome, where he contacted Zinaida.

f) Cardinal Consalvi dated his letter only "January 19," omitting the year. There are two clues to attribute this date to 1821. First, Volkonskaya arrived in Naples from Milan and a sojourn in Rome not before May of 1820. Hence, the first January she spent in Rome could not have been before 1821. The second indication is Consalvi's mention of the visit of Count Barberi, who died on August 14, 1821.[33] Thus, it can be established with certainty that this letter was written on January 19, 1821.

Letter III

One sheet, 18.5 x 24.5 cm, folded, written on one page. *Unpublished.*

Madame la Princesse,

Une lettre du Souverain d'Albano*[a]* que je reçois dans l'instant dit — Sono arrivato nel momento che i Napoletani marciano *a spron battuto* per la via Appia verso Velletri per prendere quelle posizioni.*[b]*

Il me semble qu'on ne va pas *a spron battuto* pour prendre une position, lorsque l'ennemi est à 100 lieues. On peut penser donc qu'ils viennent faire un coup de main à Rome*[c]*. *Je me hâte* de vous l'écrire, pour que vous ayez le tems de faire Vos préparatifs si vous voulez partir. Je suis avec la considération la plus distinguée.

> Ce 13 Févr[ier] 1821 à 4 heures
> Les très chauds et dévoués sentiments.
> Hercole
> Card[inal] Consalvi

a) On Tuesday, February 13, 1821, the governor of the province Albano of the Papal State, located thirteen miles from Rome, sent an urgent message to the Vatican reporting that the troops of the revolutionary Neapolitan army were approaching Rome via Velletri. This message that later proved to be totally groundless created near-panic in Rome, which is evident from the note from Cardinal Consalvi to Princess Volkonskaya.

b) Here Consalvi renders in Italian the content of the message received from the governor of Albano: "I am informed that the Neapolitans are marching at full tilt on the Appian Way toward Velletri to take up those positions."

c) The insurgence of the Neapolitan militia on July 1, 1820 was spreading quickly into a wide revolutionary movement under the leadership of General Pepe. King Ferdinand was forced to accept a new consitution, but then the members of the Holy Alliance, headed by Russia, Prussia, and Austria decided to put a swift end to this dangerous precedent, and assigned the operation to Austria.[34] On February 2, 1821, 60,000 Austrians crossed the river Po and proceeded toward Naples. The first false rumor about the counterattack of the carbonari moving in the direction of Rome began to spread on February 7th. The Prussian diplomat von Bunsen, described vividly the general state of confusion, concluding that the false rumor "was created by Consalvi himself."[35] Six days later came a second false alarm, caused by the above mentioned message of the governor of Albano. This resulted in such a panic that it was immediately decided to move the Pope, Pius VII, from Rome to Civitavecchia. When the Pope's carriage was ready to leave, there came another message refuting the initial alarming report. Consalvi's overly cautious handling of this crisis may be explained by the warning that he had received two months earlier from Metternich, who insisted that in the case of an attack on Rome by the revolutionary army, the Pope had to be immediately evacuated.[36]

Letter IV

Four pages, 18.5 x 14 cm., written on three sides. *Unpublished.*

Madame la Princess,

Je me flatte que ma très grande estime et mon véritable dévouement, ainsi que mon vif désir de vous en donner des preuves, vous soient assez connus (et je serais au désespoir si je me trompais dans mon espoir) pour que vous deviez être persuadée que je ne ferais pour vous que ce qui m'est vraiment impossible. Il y a eu un si grand nombre de places données, il y a un si grand nombre de promesses à remplir, il y a une si grande quantité de [pétitionnaires] auxquels des motifs de stricte justice obligent à devoir songer, que la volonté la plus efficace du Monde, telle que la mienne lorsqu'il s'agit de faire quelque chose pour vous, ne peut pas parvenir à réaliser ce qu'elle désire. Dans les [conditions] actuelles, je veux mieux dire dans ces moments, il y a impossibilité, et une grande, de donner une place, particulièrement à Rome, à votre protégé Maj[or] Oloué; je pourrais vous parler de vive voix, je vous en écrirais; mais je vous épargne un long decrit sur papier. Soyez pourtant persuadée, Mad[ame] la Princesse, que j'éprouve une peine *infinie* à vous donner une réponse que l'impossibilité seule m'arrache lorsqu'il est question d'une demande de votre part.[a] Mais avec tout ceci ne pensez pas que M. Oloué ne doit plus rien espérer. Laissez à moi le soin de sortir et trouver l'occasion où je puisse vous satisfaire à son égard. Si vous pensez que je pourrais l'oublier, vous pensez donc que je peux oublier ce qui me vient de votre part, et dans ce cas je vous dis que vous ne vous connaissez point, et vous ne me connaissez pas non plus. Mon dévouement à votre incomparable personne vous est garant que je n'oublierai pas M(ajor) Oloué.[b] L'Ambassadeur ne dit pas la moitié de ce que je lui dis à votre égard et ce que je lui dis n'est pas une politesse ni des compliments, mais un véritable sentiment du cœur.[c] C'est moi qui dois vous remercier de vouloir bien agréer le peu ou pour mieux dire le presque rien que je fais pour vous. Je vous prie de faire agréer mes compliments

à M. le Prince*^d* et d'agréer vous-même les sentiments que vous connaissez à votre très dévoué serviteur.

Le Card[inal] Consalvi
Rome, ce 22 octobre, 1821

a) Cardinal Consalvi's assurance of his unfailing devotion to the Princess and the desire to be of assistance became more and more insistent
with each letter. The statement about the heavy load of his responsibilities is not exaggerated, however: being Secretary of State, the Cardinal
conducted the affairs of the Vatican State almost singlehandedly, since
he enjoyed the total confidence of the ailing Pope, Pius VII.

a) *Major Olloué* — French emigré who lived in Russia for many years
and married a wealthy Russian heiress, Martyanova. Apparently Princess
Zinaida asked the Cardinal to find some position in Vatican administra-
tion for M. Olloué, who was a Catholic, and was not entirely satisfied
with his situation in Russia (Consalvi spells his name 'Oloué').

c) "L'ambassadeur" is the Austrian ambassador, Count *Antal Rudolf
Apponyi* (1782-1825) with whose wife Teresa, née Nogarola (1790-
1874), Princess Zinaida was on friendly terms. Speaking of his conversation with the Ambassador about Princess Volkonskaya, Consalvi again
lapses into unrestrained expression of his devotion and admiration.

d) The greetings to "M. le Prince" indicate that Zinaida's husband
was in Rome at that time: this was a rare occasion on which they were
together during the Princess' years of wandering about Europe.

Letter V

One page, 12 x 19.5 cm, written on both sides. *Unpublished.*

Madame la Princesse,

Ne répondez pas à ces lignes qui vous portent dans ces derniers
moments de votre présence à Rome mes vœux pour votre heureux voyage et pour votre retour, mais souvenez-vous quelque fois dans votre
absence de votre *plus* dévoué que vous laissez ici, dans l'assurance que
rien ne me sera plus à cœur que m'employer pour vous et satisfaire tant
que possible les commissions que vous voudrez bien me donner. En

vous voyant avec un vif regret éloignée de nous, je ne puis m'en consoler un peu qu'avec l'espoir de vous voir revenir en Novembre. Veuillez bien embrasser pour moi le petit Alexandre, et présentez mes compliments à la Princesse Sophie qui j'espère sera bientôt rétablie par vos services. Je m'en vais faire mon petit voyage solitaire du Dimanche, bien plus court que le vôtre que vous allez entreprendre dans ce jour, mais je n'ai pu monter en voiture sans vous passer mes regrets et mes vœux dans ces derniers instants.

Disposez, je vous [le] répète, de votre plaisir auprès de celui qui vous est devoué pour la vie.

[n.p.]
Ce 22 juin, 1823, [Rome]
Le Card[inal] Consalvi

a) From this letter, in which Cardinal Consalvi lamented about the forthcoming trip and long absence of Princess Volkonskaya, we learn the exact date of her departure: June 22, 1823 (" . . . the journey you are starting today"). As in his previous and following letters, the Cardinal expresses his affection to Zinaida as well as his willingness to help her in all possible practical matters.

b) "The little Alexander" — Volkonskaya's son, then twelve years old. "Princess Sophie," to whom Consalvi sends his greetings and wishes for a quick recovery, is Zinaida's sister-in-law, Princess Sofia Grigorievna Volkonskaya (see our note to the letter of I. I. Kozlov). This illness was apparently just a pretext for Volkonskaya's trip, since those who frequently met with Princess Sofia in Paris at that time had not mentioned her health.[37]

During the months in Paris, Princess Zinaida entertained herself much as she had in 1816, when she received a gentle reprimand from the Tsar for her appearances in private theaters.[38] It did not take her long to create a salon in Paris. We know that on July 10, 1823 she invited guests for a reading of her novel, which was to appear shortly. Zinaida became a part of the Paris social scene. She entertained in her salon with fine music and literary readings such guests as the composer Rossini, the famous actress Mlle Mars (who admired Zinaida's acting talent), writers, and statesmen who liked to conduct with her conversations on literary and political subjects.[39] As we will see from the next letter, Volkonskaya liked her life in Paris so much that she decided to spend the winter there.

Letter VI

Four pages, 19 x 23.7 cm, written on four sides. *Unpublished.*

Madame la Princess,

Je ne m'attendais pas au coup de foudre (tel a été vraiment pour moi votre lettre de Paris), qui annonce la résolution prise de passer l'hiver prochain dans cette ville et de la quitter ensuite en printems pour aller à Vienne et St. Pétersbourg, sans même dire positivement que l'hiver suivant vous reconduira à Rome, mais seulement vous bornant à une expression vague que vous désirez y revenir. Je m'étais flatté que notre climat en hiver l'emportant si gravement sur celui de Paris ... Votre santé, ainsi que celle de Madame la Princesse Sophie, vous auroit conseillé de revenir à Rome pour y passer l'hiver, ce qui auroit retardé, et peut-être empêché un éloignement, qu'il auroit fallu ne pas vous avoir connue pour ne pas sentir assez vivement. Je vous avoue, Madame la Princesse, que je le sens dans le fond de mon cœur. L'état de ma santé ne laisse pas de me faire perdre jusqu'à l'espoir de vous revoir (sic).[a] M. Berberi pourra vous dire combien je suis sensible à cette absence que vous allez faire. Il ne me reste pour tempérer la peine qu'elle me fait que l'assurance de votre part (je vous le demande au nom de cette amitié que vous avez bien voulu m'accorder) d'être desiré comme votre homme d'affaires à Rome *en tout et pour tout* dont vous pourriez avoir besoin dans cette ville, soit pour vous, soit pour tous ceux auxquelles vous pourriez prendre de l'intérêt. En exécutant vos commissions, en m'employant pour vous, je me dédommagerais quelques remédes de votre douleureuse absence. Pensez-vous qu'il y ait ici personne qui l'emporte sur moi dans l'envie de vous servir et dans le zèle de le faire de son mieux? Toutes les commissions que vous m'avez laissées en quittant Rome se trouvent déjà exécutées ou bien près de l'être: toutes celles que vous me donnerez, le seront aussi avec tout l'intérêt que vous me connaissez en tout ce qui me vient de votre part. Donnez-moi donc votre parole que je serai votre agent ici et persuadez-vous bien que loin que vos commissions puissant m'être à charge, chaque fois que vous m'en donnerez, vous me ferez un plaisir qui ira droit à mon cœur. Mlle Comtesse Barberi vous peindra les ruines de notre pauvre S. Paul que vous ne verrez pas de vos yeux. Nous le rétablirons le mieux possible malgré ce qu'il en coûtera à nos pauvres finances.[b] Nous avons caché jusqu'à

présent ce grand malheur au Pape vu l'état où il se trouve, mais il faudra
bien le lui dire dans peu [de temps]. Il s'approche de sa guérison: il est
30 jours aujourd'hui qu'il gît immobile dans la même position dans son
lit, et l'on espère que dans une vingtaine de jours il puisse se lever et
s'asseoir, et ensuite [marcher] dans un mois, restant toutefois boiteux.[c]
Veuillez bien faire agréer mes compliments à Mad[ame] la Princesse
Sophie et veuillez aussi tendrement embrasser le petit Alexandre.
Remerciez encore Mme Barberi du souvenir qu'elle me conserve. Vous
ne vous fâcherez pas, je l'espère, si quelquefois je vous déroberai pour
quelques moments à vos occupations continuelles en vous demandant
vos nouvelles qui seront toujours si chères à mon cœur. Je vous suis trop
strictement dévoué pour ne pas m'en procurer, et ce sera pour moi un
plaisir infini de voir que vous ne m'avez pas oublié *totalement*. Vous
étiez adorée ici et tout le monde vous regrette. Ayez soin de votre santé
et ne vous fatiguez vous pas beaucoup trop pour remplir tout ce que
votre incomparable cœur embrasse. Mais je m'aperçois que je vous ai
entretenue trop long[temps] avec cette lettre: pardonnez-le à mon
attachement qui ne saurait être plus grand. Je l'achève en vous répétant
que je suis ici pour vous servir *en tout* et que c'est le seul dédom-
[m]ag[em]ent que je vous demande de votre absence. Je vous baise la
main de tout mon cœur, et je vous prie de croire que personne ne vous
est plus strictement dévoué [que] moi pour la vie.

[n.d., n.p.]
[August 4, 1823][d]
Le Card[inal] Consalvi

a) Volkonskaya's decision to go from Paris straight to Russia was not
entirely to her liking either. She had postponed her homecoming as long
as she could, but this time the Tsar's insistence to put an end to this
decade of European wandering became an order impossible to disobey.
The reaction of Consalvi to Zinaida's decision, which, he says, was a
thunderbolt for him, was consistent with his previous affectionate attitude. He even uses the mild climate of Rome to talk Zinaida into spending the winter there. All this was particularly touching since the Cardinal
was very ill at that time. If earlier we referred to Consalvi's tactics used
to attract influential and wealthy foreigners, then this letter demonstrates
the undeniable sincerity of his attitude toward Volkonskaya at this time.
The offer to settle Zinaida's affairs in Rome, where she had lived for
almost three years, prompted Consalvi to embark on a lengthy, emotional discourse. Not forgetting the epistolary code of the time, one can-

not help but notice the unexpected emotional tone in the four-page letter written by the Cardinal during the most trying period of his life.

b) "Pauvre S. Paul" is the Cathedral San Paul, a magnificent granite structure with marble columns, bronze gates created by Greek artists of the time of Gregory VII, and mosaics dating from the 9th century. The Cathedral was completely destroyed by fire on July 15, 1823. Consalvi was shaken by this loss. Two weeks after the fire, he announced his decision to rebuild the cathedral. St. Paul was particularly dear to him because Pope Pius VII had spent many years there as a Benedictine monk.

c) Another sad event which the Cardinal faced those days was the severe illness of the Pope, who had fallen in his study on July 6, 1823, breaking one leg, and had remained completely immobilized ever since.

d) Unlike the first five letters from Consalvi to Princess Zinaida, this much longer communication was undated. The text of this letter, however, helps to establish its date: the Cardinal writes that the Pope had been immobilized for *exactly* thirty days. Hence this letter was written on Tuesday, August 4, 1823.

Letter VII

Two pages, 19.5 x 26 cm., written on both sides. *Unpublished.*

Madame la Princesse,

J'ai reçu presque contemporainement les deux lettres du 6 Août et du 6 Septembre, que vous m'avez ecrites, car M. de St. Priest ne m'a remis la première qu'à ma sortie du Conclave, c'est à dire à la fin de Septembre, et c'est à peu près à la même époque que j'ai pu recevoir la seconde avec les sentiments si propres à votre incomparable cœur. Vous m'avez écrit sur la mort du Pape Pie VII.[a] J'ai pu faire bien peu relativement à M. de St. Priest, ayant quitté Rome 8 jours après ma sortie du Conclave pour chercher (mais je crains en vain) dans l'air de cette campagne ce remède efficace à ma maladie que je n'ai pas trouvé dans tant de remède qu'on m'a fait prendre pendant 18 mois.[b] Je n'ai pu qu'offrir à M. de St. Priest mes maisons d'Albano et de Frascati où il avait l'intention de passer quelques jours avec Mad[ame] la Duchesse de Devonshire.[c] A mon retour à Rome après la Toussaints je tâcherai de lui montrer le mieux que je le pourrai le prix que je mets à votre recommandation à son égard.[d] Quant à votre seconde lettre, relative à la mort du Pape, vos regrets d'une personne que j'adorais et à laquelle j'ètais si pietement attaché par le long service de 23 ans, et par tant de bienfaits, et vos expressions sur mon compte si pleines de bonté et d'amitié, si flatteuses, et s'il m'est permis de me servir de cette phrase, si affectueuses, m'ont fait verser bien des larmes. J'y ai reconnu votre cœur et toute la noblesse et l'excellence de votre beau caractère. Croyez à la reconnaissance profonde et tendre que je vous en professe et soyez persuadée qu'elles ont pénétré jusqu'au fond de mon âme. Je vous prie de faire agréer tous mes remerciments à Madame la Princesse Sophie pour l'intérêt qu'elle aussi a bien voulu prendre à moi dans cette occasion et présentez lui mes plus empressés hommages. En lisant dans votre lettre l'expression que votre souvenir ne me quitte pas, j'ai été infiniment flatté qu'une personne si estimable, si aimable, que vous êtes, m'assure de me compter toujours au nombre de ses plus fidèles et plus dévoués serviteurs et amis. Oui, je le suis, et je le serai à jamais: disposez de moi comme d'une chose qui est entièrement à vous.[e] En lisant aussi que vous reviendrez à Rome, je vous prie de croire, que si je suis en vie, vous me retrouverez le même que vous m'avez trouvé la prèmiere fois. Ma personne et tout le peu que j'ai, seront à votre disposition. Veuillez bien remercier Mad[ame] Berberi et M. Berberi (dont cependant je n'ai pas reçu la lettre que vous m'annonciez) de l'intérêt qu'ils me conservent.[f] Quant à ma santé, je n'ai pas lieu d'en être content dutout. Les simptômes de mon mal, qu'on ignore toujours, sont toujours les mêmes souffrances. Le repos n'y a fait aucun bien. Vous savez sans doute que je ne suis plus dans les affaires.[g] Je crois que le mal a pris trop racine pour en guérir. Mais ce sera ce que Dieu voudra. Recevez, Madame la Princesse, l'assurance de tous les sentiments de gratitude, de dévouement, d'amitié et de confidence les plus distingués que je vous ai voués pour la vie.

> Votre plus obéissant et plus attaché ami et serv[iteur].
> Le Card[inal] Consalvi
> Montopoli en Sabine, le 10 Octobre 1823

Donnez-moi ou faites moi donner quelque fois vos nouvelles que me sont si chères.

a) The death of Pius VII on August 20, 1823 was a hard loss for Cardinal Consalvi: he was sincerely attached to the Pope whom he had served for twenty-three years. For the last three days, the Cardinal was

with the dying Pope around the clock. Himself ill, he fainted twice during his last night vigil.[42] On September 1, there was a requiem service
for the late Pope in St. Peter's. Immediately thereafter started the Conclave which ended only on September 28.

b) Consalvi received both letters from Volkonskaya, as he writes, at
the end of the month, they were handed to him after September 28th,
when he left from the Conclave. Ill and exhausted, the Cardinal was also
depressed with the results of the election: he had been on poor terms
with the new Pope, Leon XII, the former Cardinal della Genga. After the
coronation of the Pope on October 5th, Cardinal Consalvi left Rome for
his country estate in Montopoli in Sabina.[43]

c) *Duchess Devonshire*, née Lady Elizabeth Foster (1757-1824), the
second wife of Duke William Devonshire (1748-1811). An exceptionally
beautiful and intelligent woman, who remained quite handsome in her
sixties, she had lived in Italy for many years and became an important
part of the Roman social and cultural life. Her long friendship with Cardinal Consalvi surprised many people, particularly since she was a prot-
estant. Many contemporaries of Consalvi were critical of him, but the
Duchess was always his staunch admirer and supporter. In one of her
letters to Lord Byron, she wrote that "Consalvi had established a new
politics, one based on truth and openness. All Europe respects him for
this."[44]

d) *M. St. Priest* — see note "e" to letter II. In addition to his estates
in Albano and Frascati, where he was inviting St. Priest, Consalvi also
had residences in Porto D'Anzio, Tivoli, and Grotta Ferrata.

e) Cardinal Consalvi's assurance of his devotion to Zinaida, which
was a recurrant motive of his letters, received its most emphatic expression here. Apparently Volkonskaya wrote to Consalvi about her intention
to return to Rome (which she actually did five years later), and to this
the Cardinal responded that she would find him "the same as he was
when she first met him."

f) "M. et Mme. Berberi" — not to be confused with Count and
Countess Barberi. Possibly, the relatives of Volkonskaya's former secretary Barberi.

g) Consalvi, then sixty-seven, was in very poor health. Soon after this
letter to Volkonskaya, advised by his physician to spend some time at
the seashore, he moved to Porte d'Anzio where he stayed until December 23. The Cardinal was now forgotten by most of the people who earlier sought his attention. Only Cardinal Fesch remained faithful to the
former State Secretary, as well as some of his friends of Roman society.
Then came a change: on January 14, 1824, the new Pope, Leon XII,

appointed Consalvi prefect of the Congregation of the Propagation of the Faith (*Propaganda Fide*). The Cardinal was so weak at that time that he had to be carried for his last meeting with the Pope. He died ten days later, on January 10, 1824, in his estate in Porto d'Anzio. This letter, the seventh communication of Cardinal Consalvi to Princess Volkonskaya, was his last one. In his will, he left a large amount for charity, as well as some memorabilia to Duchess Devonshire, countess Albani and several other ladies from society. But no trace of any gift left to Princess Zinaida could be found.[45]

The seven letters which Cardinal Ercole Consalvi wrote to Princess Volkonskaya bear witness to their spiritual affinity and tender friendship maybe the last in the Cardinal's life. This relationship was undoubtedly a strong influence in the future life of Princess Zinaida and her decision to be converted to the Catholic faith.

NOTES ON CARDINAL CONSALVI'S FRENCH

Maintaining our principle of leaving the texts unedited, we are publishing the letters of Cardinal Consalvi without revising his French, which was not a native language for him. Besides some ordinary grammatical mistakes, the Cardinal's written French was occasionally influenced by Italian vocabulary and syntax. We are including a few examples of this type of mistake.

Instead of "trouver . . . une heure," he writes *retrouver* (analogy with Italian *ritrovare*); *symptômes* is spelled *simptômes* (Italian *sintom*); the adverb *pieusement* is replaced by *pietement* derived from Italian *pieta*; the plural of the French word *Toussaint* can be explained by the plural in Italian *l'Ognissanti*; defining the advantage of the Italian climate, Consalvi writes . . . *emportant* . . . gravement . . . (Italian *gravemento*); instead of "*designé* comme votre homme d'affaires," he uses *desiré* (analogy with Italian *desiderare*).

There is a frequent confusion of conditional, future and present verbal forms, which in some instances also have been influenced by Italian. The lack of agreement in case, gender and number occurs with such frequency that we will not attempt to list them here. Consalvi often uses complex and heavy constructions which not only violate the rules of

French syntax, but also impair clarity of meaning. This becomes particularly evident in the last two letters written when he was distressed and seriously ill.

The still unsettled rules of reforming French grammar explain the presence of then already obsolete forms such as *tems, printems, sentimens*, etc., a rather inconsistant usage of the past (*paroit, auroit*, etc.), as well as an occasional omission of the second intervocalic consanants (*verez, serons*, etc), of -t- (*les sentimens*), and of the vowel -e- (*remerciments*), etc.

LETTERS WRITTEN
TO A. N. VOLKONSKY AND A. P. GOLITSYN

In the Volkonskaya Archive there is a group of letters addressed to the son of Princess Zinaida, Alexander Nikitich Volkonsky (1811-1878). The correspondence of the Prince covers the period after 1845, when his mother, completely absorbed with her religious vocation, had withdrawn from the secular world. From this correspondence we have selected two authors: Prince Vyazemsky, whom we introduced earlier, and a complex, rather controversial figure of considerable interest, Yakov Nikolaevich Tolstoy (1791-1867). Vyazemsky's letter was dated 1859; Tolstoy's letters were written in 1858, 1863, and 1865. These letters cover the decade when Prince Volkonsky reached the peak of his diplomatic career: after a long period of minor assignments, in 1858 he became the Russian ambassador to Dresden (Saxony) and four years later was appointed the ambassador to Spain when that country was playing an important role in European affairs. Well-educated and intelligent, Prince Volkonsky was liked and respected in Russia and abroad. In spite of his mother's expectations, the Prince did not convert to Roman Catholicism, but he consistently showed tolerance towards his mother's new faith and supported her when needed. Three years after her death in 1862, Prince Volkonsky published two volumes: in the first were Princess Zinaida's literary works; in the second were collected prose and poetry dedicated to her.

Another, much smaller group of letters, unexpectedly found in the Volkonskaya Archive, was addressed to Prince Avgustin Petrovich Golitsyn (1824-1875). One of the most prominent Catholics, the Prince lived in Paris and was the editor of the prestigious French Catholic journal *Correspondant*. He occasionally undertook translations from Russian into French. One letter to Golitsyn in the Archive was sent to him by Ivan S. Turgenev, whose novel *Smoke* he had translated. Turgenev was so disappointed with Golitsyn's rendering that he decided to work on the second translation himself.

Golitsyn's distant relationship to the Volkonskys, his Catholic ties, and his frequent sojourns in Rome where he had many relatives, may explain how several letters addressed to him and to Angéle Golitsyna turned up in the Rome Archive of Zinaida Volkonskaya.

In the second volume of our study on Zinaida Volkonskaya and her circle, we will quote many other letters addressed to Prince Volkonsky.

LETTER FROM PYOTR ANDREEVICH VYAZEMSKY
TO PRINCE A. N. VOLKONSKY

On August 2/14, 1858, Prince Vyazemsky and his wife Vera Fyodorovna left Petersburg for another trip abroad. Twenty-four years had
passed since their first visit to Germany and Italy (see Vyazemsky's
letters to Volkonskaya I and II). During these years they had lost their
daughters Nadezhda and Maria, who had been with them on their first
trip. The Prince continued to write poetry and critical essays, but his
literary production became scanty, and he himself confessed to the
decline of its quality.[1] In 1855, Vyazemsky was appointed Deputy Minister of Public Education, and much of his time was taken by official
duties. Four months before their departure, however, the Prince retired,
and now, free of all official ties, he set out for a longer journey abroad,
this time without any definite plans.

The Vyazemskys devoted the first three months to visiting familiar
places and meeting old friends. Before settling for a longer stay in the
south of France, they went to Karlsbad, Dresden, Stuttgart, Baden-
Baden, Lausanne, and Geneva. On November 20/December 2, 1858,
after a brief stop in Lyon and Marseilles, they arrived in Nice. This
year-round resort, which boasted the attractions of a larger city, became
a center for Russians travelling in southern Europe. The day after their
arrival Vyazemsky was already listing in his notebook the names of the
Russians living in Nice. "Volkonskie-Sibirskie," as he called the family
of the Decembrist, Prince Sergey Volkonsky, who had recently returned
from Siberian exile, Count Kochubey, Countess Olsufieva, Prince
Sergey Golitsyn, and the poet Maykov were among their intimates. At
that time Nice was the residence of two Russian Grand Duchesses, Elena
Nikolaevna and Ekaterina Mikhaylovna. If in the 1820's and later, at the
time when he wrote the first two letters to Zinaida Volkonskaya,
Vyazemsky had had strained relations with the Tsar, he was now on
friendly terms with all the members of the imperial family. According to
his notebook, he met with the Grand Duchesses almost every other day
while in Nice. He also resumed his old relations with the Prussian writer
and diplomat, Charles Bunsen.[2] The political climate in Europe, particularly the military confrontation in Piedmont, was the subject of long
discussions in the diplomatic circles of Nice.

The sixty-seven-year-old Prince had not lost his love for travel and the
desire to witness important historical events. The present war between
Piedmont and Austria, complicated by the involvement of French troops,

fascinated Vyazemsky and drew him away from peaceful Nice to the stormy Italian roads leading to Turin and Genoa. The letters he wrote to Vera Fyodorovna while she was still in Nice reveal his involvement with the current war. "I am leading such a military life that I feel like growing a moustache," he joked.[3] His letters also contain serious observations about the situation. On May 8 Vyazemsky, started his return voyage to Nice in a mail coach: he was reluctant to go by boat ("I don't go by sea, I only glorify it").[4] On the day of his arrival, May 12, 1859, the Prince immediately related to his son Pavel his impressions of that eventful trip. "After all the noise and excitement," he concluded, "I find myself in Nice as if in a monastery, so quiet and static is the life here."[5] This "static" resort did not, however, hold the Prince for more than two weeks after his return from Genoa: on May 27, 1859, the Vyazemskys left Nice for Germany.

Two days before their departure, on May 25, the Prince wrote a letter to the son of his old friend, "Princess Zénèida," Alexander Nikitich Volkonsky, now the Russian ambassador in Dresden. Vyazemsky had known Prince Volkonsky since the latter's childhood in Moscow. And then in 1833 when the twenty-two-year-old Alexander was studying at Petersburg University, they had renewed their acquaintance, although Vyazemsky observed that it was not easy to establish a close rapport with the shy young Prince.[6] They also met in later years in Petersburg and abroad, where Volkonsky was serving as a diplomat. Their most recent meeting had been in Dresden, where the Vyazemskys had spent ten days at the beginning of their present trip, from October 4 to October 14, 1858. But the capital of Saxony had never attracted Vyazemsky. On the occasion of an earlier visit he observed: "Dresden is a new Babylon, Sodom, and Gomorrah in comparison with Karlsruhe."[7]

Four pages of yellowed paper written on two sides, 13.2 x 21 cm. *Unpublished.*

Nice, 13/25 mai, 1859

J'apprends, cher Prince, que l'on doit m'expédier des lettres et peut-être de l'argent en les adressant à la légation russe à Dresde. Veuillez bien donner vos ordres pour qu'on les garde jusqu'à mon arrivée, ou bien jusqu'à la réception d'un avis de ma part. Nous comptons quitter Nice après demain pour nous rendre à Stuttgardt par la Suisse.[a] Si vous voyez Pletneff[b] qui doit passer par Dresde, dites-lui qu'il me cherche à Genève, a l'hôtel de Métropole, ou à Stuttgardt, où Titoff pourra, en tout cas, le renseigner pour mon [itinèraire] sur mes faits et gestes.[c] J'ai toujours l'intention d'aller plus tard à Carlsbad, si toutefois Votre Excellence et Vos Excellentes veulent bien le permettre. Vous seriez bien aimable, cher Prince, de me dire un petit mot tout laconique et tout franc à ce sujet, en me le faisant venir par votre honorable collègue et mon honorable ami Titoff.[d] En tout cas, je compte toujours sur le plaisir de Vous voir à Dresde, où nous appelent nos intèrêts les plus chers et les mieux sonnants renfermés dans la cassette, confiée à votre bienveillante tutelle.[e] Présentez, je vous prie, mes hommages dévoués à la Princesse et agréez mes compliments les plus affecteux.[f]

Wiazemski

a) The plan to go to Stuttgart was realized, but it took more than five weeks because of the many stops the Vyazemskys made on the way to Switzerland. Having left Nice on May 27, 1859, they travelled to Arles, Avignon, Nimes, Montpellier, and Lyon. On June 12 they reached Geneva, where they stayed for more than two weeks before proceeding further to Stuttgart.[8]

b) *Pletnyov, Pyotr Alexandrovich* (1792-1865). Russian poet, literary critic, and journalist. Professor of Russian literature at Petersburg University (1832-1849). After Pushkin's death, he served for eight years as publisher and editor of the literary journal *Contemporary*. Pletnyov was a close friend of Zhukovsky, Vyazemsky, Gogol, and Pushkin, who dedicated to him his novel in verse *Eugene Onegin.*

c) *Titov, Vladimir Pavlovich* (1807-1891). Journalist, writer, and translator, also known under the pen name "Vladimir Kostomarov." Connected with the philosophic society "Lyubomudry." A close friend of many Russian writers, including Vyazemsky and Pushkin. In his later years, a diplomat and member of the State Council (thus, "votre collègue"). After having served as Russian ambassador to Turkey, Titov was transferred to Stuttgart, where he was stationed at the time of Vyazemsky's visits in 1858 and 1859. During his first stay in Stuttgart in October 1858, Vyazemsky spent much time with Titov, with whom he also took a trip to Baden-Baden and Stuttgart. On September 16 they visited Interlaken together. Vyazemsky corresponded with Titov and kept him informed of the events of his life — "sur mes faits et gestes," as he wrote to Prince Volkonsky. Returning to Nice from his "reconnoitering'' trip to Piedmont on May 22, Vyazemsky wrote a long letter to Titov accompanied by the verses "My Opinion on the Present War."[9]

d) At the beginning of their trip, the Vyazemskys stayed for more than a month in Karlsbad (August 30-October 3, 1858). His present request, addressed to Prince Volkonsky and apparently to his wife and daughter as well, "Votre Excellence" and "*Vos Excellentes*" (sic), implies that he expected to be invited as their houseguest in Karlsbad. But either this invitation was not extended, or the Vyazemskys themselves changed their plans, since they did not go to Karlsbad before returning to Russia. Instead, they prolonged their stay in Stuttgart, from where the Prince set out for shorter trips to Baden-Baden, Durkheim, and Heidelberg. Toward the end of their journey, Vyazemsky became tired, restless, and felt like rushing home. In one of his poems, "On the Road," he expresses hope that some day there would be airplanes, "flying rugs," which would swiftly transport people from country to country.[10] The Vyazemskys left Stuttgart via Königsberg to Petersburg, arriving on November 22/December 4, 1859.

e) "A box containing our dearest and most jingling interests" — a metaphor for the money awaiting Vyazemsky at the embassy in Dresden.

f) Wife of Alexander Volkonsky, Princess Louise, née Lilien (?-1870). It should be noted that Princess Zinaida Volkonskaya is not mentioned in this letter to her son: by this time, her complete withdrawal from the secular world was a fact known and accepted by her family and friends.

THREE LETTERS FROM
YAKOV NIKOLAEVICH TOLSTOY
TO PRINCE A. N. VOLKONSKY

In the Volkonskaya Archive there are three letters from Yakov Niko-laevich Tolstoy addressed to the Princess' son, Alexander Nikitich, and sent to him from Paris in the years 1858, 1863, and 1865. These letters are in many ways characteristic of Tolstoy, who became after 1837 one of the most controversial figures on the political and literary horizons of nineteenth century Russia.

In 1817, at the age of 26, Tolstoy became a founding member of the literary society "The Green Lamp," which included, among others, the young Pushkin, Delvig, Gnedich, Kaverin, and the future Decembrist, S. Trubetskoy. At that time, he was liked and respected by his contemporaries.[1] Pushkin, who considered Tolstoy a close friend, wrote of him: "Filosof rannij, ty bežiš' / Pirov i naslaždenij žizni; / Na igry mladosti gljadiš' / S molčanjem xladnym ukorizny." ("Early philosopher, you are escaping / The feasts and enjoyments of life; / You are observing the amusements of youth / With cold reproaching silence").[2] As for the literary works of Tolstoy, his poems, plays, and translations had not attracted serious attention. At the time, however, when written and read at the gatherings of "The Green Lamp," they were well received by those present.[3]

Early in 1821, Tolstoy turned to political activities: he became a member of the Secret Society "The Union for Social Prosperity" ("Sojuz obščestvennogo blagodenstvija"), which was closely connected with the political group later known as the Decembrists. This involvement was short, but it changed his whole life, affecting it in a rather unexpected way. Because Tolstoy went to Paris in 1823 and thus was not in Russia during the Decembrist uprising of 1825, no direct conspiracy charges were brought against him, although he later became the subject of a thorough investigation.[4] Unable to return for fear of reprisals, Tolstoy continued staying in Paris. When his financial reserves were exhausted, he found himself in an extremely difficult and humiliating situation. He was forced to borrow money knowing, however, that it would be impossible for him to return it soon, since the meager fees for his journalistic contributions hardly sufficed to cover his living expenses in Paris.[5]

The general orientation of Tolstoy's writings became ultra-patriotic. He defended Russia against the criticism of foreigners who were writing on Russian subjects, and published numerous articles attacking authors whose opinions were different from his.[6] Some of these articles were quoted in Russian periodicals. One of them, *The Moscow Telegraph*, thanking Tolstoy for being an intermediary between the Russian and French readers, asked him for literary contributions, although it was forbidden even to mention his name at that time. In an article concerning Tolstoy's review of Ancelot's book *Six Months in Russia*, Vyazemsky wrote that Russian literature should be grateful to its new "consul general," in Paris, who was defending Russian culture from the ignorant foreigners.[7]

Tolstoy did not conceal the hope that his now loyal voice would be heard in Petersburg and could help to earn him a pardon. The culmination of these efforts was his biography of Field Marshal Count Paskevich, then the Governor General in Warsaw. After the publication of this unrestrained glorification, written in rather poor taste, Tolstoy, indeed, was invited to Petersburg, and Tsar Nicholas himself offered to pay his enormous debts in Paris.[8]

In 1837, after an absence of fourteen years, Tolstoy returned to Russia.[9] There he succeeded in obtaining the position he was hoping for: a joint appointment with the Ministry of Education and with the already notorious Third Section headed by Count Benkendorf, supervised directly by the Tsar. This new post required that he continue living in Paris, where he had to write reports informing Petersburg on the political and cultural situation in France. For this he was to use his wide social connections with the French and Russian circles in France. Such obligations, diffuse and vaguely defined, had put Tolstoy in an awkward position, and he himself soon realized that people had begun to distrust him, suspecting that he had become a goverment agent.[10]

Far from his country, Tolstoy strived — or was obliged — to establish contacts with many Russians in Paris, whom he was always willing to help in various practical ways. As Vyazemsky remarked: "All Russians who came to Paris found in him an eager and experienced guide. He became a true Parisian, but at the same time remained Russian to the very core, to the marrow."[11]

The three letters to Alexander Volkonsky which he wrote during this late period are revealing of Tolstoy's changed outlook and personality. He went out of his way to help Volkonsky, Russian ambassador in Dresden at the time and later in Madrid, to resolve a practical matter: finding a good French chef. But more importantly, in the second and third letters, Tolstoy exercised his by now professional ability to write political reports. His analysis of the current situation in France and Spain show how well-informed he was, although he had a penchant for using a gossipy approach to the subjects he was discussing. Tolstoy expected that his revealing and amusing letters, interspersed with exaggerated flattery, would be well received by the Prince, from whom he was hoping to obtain some favors.

It is noteworthy that the problems of Russia in this crucial post-reform period were approached here in a detached and superficial manner (Letter No. II). Indeed, not only Tolstoy's way of life, but his views as well completely changed after 1837: all he did, said, and wrote after that time negated his former image.

Letter I

Three pages of yellowed paper, 12.5 x 20 cm. After the signature, Tolstoy's Paris address written in his hand: 34, Rue de Penthièvre. We are omitting two passages which present no interest. *Unpublished.*

Paris, le 1 Mai, 1858

Vous avez tort, mon Prince, d'élever le moindre doute à l'endroit de mes souvenirs de l'an 40 et de l'année 37.[a] Quand on a la bonne fortune de rencontrer une personne de votre mérite, l'impression qu'elle produit reste gravée en caractères indélébiles dans notre mémoire . . .

(We are omitting here a passage where Tolstoy writes of the conversations with his cousin, Jean Tolstoy, about Volkonsky. Then follows a congratulation with the important diplomatic appointment.)

. . . Je fais seulement des vœux pour que vous puissiez, dans un avenir prochain, exercer vos talents sur un théâtre plus large et plus important.[b] J'aborde maintenant la question culinaire . . .

(This lengthy part is also deleted: the following section is the answer to Volkonsky's request to help him in finding an experienced French chef for his Embassy in Dresden. Tolstoy loses himself in details describing the qualities of the chefs themselves and those whom they had previously served. It is interesting to note that their salaries ranged as high as from 1,500 to 2,400 French Francs. Tolstoy even describes the specialties of their menus. We are including here below a passage from the text exemplifying Tolstoy's presentation of his appetizing commission.)

. . . Le Sieur Lapersonne — ancien officier de la bouche du Roi Louis-Phillipe et plus tard Maître d'hôtel du Duc de Nemours qu'il a suivi dans son exil. La baronne de Seilléere, une des plus opulentes dames de Paris, où il a travaillé en dernier lieu, en fait le plus grand éloge; il passe aussi pour le premier glacier de Paris: celui-ci demande 2,000 F . . .^{c}

a) Tolstoy met Prince Volkonsky for the first time in early January 1837 in Warsaw, where he stopped on the way to Russia to call on his new patron, Count Paskevich, whose flattering biography he had recently published. This became instrumental in rescuing him from his long disgrace. The young diplomat Volkonsky was serving then in Warsaw, assigned to Count Paskevich.[12]

b) In 1858, Prince Volkonsky was the Russian Ambassador in Dresden.[13] Tolstoy probably heard the rumor about the possible appointment of the Prince to Madrid, which represented indeed a more prestigious diplomatic post, since at that time Spain played a very important role on the European political scene.

c) This paragraph shows that in addition to his political observations, which Tolstoy had to report to Russia, he became much involved with the daily life of Paris society, and was equally well-informed about its intrigues and such petty matters as the culinary specialties and salaries of successful chefs.

Letter II

Four pages, 13.5 x 20 cm. *Unpublished.*

Paris, le 30 Decembre 1862/11 Janvier 1863

Mon cher Prince,

Ne vous attendez pas à une *epistola gratulatiora*; je ne vous rendrai donc point vos aimables félicitations à l'occasion du jour de l'an; tel n'est past mon principe: je déplore, au contraire, l'usage consacré dans tous les pays du monde de se réjouir à l'occasion d'une année écoulée, de venir le dire à ses amis, à ses connaissances, et à ses supérieurs, avec jubilation et solennité pour leur rappeler qu'ils ont vécu 365 jours de plus et se sont par conséquent rapprochés de 365 pas de *l'ultima ratio.* Tout ce que je puis faire pour les personnes que j'aime et que j'estime c'est de leur dire: je vous félicite de ce que durant l'année que vient de s'écouler vous n'avez éprouvé aucun grave préjudice, que votre Santé a été satisfaisante, que vous ne vous êtes pas cassé le cou, que vous n'avez pas été la victime d'aucune trahison, d'aucune injustice humaine, — si toutefois la personne que vous congratulez a echappé à toutes ces calamités.

Mais former des vœux, c'est une mauvaise plainsanterie; car on a beau en former et des plus brillants, personne n'est là pour les mettre à exécution. Quoiqu'il en soit, si j'avais le moindre petit espoir que mes vœux seraient exaucés, je n'hésiterais pas un instant d'en adresser de fervents pour le bonheur et la prospérité de l'excellent Prince et de Madame la Princesse.[a]

Le Sieur Rayer, professeur culinaire, auteur d'une brochure sur "les conserves alimentaires," joint à toutes ces éminentes qualités celles de *craqueur émérite.* Pour le prouver, je declare que:

1e. Oncque de ma vie, je ne lui ai offer 2,500 F, n'étant d'ailleurs pas autorisé de le faire, je n'ai pu outrepasser vos instructions.

2e. Que jamais, au grand jamais, je ne lui ai offer une indemnité de 500 F; il l'aura pris sous son bonnet de cuisine. Lorsqu'il m'en a fait parler par mon Valet-de-Chambre, je lui fis répondre qu'à mon avis, il ne lui était dû qu'un mois de gage, à savoir 175 F et lui fis offrir cette somme. Vous voyez que la vérité dans la bouche de cet officier de bouche ne règne pas plus que dans son cœur; voilà pourquoi je ne serai pas fâché d'en finir avec lui.[b]

Si la Question Mexicaine vous préoccupe beaucoup, elle n'est pas moins inquiétante en-deçà des Pyrénées. Une obstination peu politique porte le maître suprême de céans à persérvérer dans son idée, nonobstant les sacrifices énormes que lui coûte cette malencontreuse expédition lointaine. Je tiens d'un employé du Ministère de la guerre que déjà 150 millions ont été dépensés à cet effet; il a ajouté que ce n'était que par le Ministère où il est employé, mais qu'on pourrait évaluer à la moitié le chiffre des dépenses de la Marine. Quant aux dépenses en chair humaine, ceci n'entra point dans les calculs des conquérants, la chair à canon est, dans ce moment-ci plus dévorée que jamais, à cause de l'art de tuer perfectionné par les progressistes modernes. Au surplus, il nous reste une consolation, c'est que tant que la guerre mexicaine durera, l'Europe pourra respirer librement, car il serait matériellement impossible de manger simultanément à deux si énormes râteliers.*c Le Journal des Débats* dans son premier pari du 8 Janvier, trace un tableau vrai mais effrayant des miséres que ravagent les provinces les plus riches de la France, misères sans remède et qui prennent des proportions désastreuses. Les murmures et les mécontentements dans la capitale se manifestent avec une recrudescence qui alarme le pouvoir.*d*

En reportant nos regards sur la *carissima patria*, un frisson de terreur nous saisit involontairement et l'on est obligé de convenir qu'il y a péril en la demeure. Toutefois sans trop exagérer le danger, on ne sauraits se dissimuler que "qui trop embrasse, mal étreint:" après l'èmacipation nous est arrivée drue comme grêle la réforme judiciaire. Louis XVIII a dit dans un language quelque peu trivial pour un Roi et que le Sieur Royer-Collard pourrait répéter: "pour faire un civet, il faut un lièvre," or, pour réformer la justice d'un vaste pays, il faut des éléments pour en reconstituer un autre. Où donc pourrait-on trouver en Russie des jurisconsultes aussi nombreux, des jurys intègres? Où sont-ils? Qui pourrait me donner leur adresse? Bref, tout est remis en question, et nous pataugeons comme des aveugles dans un ténébreux chaos.*e*

Notre ambassadeur est un charmant homme, un parfait gentleman. Je suis convaincu qu'il réussira à faire taire quelques individus, animés d'un patriotisme de *Kvas* et de *Batvinia* et qui continuent encore à maugréer à cause du nom que n'est pas Slave pur sang, d'autre jalousent son élévation subite, à cause du *chin*, préjugé que le progrès n'est pas encore parvenu à déraciner.

Je finis, en vous priant, mon Prince, de continuer à disposer de moi, que le petit malentendu qui vous a donné tant d'ennui ne vous dégoûte pas pour l'avenir, d'autant plus que j'en fais mon *mea culpa*; en effet, c'est moi qui, contrairement aux préceptes de Talleyrand ai déployé "trop de zèle." Je saurai dorénavant procéder avec moins de précipitation.*f*

Veuillez agréer l'expression de mon cordial et très respectueux dévouement.

J. Tolstoj

a) This elaborate and flowery rendering of a simple observation (why he has not been enjoying the coming of the New Year and its celebration) is characteristic of the late Tolstoy's style. He probably dwelt on this subject because he was uneasy about his own explanation given in the third paragraph.

b) Apparently the chef whom Tolstoy had recommended to Volkonsky, then Russian ambassador in Madrid, did not satisfy him, and this led to the dismissal of the "culinary professor," as he is called in this letter. Obviously embarrassed about his own handling of this matter, Tolstoy tries to turn the subject to a lighter vein, quipping that the truth does not necessarily come from the mouth of one working to fill others' mouths.

c) The affairs "beyond the Pyrenees" mentioned here were quite alarming. Napoleon III had been carried away by his ambition to increase France's national prestige, and became involved in several military operations. After the victory in the Crimean War came the Italian War of 1859, which, in spite of initial success, had not brought the desired results. In the early sixties, the foreign policy of the Second Empire became more and more adventurous. Napoleon III squandered enourmous resources in the Mexican campaign, which was a matter of prestige for him. In 1862, 40,000 French troops were sent to Mexico, but the entire operation ended in failure. We see here that Tolstoy was obtaining some help from inside informers in the French government in order to receive classified information which he used in his reports to Russia.

d) After a period of initial economic development, a distinct setback began to be felt in the early 1860's. The appearance of prosperity was still there, but the wars had exhausted the economic resources of France and affected the daily life of the people. Toward 1863, discontent was being felt all over the country. The opposition, grounded in socialist theories, had gained seats in the Senate, and many major cities were starting to vote republican.[14]

e) This ironic reference, almost in passing, to *carissima patria*, "dearest fatherland," is quite unexpected from a former member of the Secret Society. The abolition of serfdom in 1861 liberated over forty million serfs, and this required changes in local government and legislation which would come about only three years later: the reform of the courts in 1864 and the so-called *zemstva* attached to local government institutions were also established in the same year. In 1863, however, while Tolstoy was writing about the post-reform difficulties, there was indeed a rather disorderly period of transition.

Pierre Paul Royer-Collard (1763-1845) — French statesman, lawyer and philosopher. First — a moderate partisan of the Revolution, then a liberal legitimist, he occupied several elected offices, and remained a deputy until 1842, when he retired from all his posts, disillusioned with the new regime. The quotation "Pour fair un civet, il faut un lièvre" could roughly be translated as "you can't make an omelette without eggs."

f) Tolstoy refers here to *Andrey von Budberg* (1820-1881), a Russian career diplomat of German origin. His ambassadorial appointment in Paris, as Tolstoy's letter confirms, was not well received by those who were opposed to the assignment of important positions to people of foreign origin. They did not want to consider that the von Budbergs had been serving in Russia as diplomats since 1783. Tolstoy shows an ironic attitude toward this superficial patriotism, which he called of the "Kvas and Botvinya" type (a fixed expression, "kvasnoy patriotiszm"), referring to the popular Russian cider-like drink and a dish made of kvas, greens, and fish. The root of this nationalistic attitude Tolstoy also sees in the struggle for rank, for which he uses the Russian word "chin."

Letter III

Six pages of gray paper, 13.5 x 20.5 cm. *Unpublished.*

Paris, le 6 Juillet, 1865

Mon cher Prince,

Vous êtes l'homme le plus obligeant, le plus bon, le plus indulgent, le plus aimable, le plus bienveillant, le plus spiritual de tous les ministres plénipotentiaires, voire tous les ambassadeurs.[a] Vous avez eu la bonté de prendre l'initiative dans l'affaire d'un jeune homme que vous ne connaissiez que d'après le dévouement cordial et la profonde estime que vous porte son oncle, et aujourd'hui vous persévérez dans la poursuite de cette affaire, nonobstant les ennuis qu'elle doit vous faire éprouver. Oui, vous êtes la perle des envoyes et ambassadeurs, inclusivement! Voici donc les noms, prénoms et qualités du postulant:

Sergej Ivanovič Tolstoj, Lejbgvardii gusarskogo polka ad'utant Glavnogo Štaba E. I. V. i Kavaler.

Tels sont les titres de mon neveu à une rémunération, si vous parvenez à le lui faire accorder, vous ferez justice.[b]

Le tableau que vous tracez de la situation politique de l'Espagne ne saurait donner de solides garanties pour l'avenir: la sécurité du pays repose sur la fidélité de l'armée et se trouve entre les mains de leurs chefs plus ou moins ambitieux, plus ou moins turbulents, donc vous avez sous ce rapport un spécimen fort curieux en la personne du G[eneral] Prim.[c] Au surplus, tous les pays du monde offrent les mêmes inconvénients et se trouvent à peu près dans les mêmes conditions, à savoir que les destinées des Etats dépendent de la force armée, cette *ultima ratio* des insurrections. J'ai été maintes et maintes fois témoin de ces défections spontanées des troupes; il suffisait d'un bataillon pactisant avec les émeutiers, pour faire faire subitement *volte-face* à tout le reste de la troupe.[d]

J'apprends la mort du Duc de Rivas que j'ai beaucoup connu lors de son émigration sous le nom de Colonel Saavedra: je l'ai revu depuis Duc et Ambassadeur; c'était un homme de talent et d'esprit.[e]

Quant à nous, nous sommes bien tranquilles pour le moment; à en juger par les acclamations enthousiastes du bon peuple parisien à l'apparition de leur bien-aimé Empereur, il nous est permis d'espérer que tout ira à ravis.[f] Quelques différends qui ont éclaté au sein de la famille impériale ont un peu préoccupé le public, mais une ascension aéronautique a fait tout oublier et les préoccupations se sont envolées avec *le Géant*.[g] En attendant Plon-plon, on commence de l'appeler à l'armée Craint-plomb à cause de son courage équivoque, en attendant cet enfant terrible du Sénat et de la famille im[péria]le, après avoir fait *semblant* d'avoir fait une chute, pour retarder sa visite aux Tuileries, continue à bouder et va, dit on, faire un voyage de circumnavigation et tout le monde applaudit à cette lointaine pérégrination; d'aucuns chantent: "Bon voyage Monsieur Dumoulin! On vous regrettera quand vous reviendrez." On fait aussi le bruit qu'il est revenu à résipiscence qu'il reste et sera réintégré dans sa fonction de Conseiller privé.[h]

L'Impératrice paraît avoir pris au sérieux sa régence et les applaudissements populaires et ceux de la presse. Elle est fermement convaincue qu'a la mort de César, elle, Césarine, prendra en toute sécurité les rênes du gouvernement; elle ne lit donc point d'histoire? Elle pourrait bien se désillusionner en ouvrant seulement le *Moniteur* de 1813; elle y verrait que Marie-Louise, régente comme elle à cette époque, que le peuple acclamait comme la plus sage, la plus charitable des souveraines, a fini par prendre le chemin de Parme et devenir Madame Neiperg.[i]

Kolochine m'a parlé de vos cruelles souffrances; il n'est pas besoin de dire que nous y avons vivement compati.*j*

> Avec mille et mille remerciements.
> Votre bien cordialement dévoué
> J. Tolstoj

a) In 1862, Prince Volkonsky was appointed ambassador to Spain. This was an important post which promoted him to the rank of plenipotentiary minister.

b) *Sergey Ivanovich Tolstoy* (1838-1897), the nephew of Yakov Tolstoy, son of his cousin Ivan ("Jean"), whom he mentioned in his first letter to Volkonsky of May 1, 1858 in the least interesting part thus omitted. The young Tolstoy had not succeeded in achieving the career that his family expected him to have.

c) *Juan Prim* (1814-1876) — Spanish general and statesman. Prim was one of the leaders of the revolution of 1868 which resulted in the expulsion from the country of Queen Isabella II, whom he had first supported while participating in the Carlist War of 1833-39. Prim entered politics around 1841. For his involvement with the uprising, he was condemned and had to leave the country. Later pardoned, Prim became the governor of Puerto Rico. In 1861, he was commissioned to head the Spanish expedition to Mexico. At the time this letter was written, Prim returned to Spain, where he associated himself with the Progressive party. Volkonsky, then in Madrid, most likely met with General Prim.

d) Here again, Tolstoy repeats his favorite Latin expression *ultima ratio*, the last reason (see letter No. II). He also uses a French expression *volte face*, denoting a sudden turn, when he speaks about the abrupt switch of the army for the side of the insurgents.

e) *Duke de Rivas, Angel de Saaverda* (1791-1865) — Spanish politician, poet, and playwright. Around 1820, de Rivas entered politics; three years later, having been condemned to death for his extreme liberal views, he had to flee abroad. After the amnesty of 1833, de Rivas returned to Spain, where three years later he became Minister of the Interior. In 1837, however, the Duke had to flee again, this time for his conservative views, but in 1838 he was able to return to Spain. He entered then the Senate and was later appointed ambassador first to Naples and then to Paris, where he met Tolstoy.

f) The ironic mention of France's "much loved Emperor" refers to *Louis Napoleon Bonaparte* (1808-1873), the nephew of Napoleon, who was brought up in exile and, after a few unsuccessful attempts to gain power, was condemned to life imprisonment. Having managed to escape to London, Louis Napoleon returned to France after the revolution of 1848, and soon thereafter was elected to the Assembly. In December of 1848, Louis Napoleon became President of the Republic; four years later he gained absolute power and as Napoleon III headed the Second Empire in the years 1851-1870. His initially successful domestic program was, however, undermined by the course of the aggressive foreign policy which he had followed later (see notes 'c' and 'd' to letter II).

g) Tolstoy is mocking here "the affairs of the imperial family" which was losing the attention of the French people because they were preoccupied in 1865 with the latest balloon flight. "Le Géant" ("The giant") was the largest balloon in the world (over 200,000 cubic feet of gas). "The Giant" had made three ascents prior to the one mentioned here by Tolstoy. Each ascent, even the unsuccessful one, caused extraordinary enthusiasm, which overshadowed all other events of the time.

h) *Napoleon-Joseph-Charles Bonaparte* (1822-1891): son of the Ex-King of Westphalia, Emperor Napoleon's younger brother Gérôme. Prince Napoleon was nicknamed "Plon-plon" and "Crain-plon" ('Fearlead') because of his unheroic behavior during the Crimean War. Brought up and educated abroad, he returned to France only after the revolution of 1848. He was later elected to the National Assembly, then appointed Minister for the Colonies. After the death of his elder brother Gérôme, Napoleon assumed his name and was designated successor to the throne, should Napoleon III die childless. Prince Gérôme distinguished himself as an eloquent speaker, hence the comparison with Dumoulin. In 1865, his speech against France's involvement in Mexico was an embarrassment to the Emperor, and it was expected that he would suggest that his unruly cousin, as in the past, leave for one of his longer "pérégrinations" mentioned in this letter by Tolstoy.

i) Tolstoy continues to write about the events and personalities of the time in the same ironic key. In July 1865, Empress Eugenia (1826-1920) was acting as regent. Asserting that she expects after the death of Napoleon III ("César") to become France's ruler ("Césarine"), Tolstoy compares her possible fate with that of another French regent, *Marie Louise* (1791-1847), an Austrian princess, who was the second consort of the emperor Napoleon, and had also become regent for her son. After Napoleon's abdication, Marie Louise returned to Austria, and after his death she married count Adam Neipperg (1775-1829).

j) *Sergey Pavlovich Koloshin* (1822-1869) — writer and journalist. Koloshin's longer novel, *The Ulcer of Fashionable Society*, presented contemporary life in a satirical light. The collection *Our Village from*

Day to Day, which concerns peasant life, follows the tradition of the Naturalistic School. After an unsuccessful attempt to publish his own literary journal, Koloshin went abroad. He spent the last years of his life in Italy and France. While abroad, Koloshin communicated with both Alexander Volkonsky and Yakov Tolstoy.

LETTER FROM IVAN SERGEEVICH TURGENEV
TO A. P. GOLITSYN

The signed and dated letter from Ivan Sergeevich Turgenev in Volkonskaya's Archive carries no indication of its addressee. Our first assumption, that this letter was written to the Princess' son, Alexander, had to be dismissed: Prince Volkonsky was then still the Russian Ambassador in Madrid[1] whereas Turgenev's addressee was obviously living in Paris at that time. The text of the letter, until now unpublished, offers, however, some information helpful in identifying the person to whom it was written.

Dated February 21, 1868, the letter bears the address in Baden-Baden where Turgenev had been staying, with short interruptions, since 1863. The only reason the famous writer chose to live in this fashionable German resort was his desire to be close to Pauline Viardot. The celebrated singer, who was now losing her voice, had decided to move there, limiting herself to teaching and staging light opera along with occasional recitals. For more than two decades, Pauline Viardot, her husband Louis, and Turgenev had continued their menage à trois which, with the years, had become for the writer a way of life, a matter of habit. While in Baden-Baden, Turgenev was working on the French translation of his novel *The Smoke* and was writing the story "The Brigadier." Trying to help the aging Viardot establish her reputation as a teacher and stage director, Turgenev also wrote texts for her musical comedies, and sometimes even appeared in them in some odd parts — a spectacular figure, always received with curiosity by the public. During the season, he also continued to indulge in his old hobby, hunting. His correspondence with Russian, French, and German literary circles and friends was extensive during this period. This, too, helped us to determine the identity of Turgenev's addressee.

The letter, which begins with the formal "Monsieur," was written in French, with the insertion of two Russian titles: Turgenev's story "The Brigadier" and the Russian journal *European Messenger*. This suggested that the letter was written either to a Russian for whom French was the usual means of communication, or to a Russian-speaking Frenchman. Considering the second possibility, we thought that it could have been written to Prosper Mérimée, who had a good reading knowledge of Russian, but Turgenev would have not addressed him with the remote "Monsieur." Besides, his later correspondence also contradicts this assumption.

Being a subtle stylist, Turgenev was always conscious of the form of his letters. His French was grammatically impeccable, although he himself appraised it ironically as "Petersburgian French." Turgenev's literary friends, however, observed that his pure and expressive French reminded them rather of the language spoken in the French salons of the eighteenth century.[3] Although he was truly bilingual, Turgenev preferred to write in Russian not only to his Russian friends, but also sometimes to Pauline Viardot. "My friendly feelings to you," he wrote on one occasion, "could be much better expressed in our native tongue."[4] As V. Sollogub remarked, "While living abroad, Turgenev liked to use Russian — this was a real treat for him."[5]

With these observations in mind, we again went through Turgenev's letters from 1867-1868. Of his Russian correspondents who received from him letters in French, we singled out seven persons. To four of them, to whom he usually wrote in Russian, Turgenev had sent letters of recommendation in French for various people he was introducing. All four were addressed "Cher Monsieur."[6] Two others were written to Russians, for whom French was the first language and natural means of correspondence.[7] The seventh person, to whom Turgenev wrote fifteen longer letters in French, was the Russian Prince Avgustin Petrovich Golitsyn (1824-1875), a converted Catholic, essayist, and publisher of the French journal *Correspondent*, whom we believe to be the addressee of the letter in question.[8]

It was Golitsyn who translated Turgenev's novel *The Smoke* disappointing the author so much that, with the help of Mérimée, he not only corrected this unsatisfactory translation, but rewrote many parts.[9] Turgenev called Golitsyn his "translator-traditore" ("Translator-traitor"),[10] and wrote to him that " . . . it is painful to see my name on this work which . . . is swarming with mistakes and misinterpretations." The translation, Turgenev concluded, distorted the text to such an extent that "I would never finish, should I attempt to count all the mistakes."[11] In addition to this, when *The Smoke* became an object of violent political attacks in Russia, Golitsyn, not wanting to be associated with the novel, asked to remove his name from the French translation.[12] All this shows that Turgenev had reason to dislike both Golitsyn's translation and Golitsyn himself, and explains the impersonal "Monsieur," the writing of the letter in French, and the reserved tone.

Turgenev's mention in this letter of his forthcoming trip to Paris and the promise to bring a copy of the story "The Brigadier" also confirm our attribution. In one of the published letters to Golitsyn written after his trip to Paris, Turgenev returns to the same subject: he apologizes for not bringing the story himself, as promised, and informs Golitsyn that he arranged that it would now be delivered to him in Paris.[13]

A further argument in support of our conclusion about the addressee of this letter comes from the Volkonskaya Archive: we happened upon a later addition, a folder containing five short letters to Avgustin Golitsyn and one note to Angéle Golitsyna.[14] Turgenev's letter, however, was placed separately. The presence of this unexpected letter could be explained by the Catholic ties of Volkonskaya herself and those of some of her descendents, as well as by the frequent visits of Prince Avgustin Golitsyn in Rome, where several generations of his relatives resided.

This previously unpublished letter in the Volkonskaya Archive at Harvard's Houghton Library is the sixteenth known letter written by Ivan Sergeevich Turgenev to Avgustin Petrovich Golitsyn. Of the fifteen previously published letters, only two are known to be preserved in the original.[15]

Four pages of light blue paper, 14 x 21.5 cm., written on two sides. On the left side a crown and the letters 'M. A.' embossed in the paper.

Bade
Schillerstr. 7
a 21 Fevrier 1868[a]

Monsieur,[b]

Si je ne vous ai pas repondu à l'instant, c'est que je comptais aller à Paris et vous remettre en personne le No de la Revue (*Vestnik Evropy*) où se trouve ce petit récit en question.[c] La maladie d'un ami m'a retenu ici; mais j'espère pouvoir me rendre à Paris vers la fin de la semaine prochaine[d] — et j'aurai le plaisir de vous porter le "Brigadier" dés que j'y serai arrivé.[e]

Le prince Tcherkasskï* a quitté Bade depuis plus d'un mois: il est allé par Munich à Berlin où il compte passer le reste d l'hiver. Recevez, Monsieur, l'assurance de mes sentiments les plus distingués.

J. Tourguéneff

a) Turgenev always dated his letters and included his address. Once he scolded the writer Grigorovich for following the irritating Russian habit of omiting the address, hence creating confusion about the whereabouts of the addressor.[16] Thanks to this pedantic marking of his address, we know that on February 21, 1868, Turgenev lived in Baden-Baden, on Schiller Strasse 7, where he had been staying since early 1863. On March 30/April 11, 1868, ten days after his return from Paris, Turgenev moved to his own house on Thiergarten Strasse 3.

b) The formal "Monsieur" was used by Turgenev in thirteen of his fifteen letters to Golitsyn. Only in two letters did he address Golitsyn as "Mon Prince" or "Cher Monsieur."[17]

c) The title of "the story in question" is given in Russian: "Brigadir." Turgenev began the story on February 7/19, 1867 in Baden-Baden.[18] It had been published in Russian in 1868, in the January issue of the Russian journal *The European Messenger*. Turgenev devoted much attention to the story, working thoroughly on the details. As the writer Goncharov recollected, Turgenev sometimes sent urgent letters from Germany to the editor just to change or add a few words.[19]

d) Turgenev began to plan a trip to Paris in December 1867, and wrote about this in his letters, but he had to postpone the journey so many times that he himself started to joke about it: "The devil is interfering with my plans, sticking his spokes into my wheels."[20] In his letters, Turgenev gave several explanations for the delay, one of them being the illness of Louis Viardot.[21] However, the real reason was the difficult financial situation in which the wealthy Turgenev found himself at that time because of the dishonest management of his estates in Russia by his uncle Nikolay N. Turgenev, who had almost ruined him. At the beginning of January, this uncle delivered the last blow: he called an unsecured promissory note for 16,500 roubles, which his trusting nephew had left with him in case of emergency.[22] Having somehow settled his affairs, Turgenev left Baden-Baden for Paris on March 11/23, 1868. He returned there on March 20/April 1, after having spent a week in Paris, where he saw his daughter and arranged some matters with his publisher.

Golitsyin did not receive the story for translation. Soon after the publication of "The Brigadier" in Russia, Turgenev himself started working on the French translation, usually first dictating the French text to Louis Viardot ("he knew his craft"), then passing it on to Mérimée for corrections.[23] The story was published in French in issues 4, 5, and 6 of *Journal des Débats* for 1858. A few months later is apppeared, along with six other Turgenev works, in the collection *Nouvelles moscovites*.

e) On the day after his arrival in Paris, Turgenev met Golitsyn, but could not give him "The Brigadier" as promised in this letter, because he had to leave the Russian text with Mérimée who was working on the translation. He did, however, send him the story via Mérimée three months later.[25]

f) *Prince Vladimir Cherkassky* (1824-1878) — a publicist active in political life. In his youth he was close to the Slavophiles and their publication *Russian Discussion*. Together with Samarin and Milyutin, he participated in preparation for the peasant reforms, which would result in the abolishment of serfdom. Turgenev met Cherkassky in the late fifties. They were in Rome at the same time in the winter of 1858, and it is possible that their acquaintance with Golitsyn began there. Later they met both in Moscow and abroad. In the fall of 1867, when Prince Cherkassky was in Baden-Baden, Turgenev introduced him to Viardot and went hunting with him.

NOTES

[1] A detailed treatment of Volkonskaya's life and work will be offered in the second volume of this study.

[2] The note written in the hand of Volkonskaya's grandmother, M. D. Tatishcheva, which is now in the collection at Houghton Library, states that Zinaida was born in Dresden on December 3, 1789. The discrepancy in three years with the generally accepted date (December 3, 1792, Turin) could be explained by the age difference with Prince Nikita Volkonsky, who was born in 1792. The change of place was necessary because the Beloselskys lived in Turin at that time. First recorded in Roman Jakobson and Bayara Aroutunova, "An Unknown Album Page by Nikolaj Gogol," *Harvard Library Bulletin* (Cambridge, July 1972), XX, 3, p. 237.

[3] A. Gulyga, "Iz zabytogo," *Nauka i žizn'* (Moscow, 1977), III, pp. 104-107; Kant's letter to Prince A. M. Beloselsky in CGALI, f. 172, op. 1, d. 153.

[4] Zinaida never established a warm relationship with her stepmother. Characteristically, her name was not present among the memorials for those who were dear to the Princess, which she erected in her Roman villa (although among the names of statesmen and famous writers we find those of her nurse and governess).

[5] MS., Houghton Library.

[6] M. Azadovskij, "Iz materialov *Stroganovskoj Akademii*. Neopublikovannye proizvedenija Ksav'e de Mestra i Zinaidy Volkonskoj," *LN*, 1939, 33-34, pp. 206-208; MSS., Houghton Library.

[7] MSS., Houghton Library.

[8] Princess Dorothea Lieven, letter to her brother Alexander Benkendorf, September 16/28, 1813, L. G. Robinson, ed., *Letters of Dorothea Princess Lieven* (London: Longmans, 1902), p. 5.

[9] M. D. Buturlin, "Zapiski," *RA*, 1897, 1, 4, p. 641.

[10] MS., Houghton Library.

[11] F. von Gentz, *Journal* (Leipzig: 1861), p. 185; M.-H. Weil, *Les dessous du Congrès de Vienne* (Paris: Payot, 1971), I, pp. 201, 206, 229, 372, 399.

[12] MS., Houghton Library, letter to Volkonskaya from Count Moscati April 23, 1815; Rosalie Rzewuska, *Mémoires* (Rome: Cuggiani, 1939), II, p. 18.

[13] Quoted in A. N. Volkonsky commentaries in "Šest' pisem imperatora Aleksandra 1-go k knjagine Z. A. Volkonskoj," *Sbornik Russkogo Istoričeskogo Vestnika*, 1868, III, p. 312.

[14] MS., Houghton Library; (*Œuvres choisies de la princesse Zénéide Volkonsky, née princesse Béloselsky-Bélozersky* (Paris et Karlsruhe: W. Hasper, 1865), I, p. 151.

[15] N. I. Turgenev, *Pis'ma k bratu, S. I. Turgenevu* (Moscow: ANSSSR, 1936), p. 232.

[16] M. Svistunov, ed., "Griboedovskaja Moskva v pis'max M. A. Volkovoj k V. I. Lanskoj," *VE*, 1875, VIII, p. 679; R. Rzewuska (1939), p. 17; Lulu Thürheim, *Mein Leben. Erinnerungen aus Österreichs Grosser Welt* (Munich: Miller, 1914), III, p. 79, 100, 102.

[17] "Zapiska abbata Nikolja o vospitanii knjazja A. N. Volkonskogo," *RA*, 1896, I, 4, pp. 486-496.

[18] K. N. Batjuškov, "Ego pis'ma i očerk ego žizni," *RA*, 1867, II, 5, p. 1523, 1527.

[19] Zinaida Volkonskaja, "La boue d'Odessa," MS., Houghton Library; also published and commented in Nadejda Gorodetzky, "Zénaide Volkonsky, La boue d'Odessa," *Revue des études Slaves*, 1953, 30, pp. 82-86.

[20] The passport of Naumova was found later in the archive of the writer A. M. Remizov: Ja. B. Polonskij, "Literaturnyj Arxiv i usad'ba kn. Zinaidy Volkonskoj v Rime," *Vremennik. Obščestvo druzej russkoj knigi* (Paris: Povolockij, 1938), IV, pp. 163, 165.

[21] "Iz zapisok knjažny V. N. Repninoj," *RA*, 1897, II, 7, p. 489.

[22] A. Ja. Bulgakov, letter to his brother, August 19, 1818, *RA*, 1900, III, 9, p. 129.

[23] *Quatre nouvelles par la princesse Zéneide Volkonsky* ("Laure," "Deux tribus du Brésil," "Les maris mandingues," "L'enfant de Kachemyr") (Moscow: 1820), pp. 1-176; also in Volkonskaya, *Œuvres choisies* (1865), pp. 1-142.

[24] P. A. Vjazemskij, *OA*, I, pp. 318, 323.

[25] *ibid.*, pp. 319, 322, 323.

[26] Henry Beyle (Stendhal), letter to de Mareste, March 3, 1820, *Correspondance* (Paris: le Divan, 1933), V, p. 299.

[27] "Skul'ptor S. I. Gal'berg v ego zagraničnyx pis'max i zapiskax 1818-1823" *Vestnik izjaščnyx iskusstv* (St. Petersburg, 1884), II, 5, pp. 122-125; *Extracts of the Journals and Correspondence of Miss Berry*, ed. Theresa Lewis (London: 1865), III, pp. 274-276.

[28] Sosthène de La Rochefoucauld, letter to Volkonskaya, November 24, 1822, *Mémoires* (Paris: 1837), I, pp. 347-349; R. Rzewuska (1939), II, p. 17.

[29] MSS., Houghton Library.

[30] A. Ja. Bulgakov, letter to K. Ja. Bulgakov, July 28, 1824, *RA*, 1901, II, 5, p. 74.

[31] "Extrait d'une lettre au Baron Mérian en 1826," MS., Houghton Library; Volkonskaya, *Œuvres choisies* (1865), pp. 219-232.

[32] Prince P. B. Kozlovsky (1783-1840), quoted from N. Belozerskaya, "Knjaginja Z. A. Volkonskaja, " *Istoričeskij Vestnik*, 1897, LXVII, p. 952 (the letter is not dated).

[33] *Tableau Slave du cinquième siècle* (Paris: 1824); also in Volkonskaya, *Œuvres choisies* (1865), pp. 157-218.

[34] The interest of the Beloselskys in their roots has continued to the present day. Prince Sergey Sergeevich Beloselsky (1895-1979), who lived in the United States, wrote for his children a long history in English of the family's past. I am obliged to the Princess Marina Beloselsky Kasarda for bringing this manuscript to my attention.

[35] *Gazette de France*, May 31, 1824; A. Martainville, *Drapeau Blanc.* 1824, May 30. Quote from Belozerskaya, (1897), LXVII, p. 953.

[36] "Olga," otryvok, *Moskovskij nabljudatel'*, 1836, IX, pp. 308- 338; "Olga," Z. A. Volkonskaja, *Œuvres choisies* (1865), pp. 269-338.

[37] P. A. Vyazemsky, *PSS*, VII, p. 329.

[38] P. A. Vyazemsky, letter to A. I. Turgenev, February 6, 1833, *OA*, (1899), III, p. 223.

[39] B. L. Modzalevskij, "Puškin v donesenijax agentov tajnogo nadzora," *Byloe* (Petrograd: 1918), I, 29, p. 31.

[40] Adam Mickiewicz wrote for Princess Zinaida "Pokój Grecki," ("Greek room"); he also translated his "Crimean Sonnets" for her into French prose (MSS., Houghton Library).

[41] Z. A. Volkonskaya, letter to A. S. Pushkin, October 29, 1826, A. S. Puškin, *PSS* (1937), XIII, p. 229.

[42] I. I. Kozlov, letter to Z. A. Volkonskaya, November 25, 1826, MS., Houghton Library.

⁴³ M. S. Volkonsky, ed., *Zapiski knjagini M. N. Volkonskoj* (St. Petersburg: Golike, 1906), pp. xxxi, xxxii, xxxiii, 19, 20, 21; A. V. Venevitinov, "Provody knjagini Marii Volkonskoj," *RS*, 1875, XII, pp. 822-824.

⁴⁴ A. S. Puškin, "Knjagine Volkonskoj posylaja ej poemu "Cygany'"; A. S. Puškin, "Knjagine Z. A. Volkonskoj," *PSS*, III, p. 54; MS., Houghton Library.

⁴⁵ There is much information about Volkonskaya's salon in the "Letters of A. Ja. Bulgakov to his brother," *RA*, 1901, II, 5, p. 93; 1901, II, 6, pp. 164, 189, 211, 215, 223; III, 7, pp. 370, 380, 398, 410; 1901, III, 9, pp. 9, 16, 17.

⁴⁶ Two undated letters from the archmandrite Gerasim Pavsky, MSS., Houghton Library. It was recorded that not only Pavsky, but also the Metropolitan Platon frightened believers with suffering in hell for their sins: P. M. Snegirev, *Žizn' Platona, Mitropolita Moskovskogo* (Moscow: 1856), p. 540.

⁴⁷ A. S. Pushkin, letter to P. A. Vyazemsky, January 25, 1829, *PSS* (1941), XIV, p. 38.

⁴⁸ Z. A. Volkonskaja, "Aleksandru Pervomu," *Damskij žurnal*, 1826, II, pp. 74, 75; *Moskovskij telegraf*, 1826, VII, p. 3; "Na končinu Imperatricy Elizavety Alekseevny," *Damskij žurnal*, 1826, XII, p. 232; *Moskovskij telegraf*, 1826, IX, p. 3; "Iz putevyx zapisok ob Italii," *Moskovskij vestnik*, 1827, VI, pp. 392-397; "Dobrodušie," *Moskovskij vestnik*, 1827, V, pp. 372, 373; in French: *Œuvres choisies* (1865), pp. 237, 238; "Otryvok iz putevyx zapisok," *Galateja*, 1829, V, pp. 3-21; "Otryvok iz putevyx zapisok," *Galateja*, 1829, VI, pp. 88-90; "Snovidenie," *Galateja*, 1829, V, pp. 21-31.

⁴⁹ R. E. Terebinina, "Puškin i Z. A. Volkonskaja," *Russkaja literatura*, 1975, 2, p. 144.

⁵⁰ S. Durylin, "Russkie pisateli u Gete," *LN*, 1932, IV-VI, pp. 477-486. Volkonskaya's visit to Goethe will receive a detailed treatment in the second volume of this study.

⁵¹ S. A. Sobolevsky, letter to S. P. Shevyrev, July 19, 1831, *RA, 1909, II, 7, p. 500.*

⁵² S. P. Shevyrev to A. V. Venevitinov, letter from Rome, (n.d.), N. P. Barsukov, ed., *Žizn' i trudy M. P. Pogodina*, 1890, III, p. 76.

⁵³ Z. A. Volkonskaya, letter to P. A. Vyazemsky, Rome 23 Aug./4 Sept., *1830, LN*, 1952, 58, p. 98.

⁵⁴ A. I. Turgenev, letter to Z. A. Volkonskaya, December 12/24, 1832, MS., Houghton Library.

⁵⁵ M. I. Glinka, letter to Z. A. Volkonskaya, February 23, 1832, MS., Houghton Library.

⁵⁶ "Otryvki iz putevyx zapisok," *Moskovskij vestnik*, 1830, II, pp. 140-151; "Otryvok iz putevyx zapisok," *Severnye cvety*, 1830, pp. 216-227; "Otryvok iz putevyx zapisok," *Severnye cvety*, 1831, pp. 120-124; "Logogrif," *Literaturnaja gazeta*, 1830, I, 71; "Moej zvezde," *Severnye cvety*, 1832, pp. 167, 168; "Nadgrobnaja pesnja slavjanskogo gusljara," *Severnye cvety*, 1832, pp. 86, 87; "Knjazju P. A. Vjazemskomu na smert' ego dočeri," *RA*, 1867, p. 313, *Moskovskij nabljudatel'*, 1835, III, p. 113; "Otryvok skazanija ob Ol'ge," *Moskovskij nabljudatel'*, 1836, VIII, pp. 286-300, IX, pp. 308-338; "Četyre angela," *Moskovskij nabljudatel'*, 1836, VIII, pp. 116, 117; "Drugustradal'cu," *Utrennjaja zarja*, 1839, pp. 193, 194; "Pesnja Nevskaja," *RA*, 1872, 62, pp. 1979-1982; "Poslednie dni žizni Aleksandra I, " *RS*, 1878, XXI, pp. 141-150; "Extrait d'une lettre au Baron Mérian," (1826), *Œuvres choisies* (1865), pp. 221-231, pp. 249-251; in Russian, "Portret," *Dennica*, 1830, pp. 114-117.

[57] P. A. Vyazemsky, letters to his wife, May 23, 24, 25, June 1, 3, 1832, *Zven'ja* (Moscow-Leningrad): 1951, LX, pp. 369, 370, 371, 377, 380, 386, 387; Zinaida Volkonskaya, letter to Adam Mickiewicz from Botzen (Bolzano) June 6, 1832 in which she writes of her grave condition: "I am dying . . . eternity starts for your friend . . ." Archiwum literackie, XII, "Listy do A. Mickiewicza w Muzeum Adama Mickiewicza w Parizu," Warsaw, 1968, p. 214.

[58] *Scritti spirituali*, MS., Houghton Library. Nadejda Gorodetzky, who suggests that Volkonskaya was converted in 1833, richly documented Zinaida's life after the conversion: "Princess Zinaida Volkonsky," *Oxford Slavonic Papers*, 1954, V. pp. 102, 103, and "Zinaida Volkonsky as a Catholic," *The Slavic and East European Review*, London, 1960, 39, pp. 34-43; André Mazon, "Zénèide Volkonskaya la Catholique," *Festschrift für Edward Winter zum 70 Geburtstag* (Berlin: Akademie Verlag, 1967), pp. 579-590.

[59] G. G. Belli, "Sor' Artezza Zzenavida Voroshi," written in Roman dialect on January 3, 1835; G. Orioli, *Guiseppe G. Belli. Lettere Giornali Zibaldone* (Turin: Einaudi, 1962), pp. 196, 197.

[60] The relationship between Zinaida Volkonskaya and Walter Scott, as well as his poem addressed to her, will be discussed in our second volume.

[61] P. A. Vyazemsky, letter to Z. A. Volkonskaya from Hanau, September 15/27, 1824, MS., Houghton Library; also in Nina Kauchtschischwili, *L'Italia nella vita e nell'opera di P. A. Vjazemskij* (Milan: Societa Edit. e Pensiero, 1964), pp. 318-320; letter from Florence, April 12/24, 1835, MS., Houghton Library.

[62] F. Buslaev, "Rimskaja villa kn. Z. A. Volkonskoj," VE, 1896, I, I, pp. 5-32; L. Callari, *Le ville di Roma* (Rome: 1934), pp. 361- 363; Giovanni Orioli, "Zenaide Wolkonsky," *Palatino*, 1966, 4 serie, Anno X, pp. 6, 7: Carlo Pietrangeli, *Miscelanea della Societa Romana di storia Patria* (Rome: 1973), XXIII, pp. 425-430.

[63] R. E. Terebinina, "Zapisi o Puškine, Gogole, Glinke, Lermontove i drugix pisateljax v dnevnike P. D. Durnovo," *Puškin. Issledovanija i materialy* (Leningrad: "Nauka," 1978), VIII, p. 266. We will refer to this publication as Durnovo (1978).

[64] *ibid.*, pp. 256, 266.

[65] Zinaida Volkonskaya, letter to Adam Mickiewicz from Paris, November 8, 1836 written before her return trip to Rome with a short stay in Langre, *Archiwum literackie*, XII (1968), p. 213; Nadejda Gorodetzky (1954), p. 102

[66] We received from the *Vicariato di Roma* a copy of a page listing the members of the Parish of *Sts Vincenzo e Anastasio* for the year 1836, page 205, where Volkonskaya, her sister Vlasova, Vladimir Pavey, and four servants were registered as Catholics. It is significant that their names did not appear there the previous year.

[67] M. D. Buturlin, "Zapiski," RA, 1897, II, 5, p. 58.

[68] The conversion of Volkonskaya was mentioned in passing in the Eulogy to Giovanni Merlini, the spiritual father of the Princess who died in 1873: "In a miraculous way, she was called to the Catholic Church in the period ("all'epoca") of the canonization of S. Alfonso Liquori (1839)." Since the author of the Eulogy, D. Enrico Rizzoli, made other factual mistakes (i.e., Volkonskaya had been lady-in-waiting of Emperor Nicholas' wife), we decided to disregard this information accepting other, above listed sources. "Elogio di D. Giovanni Merlini, morto il 12 Gennajo 1873," Enrico Rizzoli (General-missionario). MS., Archive of the Order of the Precious Blood, Rome. See note 72.

[69] Roman Jakobson, Bayara Aroutunova (1972), pp. 239-254.

[70] V. I. Šenrok, "N. V. Gogol'. Pjat' let žizni za granicej. 1836-1841," *VE*, 1894, 8, pp. 630, 631; X. Pawel Smolikowski, *Historya zgromadzenia Zmartwychwstania Pańskiego* (Cracow: 1892-1897), II, pp. 104, 111-115.

[71] F. L. Iordan, "Zapiski," *RS*, 1891, 71, 7, pp. 247-249.

[72] P. D. Durnovo (1978), p. 273. This is further evidence that in 1837, 1838, when the Crown Prince was in Rome, Princess Volkonskaya was already converted to the Catholic faith.

[73] V. A. Zhukovsky, three notes to Z. A. Volkonskaya in Rome, January 18-30, January 26/February 7, January 30/February 11, 1839, MSS., Houghton Library.

[74] P. D. Durnovo, (1978), p. 258.

[75] *ibid.*, p. 258.

[76] G. S. Volkonsky, letter to S. G. Volkonsky, December 1811, in S. M. Volkonsky, *Archiv dekabrista S. G. Volkonskogo* (Petrograd: Golike, 1918), I, p. 374.

[77] *ibid.*, p. xxiv; P. A. Vyazemsky, letter to his wife. August 19, 1832, *Zven'ja* (1951), IX, p. 439.

[78] Dorothea v. Lieven, letter to her brother Alexander Benkendorf, February 8, 1820, L. G. Robinson, ed. (1902), p. 46.

[79] P. D. Durnovo (1978), p. 266.

[80] O. G. Basankur, "Perevodčik Puškina — Ricci," *Puškin. Vremennik Puškinskoj Komissii* (Moscow-Leningrad: ANSSSR, 1941), pp. 424- 429; E. Dmitrieva, "Moi vospominanija," *Zven'ja* (Moscow: 1950), pp. 788- 795; Nina Kauchtschischwili, *Il diario di Darja Fedorovna Ficquelmont* (Milan: Societa Editrice Vita e Pensiero, 1968), p. 73.

[81] Abbé C. de Ladou, *Monsignior Gerbet, sa vie, ses œuvres et l'école menasienne* (Paris: 1870), II., p. 162, quoting from Gorodetzky (1954), p. 102; "Zapiski arximandrita Vladimira Treleckogo", *RS*, 1889, 63, p. 566.

[82] A. N. Murav'ev, *Znakomstvo s russkimi poetami* (Kiev: 1871), p. 13.

[83] T. P. Passek, "Vospominanija," *RS*, 1878, 22, July, p. 375.

[84] Zinaida Volkonskaya, letter to Maria De Mattias, Rome, December 4, 1845, MS., Archive of the Order of Sisters Adorers of Precious Blood, Rome.

[85] "Zapiski Vladimira Treleckogo," *RS*, 1889, 63, p. 566.

[86] *Lettere della Venerabile Maria De Mattias, fondatrice delle Suore Adoratrici del Preziosissimo Sangue di N. S. G. C.* (Rome: Tragilia, 1944), I, pp. 214, 233, 264, 274, 294, 347, 350, 351, 369, 417, 433; II pp. 69, 171, 364.

[87] "Zapiski Vladimira Treleckogo," *RS*, 1889, 63, pp. 566, 567; A. Malaguti, "La Principessa Wolkonsky e Angela Molari," *Le Suore Bianche*. Primo Centenario della Fondazzione Santarcangelo di Romagnia, 3 maggio 1857-3 maggio 1957.

[88] Z. A. Volkonskaya, letter to the Pope, Pius IX, not dated, 4 pages. MS., Curia Generalizia dei Missionari del Preziosissimo Sangue, Rome.

[89] MS., Curia Generalizia dei Missionari del Preziosissimo Sangue, 4 Marzo 1834-1934. MS. La Casa Principali Dell'Instituto, Rome.

[90] Z. A. Volkonskaja, "Otryvok iz putevyx zapisok," *Severnye cvety*, 1830, p. 218.

[91] Z. A. Volkonskaya (1865), p. xiv.

[92] A. S. Puškin, *PSS* (1941) *Perepiska 1828-1831*, XIV, pp. 1-251.

[93] A. S. Pushkin, letter to N. N. Goncharova from Boldino, October 29, 1830, *PSS* (1941), XIV, pp. 118, 119.

[95] A. S. Pushkin, letter to N. N. Goncharova, October 29, 1830 from Boldino, *PSS*, XIV, pp. 118, 119, 120, 125, 130; letters to N. N. Pushkina, *ibid.*, pp. 244, 245, 246, 248, 249.

[96] The content, structure, and stylistic devices of letters in the age of Pushkin were admirably analyzed by William Mills Todd III in *The Familiar Letter as a Literary Genre in the Age of Pushkin* (Princeton, N. J.: Princeton University Press, 1976), pp. 1-230.

[97] P. A. Vyazemsky, letter to V. F. Vyazemskaya, August 3, 1826, *OA*, V, 2, p. 68.

[98] P. A. Vyazemsky, letter to his family, January 23, 1840, CGALI, f. 195, op. 1, no. 3271, 1.122. Quote from E. Gershtein, *Sud'ba Lermontova* (Moscow: GIXL, 1986), p. 120.

[99] P. A. Vyazemsky, letter to Countess Musina-Pushkina, October 18, 1837, CGADA, f. 1270, op. 1, ch. 3, no. 3319, 1, 18. Quote from E. Gershtein (1986), pp. 120, 121.

[100] P. A. Vjazemskij, *PSS*, VIII, p. 282.

[101] See note 26.

LETTERS TO PRINCESS ZINAIDA VOLKONSKAYA

Letter from Mme. De Staël

[1] A short quotation of Mme. de Staël's letter to Princess Volkonskaya appeared in André Trofimoff, *La Princesse Zéneide Wolkonsky* (Rome: Straderini, 1966), p. 38; the same short passage was quoted in Russian by R. E. Terebinina in "Puškin i Z. A. Volkonskaja," *Russkaja literatura* (Leningrad: 1975), II, p. 143.

[2] Madame de Staël, *Dix années d'exile*, ed. Gautier (Paris: Plon, 1904), p. 288.

[3] Simone Balayé, "Dans la bibiothèque de Madame de Staël," *Cahiers Staëliens*, nouvelle série (Paris: Attinger, 1970), pp. 52, 53; S. Durylin, "Gospoža de Stal' i ee russkie otnošenija," *LN*, 1939, 33-34, pp. 265-268; A. Sorel, *Gospoža Stal'* (St. Petersburg: 1892), p. 51; J. G. Galiffe, *D'un siècle à l'autre* (Génève, 1878), II, p. 312; Olga Trtnik Rossetini, "Madame de Staël et la Russie" in *Madame de Staël et l'Europe* (Paris: Bibliothèque Nationale, 1966), p. 66.

[4] Madame de Staël, *Dix années d'exile*, p. 293.

[5] *ibid.*, p. 305.

[6] *ibid.*, p. 313, 314.

[7] F. V. Rostopchin, letter to Alexander I, July 26, 1812, *RA*, 1875, II, 8, p. 400.

[8] Madame de Staël, *Dix années d'exile*, pp. 298, 314, 362.

[9] *ibid.*, p. 331.

[10] *ibid.*, p. 311, 314, 331, 362.

[11] K. N. Batjuškov, *Sočinenija* (St. Petersburg: 1885- 1887), III, p. 198.

[12] "Častnye pis'ma 1812 goda M. A. Volkovoj k V. I. Lanskoj," *RA*, 1872, pp. 2388, 2389, 2395-2397.

[13] Madame de Staël, *Dix années d'exile*, p. 318.

[14] The famous Count Orlov, as Countess Gourjeff (Gurjeva) wrote, "crawled on all fours to attract Madame de Staël to his palace, thus increasing the celebrity of his island." P. I. Ščukin, ed., *Bumagi, otnosjaščiesja do otečestvennoj vojny 1812 goda*, "Pis'ma Hélène Gourjeff," (Moscow: Tip. Mamontova, 1905), 1X, p. 303.

[15] Simone Balayé, *Les carnets de voyage de Madame de Staël* (Geneva: Droz, 1971), pp. 294-321.

[16] Madame de Staël, *Dix années*, p. 334-337.

[17] S. Durylin, *LN*, 1939, pp. 232-260; Maria Ullrichova, ed. *Lettres de Madame de Staël conservées en Bohême* (Prague: Academie Tchéchoslovaque des Sciences, 1960), p. 266; George Solovieff, "Madame de Staël et ses correspondants russes," *Cahiers Staëliens, nouvelle série*, 1962, no, 2, pp. 9-17.

[18] *Arxiv dekabrista S. G. Volkonskogo*, S. M. Volkonskij, ed. (Petrograd: Golike, 1918), pp. 378, 381; "Častnye pis'ma 1812 goda," *RA*, 1872, p, 2397.

[19] "Iz materialov "Stroganovskoj Akademii," *LN*, 33-34, pp. 206-208.

[20] Norman King, "Un récit inédit du grand voyage de Madame de Staël (1812-1813)," *Cahiers Staëliens*, nouvelle série, (1966), no. 4, pp. 11, 13.

[21] P. I. Ščukin, ed. (1905), IX, p. 302.

[22] CGALI, f. 46, ed. xr. 560, 11, 409-410. Quote from R. E. Terebinina, "Puškin i Z. A. Volkonskaja," *Russkaja literatura* (Leningrad: 1975), II, p. 143.

[23] "Častnye pis'ma 1812 goda," *RA*, 1872, p. 2397.

[24] "Zapiski grafa M. D. Buturlina," *RA,*. 1897, 1, 2, p. 640; *Mémoires de la comtesse de Boigne née D'Osmond* (Paris: Mercure de France, 1971), p. 274.

[25] A. N. Volkonskij, "Poezdka fligel' ad'jutanta knjazja N. G. Volkonskogo k Napoleonu v 1808 godu," *RA*, 1874, 1, 1, pp. 1047-1050.

Letter from E. A. Baratynsky

[1] N. Maksimov, "Evgenij Abramovič Baratynskij po bumagam Pažeskogo Korpusa," *RS*, 1870, 11, pp. 201-207.

[2] E. A. Baratynsky, Letter to N. V. Putyata, Fall 1825, CGALI, f. 394, op. 1, ed. xr. 80. Quoted from Geir Kjetsaa, *E. A. Baratynskij, Žizn' i tvorčestvo* (Oslo-Bergen-Tromsö, Universitetsforlaget, 1973), p. 113; Letter to N. V. Putyata of January 1826, *RA,* 1867, I, p. 274.

[3] P. A. Vyazemsky, letter to A. Turgenev, October 15, 1828, *OA* III, p. 179; P. A. Vyazemsky, letter to Pushkin, A. S. Puškin, *PSS*, XIII, p. 276.

[4] E. A. Baratynsky, letter to N. M. Konshin, December 19, 1826, *RS*, 1908, 12, p. 759.

[5] N. Barsukov, *Žizn' i trudy M. P. Pogodina* (St. Petersburg: 1889), II, p. 37; N. D. Ivančin-Pisarev, "Al'bom avtografov," *SiN*, 1905, X, p. 505; D. L. Mordovcev, *Russkie ženščiny novogo vremeni* (St. Petersburg: 1874), p. 264; P. A. Vjazemskij, *PSS* (St. Petersburg: 1882), VII, p. 329; T. P. Passek, "Vospominanija," *RS*, 1873, 3, p. 315; E. A. Baratynsky, letter to Mukhanov, October 29, 1826, *RA*, 1895, III, 9, p. 125.

[6] "Iz carstva vista i zimy," almanac *Podsnežnik* (St. Petersburg: 1892), p. 151; E. A. Baratynskij, *Polnoe sobranie stixotvorenij* (Leningrad: Sov. Pisatel', BBP, 1957), p. 144.

[7] "Kuplety na den' roždenija knjagini Zinaidy Volkonskoj v ponedel'nik 3-go dekabrja 1828 goda, sočinennye v Moskve kn. P. A. Vjazemskim, E. A. Baratynskim, S. P. Ševyrevym, N. F. Pavlovym i I. S. Kireevskim," *ibid.*, pp. 314-316.

[8] E. A. Baratynskij, *Stixotvorenija* (Moscow, 1835), I-II. Collection of Baron V. K. Lemmerman, Rome; now at Houghton Library, Harvard University.

[9] Z. A. Volkonskaya, letter to P. A. Vyazemsky from Rome, March 4, 1830, *LN*, 1952, 58, p. 98; Vyazemsky, letter to A. Turgenev, January 1, 1829, *Arxiv brat'ev Turgenevyx* (Petrograd: 1921), I, 6, p. 77.

[10] E. A. Baratynsky, letter to N. V. Putyata from Naples, April/May 1844, *RA*, 1867, p. 296.

[11] "Djad'ke-ital'jancu," E. A. Baratynskij, (1957), p. 203.

[12] Geir Kjetsaa (1973), pp. 564-637.

[13] E. A. Baratynskij, "Istorija koketstva," *Severnye cvety*, 1825, pp. 109-111; E. A. Baratynskij, *PSS*, M. L. Gofman, ed. (Petrograd: Akademija Nauk, 1916), 11, pp. 204-207.

Letter from I. I. Kozlov

[1] N. M. Danilov, "Materialy dlja polnogo sobranija sočinenij I. I. Kozlova," *IORJaiS*, 1915, XX, 2, p. 102; A. Xomutov, "Iz bumag poeta I. I. Kozlova," *RA*, 1886, 1, 2, pp. 177-202.

[2] V. A. Zhukovsky, introduction to Kozlov's poem *Chernets: Puškin i ego sovremenniki* (St. Petersburg, 1911), XIV, p. 63.

[3] P. A. Vyazemsky, letter to V. F. Vyazemskaya, January 5, 1832, *Zven'ja* (Moscow: Goskultprosvetizd, 1951), IX, p. 243.

[4] K. Ja. Grot, "Dnevnik I. I. Kozlova," *SiN*, 1906, XI, pp. 39-66; A. Xomutov (1866), pp. 181-192.

[5] K. Ja. Grot (1906), pp. 48, 51, 52, 56-58; N. V. Solov'ev, *Istorija odnoj žizni; A. A. Voejkova* (Petrograd, 1915), 1, pp. 94-97, 100-102; K. Ja. Grot," K biografii I. I. Kozlova," *IORJaiS*, 1904, IX, 2, pp. 75, 76.

[6] I. I. Kozlov, "Knjagine Z. A. Volkonskoj, *Polnoe sobranie stixotvorenij* (Leningrad: Sovetskij Pisatel', *BBP*, 1960), pp. 103, 104. This poem first appeared, unattributed, in *RA*, 1900, 1, 2, p. 311 under the title "K kn. Z. A. V-oj." The publisher of the *Russian archive*, P. Bartenev, commented upon this title that "It was indeed addressed to the Princess Zenaida Aleksandrovna Volkonskaya. Whose it is, however, we don't know. It was found in the Mukhanov's estate papers and was then placed in the museum of I. P. Shchukin."

[7] K. Ja. Grot (1906), p. 46.

[8] *ibid.*

[9] I. I. Kozlov, *PSS* (1960), p. 103.

[10] I. I. Kozlov, "Portugal'skaja pesnja," *ibid.*, p. 138. Dargomyzhsky's composition, entitled "Privet," appeared in 1828, published by M. Bernard.

[11] P. A. Vyazemsky, letter to I. I. Kozlov, January 2, 1828, in A. Khomutov (1896), p. 183.

[12] Now in Houghton Library.

[13] A. G. Laval, letter to I. I. Kozlov, February 10, 1831 in Khomutov (1886), p. 317.

[14] I. I. Kozlov, "Pesnja solov'ja" ("Pridi, pridi ..."). The manuscript is in the Houghton Library. A complete text of this poem will appear in the second volume of this work.

[15] Z. A. Volkonskaja, "Ty arfa stradan'ja ..." First published in the almanac *Utrennjaja zarja*, 1839, p. 139. The manuscript is now in the Houghton Library.

[16] I. I. Kozlov, "Knjagine Z. A. Volkonskoj (v otvet na ee poslanie)," *PSS* (1960), p. 301.

[17] I. V. Kireevskij, *PSS* (Moscow: Put', 1911), 11, p. 27.

[18] M. A. Venevitinov, "K biografii poeta D. V. Venevitinova," *RA*, 1885, I, 1, p. 127.

[19] Z. A. Volkonskaya, letter to A. S. Pushkin, October 29, 1826, A. S. Puškin, *PSS,* *XIII, p. 299.*

[20] K. Ja. Grot (1906), pp. 41, 42.

[21] K. Ja. Grot (1904), p. 90.

[22] *Černec, kievskaja povest'. Sočinenie Ivana Kozlova* (St. Petersburg, 1825).

[23] I. I. Kozlov, letters to A. A. Voeykova: N. V. Solov'ev, *Istorija odnoj žizni* (1916), 11, pp. 27-29, 36, 50; Xomutov (1886), pp. 179, 188, 193; I. I. Kozlov, letter to A. S. Pushkin, May 31, 1825, A. S. Puškin: *PSS* (1937), X111, p. 176.

[24] Benjamin Constant, *Adolphe* (Paris: Garnier, 1955), pp. 19-22.

[25] P. A. Vyazemskij, *Adolf, PSS,* 1886, X, p. iii.

[26] P. A. Vyazemsky, letter to V. F. Vyazemskaya, September 6, 1826. *OA,* V, 2, p. 90.

[27] A. S. Pushkin, letter to A. I. Turgenev, July 14, 1824, A. S. Puškin, *PSS* (1937), XIII, p. 103.

[28] P. A. Vyazemsky, letter to I. I. Kozlov, July 9, 1827 in Khomutov, *RA,* 1886, 1, 2, pp. 184, 185. "Your Princess" — Natalya Dolgorukaya in Kozlov's poem of the same name.

Letter from M. I. Glinka

[1] This letter, the manuscript of which is in the Houghton Library of Harvard University, was published by I. S. Zilbershtein, "Novonajdennoe pis'mo M. I. Glinki k Z. A. Volkonskoj," *Pamjati Glinki. Issledovanija i materialy* (Moscow: Ak. Nauk, 1958), pp. 441-456. This thorough and informative publication needs, however, some additions and corrections. One of them: this manuscript was never in the Columbia University Library.

[2] M. I. Glinka, "Zapiski," in *PSS* (Moscow: Izd. Muzyka, 1973) I, pp. 242, 243.

[3] *Ibid.,* p. 249.

[4] A. N. Strugovščikov, "M. I. Glinka. Vospominanija," *RS,* 1874, 9, pp. 715, 716.

[5] M. I. Glinka (1973), pp. 211, 240.

[6] *Ibid.,* p. 249.

[7] Hector Berlioz on Glinka, *Journal des Débats,* 1845, April 16.

[8] I. S. Zilbershtein in his article asserts: "There is no information about their (Volkonskaya and Glinka's) acquaintance. There is not a single word about Glinka's meeting Volkonskaya in the memoirs of his contemporaries, and she is not mentioned in the biography of the great composer . . . All this confirms our assumption that Glinka did not meet Volkonskaya in the twenties, when she was living in Russia." Zilbershtein, 1958, p. 448.

[9] M.P. Pogodin, "Vospominanija o S. P. Ševyreve," *Žurnal Ministerstva Narodnogo Prosveščenija,* 1869, 141, p. 405; V. V. Stasov, letter to N. F. Findeizen, May 26, 1893 in *Ežegodnik Imperatorskix Teatrov,* 1912, XI, p. 8.

[10] M. I. Glinka (1973), p. 234.

[11] N. P. Barsukov, *Žizn' i trudy M. P. Pogodina* (Moscow: 1889), II, p. 67; E. A. Baratynskij, *Materialy k ego biografii. Iz Tat'evskogo arxiva* (Petrograd: Izd. Imp. Ak. Nauk 1916), pp. 79, 111, 125.

[12] The house concerts held by Count A. Soymonov were mostly devoted to vocal music since the young countess was an accomplished singer schooled in Florence by the

famous Manielli. They attracted Moscow music lovers particularly during the years when Volkonskaya lived there. *RA*, 1897, III, 9, p. 549.

[13] "Pis'ma N. F. Pavlova k A. A. Kraevskomu," *RA*, 1897, I, 3, p. 455.

[14] *Liričeskij al'bom na 1829 god*, izdan M. Glinkoju i N. Pavliščevym (St. Petersburg, 1829). This copy from Princess Volkonskaya's Roman library is now at the Houghton Library of Harvard University.

[15] M. I. Glinka, letter to S. P. Shevyrev, November 10, 1831 "Iz bumag Ševyreva," *RA*, 1878, 1, 2, p. 59.

[16] M. I. Glinka (1973), p. 250.

[17] M. I. Glinka, letter to Shevyrev, *RA*, 1878, 1, 2, pp. 59, 60.

[18] B. V. Asaf'ev, *M. I. Glinka* (Moscow: Izd. Muzyka, 1950), p. 71.

[19] M. I. Glinka (1973), pp. 250-252.

[20] *ibid.*, p. 251.

[21] V. A. Sollogub, *Vospominanija* (Moscow-Leningrad, Academia, 1931), p. 205.

[22] M. I. Glinka, letter to Shevyrev, *RA*, 1878, I, 2, p. 59; M. I. Glinka, *Zapiski* (1973), p. 252.

[23] I. S. Zilbershtein failed to make a distinction between Palazzo Poli on via Poli, in the center of Rome, where the Princess rented a large apartment, and her own villa in Lateran (then almost out of town), which in 1832 was being built and where Volkonskaya moved only in 1833. Volkonskaya corresponded with many of her old friends, as stated in Zilbershtein's article. Two names, however, have to be excluded from those listed there: Mme. de Staël, who died twelve years before Zinaida's arrival in Rome and Count Ricci, who left Russia in 1829 for Rome, and while there, was in constant contact with the Princess. Zilbershtein, 1958, p. 445.

[24] Dnevnik P. D. Durnovo in Puškin, *Issledovanija i materialy* (Leningrad: "Nauka," 1978), VIII. p. 256.

[25] M. I. Glinka (1973), p. 252.

[26] *ibid.*, p. 249.

[27] *ibid.*, p. 252.

[28] *ibid.*, p. 251, 259; Stendhal, *Vie de Rossini* (Paris: Le Divan, 1928), pp. 79, 80, 120, 129; F. Mendelssohn, *Letters* (New York: 1868), p. 149; F. Vigel', "Zapiski," *RA*, 1892, 1, 1, p. 132.

[29] S. A. Sobolevsky to S. P. Shevyrev, letter of November 14, 1832, *RA*, 1909, 11, 7, p. 509.

[30] "Al'bom avtografov N. D. Ivančina-Pisareva," *Starina i novizna* (Moscow: 1905), X, pp. 527-533.

[31] Roman Jakobson and Bayara Aroutunova, "An Unknown Album Page by Nikolaj Gogol," *Harvard Library Bulletin* (Cambridge: July 1972), XX, 3, pp. 236-239.

[32] M. A. Vlasova, entry in the album of Z. A. Volkonskaya, MS, Houghton Library.

[33] O. G. Bazankur,"Perevodčik Puškina-Ricci," *Puškin. Vremennik Puškinskoj komissii* (Moscow-Leningrad: Ak. Nauk SSSR, 1941), pp. 425-429; "Pis'ma A. Ja. Bulgakova k bratu," *RA*, 1900, III, 12, pp. 567, 570-573; RA, 1901, II, 7, pp. 399, 409; *RA*, 1903, III, 9, p. 142; "Zapiski M. D. Buturlina," *RA*, 1897, II, 8, p. 549; M. Dmitrieva, "Moi vospominanija," *Zven'ja* (Moscow: 1950), VIII, p. 788, 792.

[34] N. M. Rozhalin, *Gete, "Stradanija Vertera," (Moscow: 1828, 1829), I, II*; his articles appeared in *Moskovskij vestnik*, 1827, nos. 1, 4, 5, 6, 15, 16; 1830, 1; *VE*, 1825, no. 144, 7.

[35] S. Durylin, "Russkie pisateli u Gete v Veimare," *LN*, 1932, 4-6, pp. 422-444; S. P. Shevyrev, letter to A. P. Elagina, May 29, 1829, *RA*, 1879, I, 1, p. 138, 139.

[36] I.A . Byčkov, ed., *Dnevnik V. A. Žukovskogo* (1901), entry of January 18/30, 1838, p. 460: "Gogol's birthday — at Volkonskaya's. Singing Ricci, Capaldi, Corsini." (The spelling varies: Capaldi-Capalti).

[37] M. I. Glinka, see note no. 17 here.

[38] Album of M. A. Vlasova, entry of March 3, 1832, MS., Houghton Library.

[39] *Arxiv Raevskix* (St. Petersburg: Alexandrov, 1912), IV, pp. 372, 389, 548 (letter of A. M. Raevskaya to E. N. Orlova of December 14/26, 1856); also a letter addressed to Marie Ricci, Rome, Via Borgognoni 96.

Letter from A. I. Turgenev

[1] A. S. Pushkin, letter to P. A. Vyazemsky, August, 1831, and to F. N. Glinka, November 21, 1831 in A. S. Puškin, *PSS*, XIV, pp. 216, 241.

[2] A. I. Turgenev, letters to P. A. Vyazemsky, April 28, 1833, and December 17, 1833, *Arxiv brat'ev Turgenevyx* (Petrograd: Ak. Nauk, 1821), 1, 6, pp. 216, 372.

[3] Stendhal, *Correspondance* (Paris: Le Divan, 1834), V111. pp. 42, 49-51, 53-56, 61, 62, 65.

[4] C. Bunsen, *Aus seinen Briefen* (Leipzig, 1868), pp. 393, 394; François Michel, *Etudes Stendhaliènnes* (Paris: Mercure de France, 1957), p. 349; Chateaubriand, quoted by Vyazemsky, *OA*, 1899, 111, p. 224.

[5] A. I. Turgenev, *Akty istoričeskie otnosjaščiesja k Rossii, izvlečennye iz inostrannyx arxivov i bibliotek A. I. Turgenevym* (St. Petersburg, 1841-1842), pp. 1, 11.

[6] P. A. Vjazemskij, "Iz staroj zapisnoj knižki," *RA*, 1875, 1, 1, pp. 64, 65; also: letters to A. I Turgenev, November 20, 1826 and September 4, 1832, *Arxiv brat'ev Turgenevyx* (1921) pp. 47, 104.

[7] *ibid.*, pp. 124, 129, 185, 186, 226.

[8] I. A. Byčkov, ed., *Dnevnik V. A. Žukovskogo* (St. Petersburg: 1901), pp. 277-279, 283, 288, 290, 295.

[9] A. I. Turgenev, letter to P. A. Vyazemsky, December 12/24, 1832, *Arxiv brat'ev Turgenevyx* (1921), pp. 122-128.

[10] A. I. Turgenev, letter to N. I. Turgenev, November 22, 1827, *Pis'ma A. I. Turgeneva N. I. Turgenevu* (Leipzig, 1872), p. 270; letter to P. A. Vyazemsky, December 12/24, 1832, *Arxiv brat'ev Turgenevyx* (1921), p. 124.

[11] *ibid.*, p. 137.

[12] *ibid.*, p. 124.

[13] Z. A. Volkonskaja, "Putevye zametki. Veimar — Bavarija — Tirol'," *Severnye cvety*, No. 6, 1830, pp. 116-227.

[14] *ibid.*, pp. 53, 75, 124.

[15] *ibid.*, p. 124.

[16] V. A. Zhukovsky, letter to A. I. Turgenev, October 19/31, 1832, *RA*, I, 2, pp. 266, 267; A. I. Turgenev, letters to P. A. Vyazemsky, December 12/24, 1832, December 31/January 12, 1833, and April 12/24, 1833, *Arxiv brat'ev Turgenevyx*, (1921), pp. 125, 141, 183, 184.

[17] A. I. Turgenev, letter to K. Ja. Bulgakov, April 10, 1833, *Arxiv brat'ev Turgenevyx* (1921), pp. 181, 182.

[18] A. I. Turgenev, "Pis'mo iz Pariža," *Evropeec*, 1832, No 2, pp. 272-280.
[19] A. I. Turgenev, letters to P. A. Vyazemsky, January 18/30, 1833, January 24/February 5, 1833, *Arxiv brat'ev Turgenevyx* (1921), VI. pp. 149, 150, 156.

Two Letters from P. A. Vyazemsky

[1] P. A. Vjazemskij *Polnoe sobranie sočinenij v 12 tomax* (St. Petersburg: 1878), 1, p. x; *RA*, 1875, 111, 9, pp. 441, 442.
[2] P. A. Vyazemsky letter to A. I. Turgenev, September 30, 1819, *OA* (St. Petersburg: 1899), 1, p. 318.
[3] *ibid.*, pp. 322, 323.
[4] Z. A. Volkonskaya, letter to P. A. Vyazemsky, September 20, 1826 in *LN*, 1952, 58, p. 52.
[5] Z. A. Volkonskaja, "Aleksandru Pervomu," *Moskovskij telegraf*, 1826, no 1, p. vii; "Na smert' Imperatricy Elizavety Alekseevny," *Moskovskij telegraf*, 1826, no. 2, p. ix.
[6] P. A. Vjazemskij, "Zapiska o knjaze Vjazemskom, im samim sostavlennaja," *Zapisnye knižki* (Moscow: Ak. Nauk, 1963), p. 154; *OA* (1899), 111, p. 211, 212.
[7] P. A. Vyazemsky, letter to A. I. Turgenev, February 6, 1833, *OA* (1899), 11, p. 223.
[8] P. A. Vjazemskij, "Iz staroj zapisnoj knižki," *RA*, 1873, II, 6, 1085.
[9] A. Z. Volkonskaya, letter to P. A. Vyazemsky, *LN*, 1952, 58, p. 98.
[10] P. A. Vyazemsky, letter to A. I. Turgenev, February 6, 1833, *OA* (1899), 111, p. 223.
[11] P. A. Vjazemskij, *Zapisnye knižki*, 1963, pp. 222, 223.
[12] P. A. Vyazemsky, letter to V. F. Vyazemskaya, April 21-22, 1828, in A. S. Puškin, *PSS* (1941), XIV, pp. 12, 13, 14.
[13] P. A. Vyazemsky, letter to P. P. Vyazemsky, August 16-28, 1834, CGALI, m. 4108, ff. 26-29, quote from Nina Kauchtschischwili, *L'Italia nella vita e nell'opera di P. A. Vjazemskij* (Milan: Societa edit. vita e pensiero, 1964), p. 265.
[14] *Ibid.*, p. 276; also: V. A. Zhukovsky, letter to A. I. Turgenev, October 8, 1834, *RA*, 1895, III, 11, p. 284.
[15] P. A. Vyazemsky, letter to P. P. Vyazemsky, December 4/16, 1834, CGALI, m. 4108, ff. 26-29. Quote from N. Kauchtschischwili, p. 280.
[16] *Ibid.*, p. 281.
[17] P. A. Vyazemsky, letter to P. P. Vyazemsky, December 4/16, 1834, *ibid.*, p. 284 f.
[18] P. A. Vyazemsky, letter to A. S. Pushkin, August 24, 1831, in A. S. Puškin, *PSS* (1941), XIV, p. 214.
[19] P. A. Vyazemsky, letter to P. P. Vyazemsky, December 4/16, 1834. Quote from N. Kauchtschischwili, p. 281 f.; also: Stendhal, letter to Vyazemsky, in *Correspondance* (Paris: Pléiade, 1967), II, pp. 771, 929 f.; V. Nečaeva, S. Durylin, "P. A. Vjazemskij i Francija," *LN* (Moscow: 1937), 31-32, p. 124; T. Kočetkova, "Stendal' i Vjazemskij," *Voprosy literatury* (1959), VII, pp. 148-155.
[20] P. A. Vyazemsky, letter to P. P. Vyazemsky, December 4/16, 1834, in N. Kauchtschischwili, p. 284.
[21] G. Orioli, "Zenaide Wolkonsky," in *Palatino*, 1966, No. 2, p. 6 f.; E. Colombi, "Zenaide Wolkonsky a Palazzo Poli," *Orazio*, 1956, no. 5-6, pp. 33-37.
[22] P. A. Vyazemsky, letter to P. P. Vyazemsky, February 21, 1835, in N. Kauchtschischwili, pp. 289-292.

[23] P. A. Vjazemskij, *Zapisnye knižki* (Moscow: 1963), p. 229.

[24] *ibid.*, p. 229.

[25] Z. A. Volkonskaja, "Knjazju P. A. Vjazemskomu na smert' ego dočeri," *Moskovskij nabljudatel'* (Moscow, 1835), II, p. 113. Three years later, on June 25, 1838, Gogol wrote to Vyazemsky, then in Petersburg, about his visit to the cemetery with Princess Volkonskaya: "There are bushes of roses on the grave which is so dear to your heart. I went there once more ... and was again pleased to see that this grave is not orphaned." N. V. Gogol to P. A. Vyazemsky, Rome, June 25, 1838, N. V. Gogol', *PSS* (Moscow: 1937-1952), XI, p. 156.

[26] P. A. Vyazemsky, letter to A. I. Turgenev, June 30, 1835, *OA*, III, p. 267.

[27] This letter, whose manuscript is now in the Houghton Library, was published in full in Nina Kauchtschischwili's extremely interesting book (1964). We have corrected a few readings of the text (marking them in bold print in square brackets) and offered some additional information.

[28] V. A. Zhukovsky, letter to A. P. Elagina, in K. K. Zeidlic, *Žizn' i poezija Žukovskogo* (S. Petersburg: 1883), p. 161.

[29] P. A. Vyazemsky, letter to P. P. Vyazemsky, September 19, 1834, CGALI, m. 4108, ff. 9, 10. Quoting from N. Kauchtschischwili (1964), p. 267.

[30] P. A. Vjazemskij, "Zapiska o knjaze Vjazemskom" (Moscow: 1963), pp. 146-164.

[31] P. A. Vyazemsky, letter to Petersburg from Munich, October 27/November 8, 1834, CGALI, m. 4108, ff. 24, 25. Quoting from N. Kauchtschischwili (1964), pp. 277, 278.

[32] P. A. Vyazemsky, letter to P. P. Vyazemsky,October 14/26, 1834, CGALI, m. 4108, ff. 3-6. Quoting from N. Kauchtschischwili (1963), p. 275.

[33] P. A. Vyazemsky, letter to V.F. Vyazemskaya, April 12, 1835, CGALI, m. 3269, ff. 73, 74. Quoting from N. Kauchtschischwili, pp. 293, 294.

[34] A. I. Turgenev, letter to P. A. Vyazemsky, October 23, 1834, *OA*, (1899), 111, p. 260.

[35] P. A. Vjazemskij, "Kuplety, petye na semejnom prazdnike Okulovyx," *PSS* (1880), IV, pp. 65, 66; "Darje Alekseevne Šypovoj, uroždennoj Okulovoj," *PSS* (1880), IV, pp. 103-105.

[36] P. A. Vyazemsky, letter to A. I. Turgenev, June 30/July 12, 1835, *PSS*, X, p. 267.

[37] P. A. Vyazemsky, letter to I. I. Dmitriev, June 17, 1837, *RA*, 1868, 1, 4, p. 655.

[38] René Galland, "Francuzskij jazyk pisem kn. P. A. Vjazemskogo," *Russkij literaturnyj arxiv* (New York: Rausen, 1956), pp. 54, 55; also see here the section on the French writing of Tsar Alexander I.

Three Notes from V. A. Zhukovsky

[1] Carl v. Zeidlitz, *Wasily Andreevisch Joukovsky* (Mitau: 1870), p. 148.

[2] Zhukovsky's social contacts in Rome were recorded in his diary: V. A. Žukovskij, *Dnevniki*, ed. I. A. Byčkov (St. Petersburg: 1901), pp. 446, 447, 454-459, 464, 466.

[3] *ibid.*, pp. 447-449, 457, 462; N. V. Gogol', *Polnoe sobranie sočinenij* (Moscow-Leningrad: Ak. Nauk, 14 vols, 1937-1952), X1, p. 197.

[4] N. V. Solov'ev, "Poet-xudožnik V. A. Žukovskij," in *V. A. Žukovskij* (St. Petersburg: Russkij bibliofil, 1913), pp. 69-71; Žukovskij, *Dnevniki*, pp. 449-453, 456, 457, 460-463.

[5] V. A. Žukovskij, *Dnevniki*, p. 447.

[6] "My počti ves' den' vmeste osmatrivali Rim s utra do noči." N. V. Gogol', letter to V. N. Repnina, January 18, 1839, in N. V. Gogol, *PSS*. X1, p. 195.

[7] A. I. Turgenev, letter to P. A. Vyazemsky, April 21, 1839 in *OA*, 1899, 1V, p. 70, 71.

[8] V. A. Zhukovsky, letter to I. I. Kozlov, February 9/21, 1839 in *RA*. 1867, 1, p. 842.

[9] V. A. Zhukovsky, letter to A. I Turgenev, end of 1825, in *RA*, 1895, 111, 9, p. 200.

[10] V. A. Žukovskij, *Dnevniki*, pp. 277-279, 283, 288, 290, 294, 295.

[11] *ibid.*, pp. 447-449, 455, 458, 459, 463, 464, 466.

[12] *ibid.*, p. 464.

[13] *ibid.*, p. 463.

[14] *ibid.*, p. 462.

[15] *ibid.*, p. 463.

[16] In 1974, this book was still in Baron V. K. Lemmerman's collection in Rome among books and paintings which belonged to Princess Zinaida Volkonskaya.

[17] V. A. Žukovskij, *Dnevniki*, p. 464.

[18] *ibid.*, pp. 457, 464.

[19] *ibid.*, p. 466.

[20] *ibid.*, p. 464.

[21] *ibid.*, pp. 464-466; N. V. Gogol', letter from Rome to A. S. Danilevsky, February 2, 1838, in *PSS*, XI, pp. 121-123; letter of P. A. Vyazemsky to his son, February 21/March 5, 1835, in N. Kauchtschischwili, *L'Italia nella vita e nell'opera di P. A. Vjazemskij* (Milan: Societa editrice vita e pensiero, 1964), pp. 289-291.

[22] V. A. Žukovskij, *Dnevniki*, p. 266.

[23] Z. A. Volkonskaja, "Synu i drugu. Četyre angela," *Moskovskij nabljudatel'*, 1836, I, 8, pp. 116-117.

[24] V. A. Žukovskij, *Dnevniki*, p. 428.

[25] See above (note 9).

[26] As this book went to press, the text of three notes by Zhukovsky had been published by V.M. Fredkin in *Propavšij dnevnik Puškina* (Moscow: "Znanie" 1991), pp. 142-144. The text of Zhukovsky's short letters has no commentary, is undated, and errs from the original in four instances.

Fifteen Letters from Alexander I

[1] A. N. Volkonskij, "Šest' pisem imperatora Aleksandra 1-ogo k knjagine Z. A. Volkonskoj," *Sbornik russkogo istoričeskogo vestnika*, 1868, III, pp. 310-314.

[2] P. B.(artenev), "O knjagine Z. A. Volkonskoj," *RA*, 1867, III, 10, p. 310; "Zapiska abbata Nikolja," *RA*, 1895, I, 4, p. 495; "Al'bom Ivančina-Pisareva," *SiN*, 1905, X, p. 505; D. Mordovcev, *Russkie ženščiny novogo vremeni* (St. Petersburg: 1874), p. 261; S. M. Volkonskij, ed., *Arxiv dekabrista S. G. Volkonskogo* (Petrograd: Golike, 1918), I, p. XL.

[3] Velikij Knjaz' Nikolaj Mixajlovič, *Imperator Aleksandr I.* (St. Petersburg: Exsp. Gos. Bumag. 1912), I, p. v.

[4] N. Barsukov, *Žizn' i trudy M. P. Pogodina* (St. Petersburg: 1889), II, p. 36; N. A. Belozerskaja "Knjaginja Z. A. Volkonskaja," *Istoričeskij vestnik*, 1897, LXVII, p. 942; V. V. Veresaev, *Gogol' v žizni* (M.-L.: "Akademia," 1933), p. 514f.

[5] A. de Caulaincourt, "Nouvelles et on dit de Saint-Pétersbourg" in Grand-Duc Nicolas Mikhailowitch, *Les relations diplomatiques de la Russia et de la France* (St. Petersburg: 1908), VI, pp. 37, 67, 82, 110-113, 124-127, 184; R. S. Edling, "Iz zapisok," *RA*, 1887, I, 1, pp. 212, 213; R. Rzewuska, *Mémoires* (Rome: Cuggiani, 1939), I, pp. 247, 248, II, pp. 96, 97; F. F. Vigel', *Zapiski* (Moscow: "Krug," 1928), p. 39.

[6] Grand-Duc Nicolas Mikhailowitch, *Correspondance de L'Empereur Alexandre 1er avec sa soeur La Grande Duchesse Catherine* (St. Petersburg: Manufacture des papiers de L'État, 1910), pp. 3, 6, 7, 46, 47, 59.

[7] N. V. Solov'ev, *Istorija odnoj žizni* (Petrograd: "Sirius," 1915), I, p. 140; R. Rzewuska (1939), I, pp. 258-267.

[8] A. Czartorysky and Queen Hortense are quoted in V. I. Timirjazev, "Inostrancy o Rossii," *Istoričeskij vestnik*, 1908, 62, p. 1053; Karl von Nostitz, "Diary" in Frederick Freksa, ed. *A Peace Congress of Intrigue* (New York: The Century, 1919), p. 114; F. Gentz, *Journal* (Leipzig: 1861), p. 185; L. Thürheim, *Mein Leben. Erinnerungen aus Österreichs Grosser Welt.* (Munich: Georg Müller, 1913), II, pp. 92-95.

[9] *Kamer-Fur'erskij Žurnal*, 1811, VII-XII (St. Petersburg: 1910) pp. 360, 439.

[10] M. Svistunov, ed. "Griboedovskaja Moskva v pis'max M. A. Volkovoj k V. I. Lanskoj," *VE*, 1874, VIII, p. 596; Letter of Madame de Staël to Z. Volkonskaya of August 1812, MS., Houghton Library.

[11] Quoted in A. I. Mixajlovskij-Danilevskij, *PSS* (St. Petersburg: 1850), VII, pp. 276, 322.

[12] A. de Caulaincourt, *Mémoires* (Paris: Plon, 1933), II, p. 221.

[13] A. S. Šiškov, *Zapiski, mnenija i perepiska* (Berlin: 1870), I, pp. 187, 188.

[14] M. I. Goleniščev-Kutuzov, letter to E. M. Tisenhausen, *SiN* 1874, X, p. 377.

[15] F. Rippold, ed., *Erinnerungen aus dem Leben des General Feldmarschals Herman von Boyer* (Leipzig: 1890), III, p. 16.

[16] A. S. Šiškov (1870), p. 188.

[17] N. K. Šil'der, *Imperator Aleksandr Pervyj* (St. Petersburg: Suvorin, 1905), III, p. 513, 514.

[18] Grand-Duc Nicolas Mikhaîlowitch (1910), p. 151.

[19] A. de La Garde-Chambonas, *Souvenirs du Congrès de Vienne* (Paris: H. Vivien, 1901), p. 91; V. I. Timirjazev, (1908), p. 112.

[20] P. E. Ščegolev, ed., *Vospominanija brat'ev Bestuževyx* (Petrograd: "Ogni," 1917), p. 217; A. Turgenev, letter to A. Bulgakov, April 20, 1817, *Pis'ma A. I. Turgeneva Bulgakovym* (Moscow: Gos. Soc.-Econ. Izd., 1939), p. 157; P. A. Vjazemskij, *Zapisnye knižki* (Moscow: Akad. Nauk, 1963), p. 154; also — letter to his wife, February 2, 1832, *Zven'ja* (Moscow: GIZ, 1951), IX, p. 277; S. G. Volkonskij, *Zapiski* (St. Petersburg: Sinod. Tip., 1902), p. 379.

[21] John Quincy Adams, *Memoirs* (Philadelphia: 1874), p. 94; A. de Caulaincourt (1908), VI, p. 15; A. de la Garde-Chambonas (1901), pp. 91, 92.

[22] Grand-Duc Nicolas Mikhailowitch (1910), pp 159, 160, 183, 186, 187.

[23] F. R. Chateaubriand, *Congrès de Verone* (Paris: 1838), I, p. 114.

[24] E. Chapuisat, ed., *Journal de Y. G. Eynard.* (Paris: Plon, 1914), pp. xviii, xvix; La Garde-Chambonas (1901), I, pp. 200, 412-418; II, p. 77; "Iz zapisok grafini Edling," *RA*, 1887, I, 3, p. 412; F. V. Gentz, *Journal* (Leipzig: 1861), pp. 185-190; A. Fournier, *Die Geheimpolizei auf dem Wiener Kongress* (Vienna: F. Tempinsky, 1913), p. 154; R. Rzewuska, *Mémoires* (1939), I, pp. 248-258; M. H. Weil, *Les dessous du Congrès de Vienne* (Paris: Payot, 1917), I, pp. 193, 210, 205, 318, 443, 446, 558.

[25] Sophia G. Volkonskaya, letter to Mlle. de Cochelet, London, June 11/23, 1814, Mlle. de Cochelet, *Mémoires* (Bruxelles: 1837), II, p. 16; III, pp. 41-43.

[26] K. Metternich, *Mémoires* (Paris: 1881), III, p. 500.

[27] M. D. Nesselrode to N. D. Guriev, February 2, 1824, in Šil'der, *Imperator Aleksandr Pervyj* (St. Petersburg: 1905), IV, pp. 560-562; Velikij Knjaz' Nikolaj Mixajlovič (1912), I, 2, pp. 304-307.

[28] "Pis'ma K. Ja. Bulgakova k ego bratu," *RA*, 1903, II, 5, p. 63; H. Schnitzer, *Histoire intime de la Russie sous les Empereurs Alexandre et Nicholas* (Paris: 1847), II, pp. 22-26; P. A. Vjazemskij, *PSS*, VII, pp. 451, 452; Velikij Knjaz' Nikolaj Mixajlovič (1912), I, 2, pp. 296-309, 316-320.

[29] Z. A. Volkonskaja, "Aleksandru Pervomu," *Damskij Žurnal*, 1826, pp. 74-75; "Poslednie dni žizni Aleksandra I. Rasskazy očevidcev, zapisannye knjagineju Z. A. Volkonskoju," *RS*, 1878, XXI, 1, pp. 139-150.

[30] S. Durylin, "Russkie pisateli u Gete v Veimare," *LN*, 1932, 4-6, pp. 477; MSS. Goethe- und Schiller-Archive in Weimar (See Volume II of this study).

[31] A. Bogdanovič *Istorija carstvovanija imperatora Aleksandra Pervogo i Rossii ego vremeni* (St. Petersburg: 1869), IV, pp. 56-85; N. Šil'der (1905), III, pp. 148-152.

[32] N. Šil'der (1905), III, pp. 154, 155; C. Joneville, *Life and Times of Alexander I* (London: 1875), II, p. 275.

[33] A. Bogdanovič (1868), IV, pp. 84, 87, 98, 101-114.

[34] Vel. Knjaz' Nikolaj Mixajlovič (1912), I, 1, pp. 144, 145.

[35] *Recollections of Caulaincourt, duc of Vicenza* (London: 1838), I, pp. 168, 169; E. Cazalas, ed., *Mémoires du General Bennigsen* (Paris: H. Charles-Lavauzelle, 1907), III, pp. 222-227.

[36] N. Šil'der (1905), III, p. 154; A. Bogdanovič (1869), IV, pp. 115, 116.

[37] S. M. Volkonskij, ed. (1918), I, p. x.

[38] Letter of May 28, 1813 in Grand-Duc Nicolas Mikhaïlowitch (1910), p. 153.

[39] Alexander went to Opotschno to meet his sister, the Grand Duchess Ekaterina on June 4/16 as registered in Shil'der (1905), III, p. 154; Grand-Duc Nicolas Mikhaïlowitch (1910), pp. 154, 155.

[40] A. N. Volkonskij (1868), III, p. 312.

[41] A. Bogdanovič (1869), IV, pp. 161-179; N. Šil'der (1905), III, pp. 161-164; Bennigsen (1907), III, pp. 238-240.

[42] A. Bogdanovič (1869), IV, pp. 190-202; Caulaincourt (1838), 1, pp. 205-220; C. Joyneville (1875), II, p. 303; N. Šil'der (1905), III, pp. 165, 166.

[43] A. S. Šyškov, *Kratkie zapiski* (St. Petersburg: 1831), pp. 161, 162.

[44] A. Bogdanovič (1869), IV, pp. 348, 349.

[45] Caulaincourt (1839), I, pp. 239, 241, 245, 246; N. Šil'der (1905), III, pp. 170-174; T. Bernhardi, *Denkwürdigkeiten aus dem Leben des Carl F. Grafen von Toll* (Leipzig: 1857), III, pp. 420-423; Bennigsen (1907), III,. pp. 241-245.

[46] Vel. Knjaz' Nikolaj Mixajlovič (1912), I, p. 152.

[47] C. Joyneville (1875), II, p. 314.

[48] See note no. 22.

[49] N. Šil'der (1905), III, pp. 180-182; A. Bogdanovič (1869), IV, pp. 346-353.

[50] Z. A. Volkonskaja, "Couplets à Spada,": "Iz materialov Stroganovskoj Akademii," publ. M. Azadovskij, *LN*, 33-34, pp. 209, 210; A. F. Šidlovskij, "Pis'ma Tepljakovu," *RS*, 1896, 85, pp. 670-677.

[51] *Le Portefeuille de la Comtesse D'Albany* (Paris: 1902), p. 609; Theresa Lewis, ed., *Extracts of the Journals and Correspondence of Miss Berry* (London: 1865), III, pp. 344, 345; *Mémoires de Mlle de Cochelet (1836-1838)*, I, pp. 384-386; II, pp. 15, 16, 216-219; S. G. Volkonskij (1902), I, pp. 337-340.

[52] S. G. Volkonskij, (1902), I, p. 379; P. A. Vjazemskij, *Zven'ja* (1951), IX, p. 277; Mlle. de Cochelet, II, pp. 163, 164.

[53] M. H. Weil (1917), p. 205; Graziano Giachetti, *Der Wiener Kongress* (Bern: Hallwag, 1945), p. 66,

[54] See above no. 51.

[55] N. Šil'der (1905), IV, pp. 71-74.

[56] Metternich, private letter quoted by M. Paléologue, *Alexandre 1er* (Paris: Plon, 1937), pp. 277, 278.

[57] Velikij Knjaz' Nikolaj Mixajlovič (1912), I, 2, pp. 291, 294, 470; also in II, appendix, pp. 210-214; Conte della Scarena, Reminiscences in *La Civilita Cattolica*, 1878, XII, 633.

[58] Nikolaj Turgenev, Dnevniki, *Arxiv Brat'ev Turgenevyx, 1811- 1816* (St. Petersburg: 1913), III, p. 301.

[59] A. de Caulaincourt, "Nouvelles et on dit" (1908), VI, p. 110.

[60] *Arxiv Knjazja Voroncova* (Moscow: 1890), XXXVI, p. 240; ibid., (Moscow: 1893), XXIX, pp. 8, 10, 11; Polovtsoff, *Correspondance diplomatique* (St. Petersburg: Societé Imp., 1907), p. 379.

[61] P. A. Vjazemskij, *PSS*, II, pp. 85-111, IX, p. 107.

[62] "Zapiski Bestuževa," *RA*, 1881, XXXII, p. 598; I. K. Luppol, ed., *Pis'ma A. Turgeneva Bulgakovym* (Moscow: Ekonom. Izd., 1939), p. 157; *Arxiv Gosudarstvennogo Soveta* (St. Petersburg, 1875), IV-1, pp. 473-476 (1876), IV-2, pp. 558-578.

[63] Rasskazy knjazja A. N. Golicyna. "Iz zapisok Yu. N. Barten'eva" *RA*, I, 2, pp. 100, 101.

[64] Conversation with Chateaubriand, quoted in N. Šil'der (1905), IV, p. 259.

[65] P. A. Vjazemskij, *PSS*, VII, pp. 451, 452.

[66] "Pis'ma A. Ja. Bulgakova k bratu," *RA*, 1901, II, 5, p. 52.

[67] P. M. Volkonskij, "Pis'ma I. V. Vasil'čikovu," *RA*, 1875, II, 5, pp. 49, 70-83; Velikij Knjaz' Nikolaj Mixajlovič (1912), 1, 2, pp. 304-307, 318, 319, 330; Šil'der (1905), IV, pp. 560, 561.

[68] Grand-Duc Nicholas Mikhaïlowitch, *L'Imperatrice Elisabeth* (St. Petersburg: 1909), III, p. 504.

[69] *Tableau Slave du V-me Siècle* had two editions in Paris: first in 1820, second in 1824. The translation of this work by Shalikov appeared in *Ladies' Journal (Damskij Žurnal)* in 1822, followed by polemics concerning Shalikov's translation.

[70] Šil'der (1905), IV, pp. 184-187; Metternich, *Mémoires* (1881), 111, pp. 373, 374, 377; Velikij Knjaz' Nikolaj Mixajlovič (1914), 11, pp. 254-264; *Vosstanie dekabristov*, (Moscow: GIZ, 1926), 11, pp. 67, 69.

Seven Letters from Cardinal Ercole Consalvi

[1] J. Crétineau-Joly, ed., *Mémoires du Cardinal Consalvi* (Paris: 1866), I, p. 28.

[2] Quoted in Engelbert Fischer, *Cardinal Consalvi* (Mainz: 1899), p. 325.

[3] Adrien Boudou, *Le Saint Siège et la Russie. Leur relation diplomatique au XIX siècle, 1814-1847* (Paris: Plon, 1922) pp. 38, 39; John T. Ellis, *Cardinal Consalvi and Anglo-Papal Relations* (Washington, D. C.: The Catholic University of America Press, 1942), pp. 21-33; Richard Wichterich, *Sein Schicksal war Napoleon. Leben und Zeit des Kardinal-staatssekretär Ercole Consalvi* (Heidelberg: F. H. Kerle, 1951), pp. 299, 300, 302. We doubt that Consalvi met the Princess in 1813 when she was in Rome for a short time.

[4] P. G. A. Angelucci, *Il grande Segretario della Santa Sede* (Rome: Scuola typ. Pio X, 1924), p. 49; Crétineau-Joly (1866) I, pp. 36, 37, 83, 84; Ellis (1942), pp. 24-27.

[5] Charles Nicoullaud, ed., *Mémoires de la Comtesse de Boigne* (Paris: Plon, 1907), II, pp. 280, 405.

[6] A. Boudou (1922), pp. 45-48; E. Fischer (1899), pp. 28, 104-113; P. Ilario Rinieri, *Corrispondenza inedita dei Cardinali Consalvi e Pacca del tempo del Congresso di Vienna* (Torino: Unione Typografico, 1903), pp. 583, 704-710, 718, 738-745.

[7] J.-G. Eynard, *Journal* (Paris: Plon, 1924) I, pp. 17-19; II, p. 96; August Fournier, *Die Geheimpolizei auf dem Wiener Kongress* (Wien: Tempsky, 1913), pp. 120, 181, 246-248, 287, 353; Albert Sorel, *L'Europe et la révolution française* (Paris: Plon, 1897-1906), VIII, pp. 358-360, 373; Maurice-Henri Weil, *Les dessous du Congrès de Vienne* (Paris: Payot, 1917) I, pp. 35, 45-50; R. Wichterich (1951), pp. 310-317.

[8] A. Boudou (1922), pp. 48-52.

[9] "Diario del Marchese di San Marzano" quoted in I. Rinieri (1903), p. LIV.

[10] Excerpts from the notes of Prince de Ligne, quoted in R. Wichterich (1951), p. 311.

[11] A. Fournier (1913), p. 469.

[12] A. Boudou (1922), pp. 37-63, 64-89; Massimo D'Azeglio, *Recollections* (London: 1868) II, p. 127; "La Russia e l'arbitrato della Santa Sede," *La Civiltà Cattolica*, 1899, February issue; Ilario Rinieri (1903), pp. 115, 130, 132, 600, 642-647.

[13] A. Boudou (1922), pp. 132, 133; *La Civiltà Cattolica*, December 4, 1876; Velikij Knjaz' Nikolaj Mixajlovič, *Imperator Aleksandr I* (St. Petersburg: Exped. Gos. Bumag, 1912), I, p. v.

[14] A. Boudou (1922), p. 149.

[15] J. Crétineau-Joly (1866), I, p. 59.

[16] M. D'Azeglio (1868) II, p. 128.

[17] Russian ambassador A. Italinski (1743-1827) to Cardinal Consalvi, letters of December 4, 1822 and April 9, 1823 in the private papers of Ercole Consalvi. MSS., Congregation of the Propagation of the Faith (*Propaganda Fede*), Rome. Folder XXXII, items 3, 4. About Italinsky and his mission in Rome — A. Boudou (1922), pp. 79-81, 88-90.

[18] J. Crétineau-Joly, I, p. 65; quoted in L. Fischer (1899), pp. 291, 292.

[19] Laure Junot Duchesse D'Abrantès, *Mémoires* (Paris: J. de Bonnot, 1969), XV, p. 206; A. C. Lenormant, ed. *Souvenirs et correspondance tiré de papiers de Madame Récamier* (Paris: 1859), II, pp. 50, 51; Lulu Thürheim, *Mein Leben. Erinnerungen aus Österreichs Grosser Welt* (Munich: Müller, 1914), pp. 178, 179.

[20] L. Thürheim (1914), p. 100.

[21] Comtesse de Boigne (1907), I, p. 280.

[22] H. Beyle (Stendhal), letter to A. de Marest of March 26, 1820, *Correspondance* (Paris: Bibliothèque de Pléiade, 1967) I, p. 1016.

[23] M. D'Azeglio (1868) II, pp. 126, 127.

[24] Mlle Cochelet, *Mémoires* (Bruxelles:1838) II, p. 196; Duchesse D' Abrantès (1969) XV, p. 609; Lady Theresa Lewis, ed., Miss Berry, *Extracts of the Journal and Correspondence* (London: 1863), III, pp. 330, 344, 345.

[25] Diego Angeli, *Roma Romantica* (Milan: S. A. Fratelli Traves, 1935), pp. 212-215; A. Cametti, *Memorie storiche dell'Accademia Filarmonica Romana*, 1924), pp. 43, 49, 50; Miss Berry (1863), pp. 274-276, 330; Rosalie Rzewuska, *Mémoires* (Rome: Cuggiani, 1950), pp. 16-18.

[26] MSS. Houghton Library: two unpublished letters of Archimandrite Gerasim Pavsky (1797-1866) to Volkonskaya written in Moscow, most likely between 1827 and 1828, after her rupture with Barbieri and involvement with Count Ricci which caused a divorce from his wife, Zinaida's good friend.

[27] MS. Houghton Library: Cardinal Consalvi's letter of October 10, 1823 (the full text of this letter is included here).

[28] This part of the correspondence of Cardinal Consalvi in his private archive in *Propaganda Fede* in Rome was not made available to us.

[29] Henri Beyle (Stendhal), letter to A. de Mareste, March 3, 1820 in *Correspondance* (Paris: Bibliothèque de Pléiade, 1962), I, p. 1003.

[30] Stendhal, "La vie de Rossini," in *Œuvres complètes* (Paris: P. Larrive, 1954), II, p. 436.

[31] Miss Berry (1863), pp. 284, 285.

[32] Friedrich von Gentz, *Depêches inédites* (Paris: 1876); *Tagebücher* (Leipzig: 1873); *Schriften und Briefe aus den Jahren 1815-1832* (Munich: H. von Eckhardt, 1921).

[33] See above note no. 29; Miss Berry (1863), p. 274.

[34] Francis Bunsen, *Vie et lettres de la Baronne Bunsen* (Geneva- Paris: 1895) I, p. 50; F. von Gentz (1921), pp. 91-96.

[35] Ch. J. von Bunsen, *Aus seinen Briefen* (Leipzig: 1868), pp. 170, 171; Viscount Castlereagh, *Correspondence, Dispatches and other Papers* (London: 1853), VII, pp. 272, 284, 340, 375.

[36] K. Metternich, letter to Cardinal Consalvi, December 13, 1820, quoted in Crétineau-Joly (1866), I, p. 140.

[37] Mémoires de Vicomte de La Rochefoucauld (Paris:1837), I, pp. 373, 374, 380.

[38] Letter of Alexander I to Volkonskaya of May 24, 1814, MS. Houghton Library; Miss Berry (1865), p. 330.

[39] Miss Berry (1863), pp. 330, 331; R. Rzewuska (1950), II, p. 17.

[40] See note (a) to Consalvi's letter no. 1.

[41] F. Bunsen (1895), I, pp. 207, 208; E. Fischer (1899), p. 332, 333.

[42] F. Bunsen (1895), pp. 196, 212, 213; E. Fischer (1899), p. 333; Ernest Daudet, *Diplomates et hommes d'Etat contemporains. Le Cardinal Consalvi.* (Paris: 1866), pp. 182, 288; A. Lenormant, ed. (1859), II, pp. 50, 52, 53.

[43] Léon Pélissier, ed., *Le Portefeuille de la Comtesse D'Albany* (Paris: A. Fontemoing, 1902), pp. 601-609.

[44] Elizabeth, Duchess of Devonshire to Lord George Byron, letter of August 17, 1821, in *The Two Duchesses* (London: 1898), p. 440; L. Thürheim (1914), III, p. 176; A. Lenormant, ed. (1859), II, pp. 50-55.

[45] Crétineau-Joly (1866), I, pp. 192-198.

LETTERS TO PRINCE A. N. VOLKONSKY

Letter from P. A. Vyazemsky to A. N. Volkonsky

[1] E. G. Gerštein, *Sud'ba Lermontova* (Moscow: GIXL, 1986), pp. 121, 336n.

[2] P. A. Vjazemskij, "Staraja zapisnaja knižka," *PSS* (1886), X, pp. 112-218.

[3] P. A. Vyazemsky, letter to V. F. Vyazemskaya, May 4, 1859, in Nina Kauchtschis-chwili, *L'Italia nella vita e nell'opera di P. A. Vyazemskij* (Milan: 1964), p. 314.

[4] Letter to A. I. Turgenev, June 2, 1833, *OA*, 111, pp. 223-228.

[5] P. A. Vyazemsky, letter to P. P. Vyazemsky, May 12, 1859, in Nina Kauchtschisch-wili, (1964), p. 315.

[6] P. A. Vyazemskij, *PSS*, X, p. 100.

[7] *ibid.*, pp. 219-227, 235.

[8] *ibid.*, p. 226.

[9] *ibid.*, pp. 228, 237.

[10] P. A. Vyazemskij, *PSS* (1887), X1, pp. 297, 298.

Three Letters from Ya. N. Tolstoy

[1] B. L. Modzalevskij, "Jakov Nikolaevič Tolstoj" (St. Petersburg: *RS*, 1899, No. 9, 10, pp. 5, 11-14; P. E. Ščegolev, "Iz dvadcatyx godov. K biografii Ja. N. Tolstogo," *Puškin i ego sovremenniki. Materialy i issledovanija* (St. Petersburg: Ak. Nauj, 1904), II, pp. 65-67; A. S. Pushkin, letter to Ya. Tolstoy, Sept. 26, 1822, *PSS* (1937), XIII, pp. 46-48; letter to Bestuzhev, January 12, 1824, *ibid.*, p. 62, 84.

[2] A. S. Puškin, "Stansy" (1819), *PSS*, 11, p. 109.

[3] Ja. N. Tolstoj, *Moe prazdnoe vremja ili sobranie nekotoryx stixotvorenij* (St. Peters-burg: 1821); translation in verse of Tibullus' 5th elegy, *Žurnal drevnej i novoj sloves-nosti*, 1818, October 22-25; adaptation of two French plays, staged but unpublished: "Mnimye razbojniki, ili sumatoxa v traktire," "Neterpelivyj"; translations of Pushkin's poem "Černaja Šal'" *Sovremennik*, 1857, IV, p. 267; B. L. Modzalevskij (1899), pp. 15-21.

[4] B. L. Modzalevskij (1899), pp. 21-23, 28-38; P. E. Ščegolev, "Zelenaja lampa," *Puškin i ego sovremenniki* (1908), VII, pp. 19-28, 36; N. I. Turgenev, *La Russie et les Russes* (Paris: 1847), 1, pp. 197- 199; A. E. Rozen, *Zapiski dekabrista* (Leipzig: 1870), pp. 66, 67.

[5] Modzalevskij (1899), pp. 25, 35.

[6] Ja. Tolstoj, "Quelques pages sur l'Anthologie russe pour servir de réponse à une critique de cet ouvrage insérée dans le "Journal de Paris" (Paris: 1824), in this review Tolstoy defends the originality of Krylov's fables; J. Tolstoj, "Resumé de l'historie de Russie," *Revue Encyclopédique*, 1825. XXVI, pp. 531-534; Tolstoy's articles on con-temporary Russian literature appeared in *Revue Encyclopédique*, XXI, XXVI, XXXI, XXXVIII, XLIV; J. Tolstoj, "Six mois suffisent-ils pour connaître un pays, un observa-tion sur l'ouvrage de M. Ancelot, intitulé *Six mois en Russie*"; Tolstoy's longer review of a book criticizing the article of general Jomini appeared in Paris in 1829; Jacque Tol-stoj, "Lettre d'un Russe à un Russe; simple réponse au pamphlet de Mme la Duchesse d'Abrantès, *Catherine II*' (Paris: 1835); Ja. N. Tolstoj, "La Russie en 1839, revée par Mr. de Custin" (Paris: 1844), pp., 1-112.

⁷ P. A. Vjazemskij, *Zapisnaja knižka*: July 30, 1826 (Moscow: Ak. Nauk, 1963), p. 134, No. 418; P. A. Vyazemsky's letter to A. I. Turgenev was quoted by V. A. Zhukovsky, *RA*, 1895, IV, 10, p. 231; see also *Moskovskij telegraf*, XV, pp. 216-232, XVI, pp. 154, 164- 178; B. L. Modzalevskij (1899), pp. 29-33.

⁸ "Zapiska o tajnyx obščestvax Ja. N. Tolstogo," July 26, 1826; P. E. Ščegolev (1904), pp. 29-34; S. A. Ščeglov, "Perepiska Ja. N. Tolstogo s A. I. Turgenevym," *Pamjati dekabristov* (Leningrad: Ak. Nauk, 1926), II, pp. 164-178; B. L. Modzalevskij (1899), pp. 29, 30; J. Tolstoj, *Essai biographique et historique sur le feldmaréchal prince de Varsovie compte Paskevitch de Erivan* (Paris: 1835), pp. 1-235; this biographie had been translated into Polish by V. Zająozkowski and published in Warsaw; first and second editions appeared in 1840, third in 1841.

⁹ Tolstoy's letters to his brother of October 14, 1827, September 8, 1829, August 30, 1830 in Modzalevskij (1899), pp. 29, 30, 36, 38, 42.

¹⁰ B. L. Modzalevskij (1899), pp. 44-49; *Zapiski Ivana Golovina* (Leipzig: 1859), pp. 77, 78, 112-114; "Iz zapisok V. A. Muxanova," *RA*, 1897, I, 1, p. 51; *RA*, 1897, I, 2, p. 278; E. Tarle, "Donesenija Jakova Tolstogo iz Pariža v III Otdelenie," *LN*, 1937, 31-32, pp. 563-565; A. I. Turgenev, letter to N. I. Turgenev from St. Petersburg about Tolstoy's appointment with a salary of 3,000 rubles, *Puškin i ego sovremenniki* (1908), VI, p. 85. Tolstoy was recommended for this position by Elim Meshchersky, *LN*, 1939, 32-33, pp. 383, 450, 478. Tolstoy himself wrote to Paskevich that to have an agent in Paris whose task would be to "influence the French press, three things are needed: money, money, money." E. Tarle, *LN*, 1937, 31-32, pp. 567.

¹¹ P. A. Vjazemskij, *PSS* (1878), I, p. 245.

¹² V.V. Il'in, "Vospominanie o knjaze A. N. Volkonskom," *RA*, II, 3, p. 252.

¹³ *ibid.*, pp. 252, 253.

¹⁴ At that time, Tolstoy had an emphatically negative attitude toward all kinds of revolutionary movements be they Hungarian, Spanish uprisings, or the French revolution of 1848. This is clearly expressed in the second volume of Tolstoy's biography of Paskevich and in his *Relation des opérations de l'armée russe en Hongrie sous les ordres du feld-maréchal prince de Varsovie compte Paskevitch d'Erivan.*

Letter from I. S. Turgenev to A. P. Golitsyn

¹ Soon after the death of A. N. Volkonsky, there appeared an article about him by his friend, General Il'in, who wrote: "After the revolution and the departure of the Queen from Spain in 1867, the Prince, following the Imperial order, went to Paris." Il'in obviously had confused the dates: the Spanish revolution took place in the middle of September 1868, and Queen Isabella left Spain for France on September 30, 1868. Hence, Prince Volkonsky could not have been in Paris in February 1868.

² Prosper Merimée, *Correspondance général*, 2me série (Toulouse: F. Privat, 1961), XIII, pp. 546, 547; XIV, pp. 44, 66, 95-98, 112-115, 121-123, 169-171.

³ V. Giraux, *Essai sur H. Taine* (Paris: 1901), p. 190.

⁴ I. S. Turgenev, letter to S. A. Miller, March 6/18, 1853 in *PSS* v 28 tomax (Moscow-Leningrad: Izd. Nauka, 1960-1968), *Pis'ma*, II, p. 131.

⁵ V. Sollogub, *Vospominanija* (Moscow-Leningrad: Academia, 1931), p. 445.

⁶ Turgenev's French letters to his Russian correspondents: M. N. Katkov, July 26/August 7, 1866, *Pis'ma*, VI, p. 91; V. F. Odoevskij, September 29, 1867, *Pis'ma*, VI,

p. 310; M. N. Stasjulevič, September 29, 1867, *Pis'ma*, VI, p. 312; F. I. Tjutčev, September 29, 1867, *Pis'ma*, VI, p. 313; B. N. Čičerin, September 29, 1867, *ibid*. The first of these short notes introduced the cellist B. Cossman, the other four were written on behalf of the American diplomat and writer Eugene Schuyler, then stationed in Moscow.

[7] I. S. Turgenev, letter to Albert N. Turgenev, March 22/April 3, 1869, *Pis'ma*, VII, p. 346; and to E. F. Raden of May 9/21, 1866, *Pis'ma*, VI, p. 76.

[8] Turgenev's fifteen letters to A. P. Golitsyn cover a span of approximately ten months, from June 19/July 1, 1867 to April 12/24, 1868: *Pis'ma* VI, pp. 281, 282, 283, 288, 296, 297, 299, 304-306, 325, 338, 343, 348; *Pis'ma*, VII, pp. 118, 129.

[9] I. S. Turgenev, letters to A. P. Golitsyn, *Pis'ma*, VI, pp. 281, 282, 288, 289, 296, 305, 338, 567, 568; to Jules Hetzel, *Pis'ma*, VII, p. 333.

[10] I. S. Turgenev, letter to Pauline Viardot, March 14/26, 1868, *Pis'ma*, VII, p. 96.

[11] I. S. Turgenev, letter to A. P. Golitsyn, July 14/26, 1867, *Pis'ma*, VI, pp. 288, 289.

[12] I. S. Turgenev, letter to Jules Hetzel, February 13/25, 1868, *Pis'ma*, VII, p. 63.

[13] I. S. Turgenev, letter to A. P. Golitsyn, April 12/24, 1868, *Pis'ma*, VII, pp. 118, 119.

[14] Letters to A. P. Golitsyn from Alfred Pierre Faloux, Joseph Hippolyte Guilbert, Ernest Naville, and August Haxthausen; also a note to Angéle Golitsyna from Sophie Svetchina, Houghton Library, Harvard University.

[15] I. S. Turgenev, letter to A. P. Golitsyn of July 14/26, 1867 in *Pis'ma*, VI, pp. 288, 289; the original of this letter is in the Houghton Library, Harvard University; the original of the April 12/24, 1868 letter, published in *Pis'ma*, VII, pp. 118, 119, is in the private collection of I. S. Zilbershtein.

[16] I. S. Turgenev, letter to D. V. Grigorovich, January 25/February 6, 1881, Turgenev, *Pis'ma*, XIII, 1, p. 48.

[17] I. S. Turgenev, letters to A. P. Golitsyn of August 19/31, 1867 and of September 3/15, 1867, *Pis'ma*, VI, pp. 299, 306.

[18] Written on the cover of the first draft, in Bibliothèque national, Collection Slave, 84.

[19] I. A. Goncharov, letter to M. M. Stasyulevich, *PSS* v vos'mi tomax (Moscow: GIXL, 1955), VIII, p. 395.

[20] I. S. Turgenev, letter to Maxim Ducamp, February 6/18, 1868, *Pis'ma*, VII, p. 53.

[21] I. S. Turgenev, *Pis'ma*, VII, pp. 15, 28, 32, 33, 35, 38, 39, 43, 52, 53, 63, 69.

[22] I. S. Turgenev, letters to N. A. Kishinsky, April 25/May 7, 1867, June 17/29, 1867, December 9/21, 1867, *Pis'ma*, VI, pp. 238, 290, 291; VII, pp. 10, 18, 90.

[23] I. S. Turgenev, letter to Jules Hetzel, May 30/June 11, 1868, *Pis'ma*, VII, p. 147.

[24] *Nouvelles moscovites* (Paris: J. Hetzel, 1869).

[25] Prosper Mérimée, *Correspondance générale*, VIII, p. 169.

INDEX

Albany, Louise (née Stolberg), 136, 151

Alexander I, Tsar of Russia: and Volkonskaya (1810–1825), 17–27, 37, 41, 44,
75, 92–132; Napoleon, 44, 100, 103,
109, 111; on the battlefields: Bautzen,
100, 103, 104, Dresden, Kulm, 106,
107, Leipzig, 110, 111; congresses:
Vienna, 20, 98, 118, Laybach, Troppau, Verona, 23, 24, 98, 121, 124;
Metternich, 98, 121, 122, 124; policy
towards Rome, 122, 133–136; last
years (1822–1825), 98, 99, 124–126,
128, 129

Alexander II, 32, 86, 87, 90

Alopeus, D.M., 121, 122

Alopeus, Jannette (née Wenkstern), 120,
121, 122

Ancelot, Jaque Arsène F.P., 160

Apponyi, Antal Rudolf, 140, 143, 144

Arakcheev, A.A., 98, 101, 125, 129

Arndt, E.M., 44

Aufresne, Mme. Rival, 113, 115, 116

Baratynskaya, N.L., 49

Baratynsky, E.A., Moscow years 1824–
1826, 49–52; in Volkonskaya salon,
26, 28, 49–51; "History of Coquetry"
("Istoriya koketstva"), 51, 52

Barberi, Giovanni, 140, 141, 146, 147

Barbieri, Michelangelo, 20–24, 27, 28,
137

Bartenev, P.I., 47

Barteneva, P.A., 53

Batyushkov, K.N., 22, 44

Beethoven, Ludwig van, 140

Belli, Giuseppe Gioacchino, 36, 78

Bellini, Vincenzo, 60, 64, 67

Beloselskaya, A.G. (née Kozitskaya), 18,
44–47, 54, 56, 58, 93, 123, 130

Beloselskaya, V. Ya. (née Tatishcheva),
18

Beloselsky-Belozersky, A.M., 17, 25, 75,
115

Benkendorf, A. Kh., 38, 160

Bentinck, William, 44

Berlioz, Hector, 61

Berry, Mary, 27, 81, 180

Boigne, Eléonore Adélaide d'Osmond,
47, 118, 134, 136, 137

Bonaparte, Maria Letizia (née Ramo-
lino), 77

Bonaparte, Napoleon-Joseph-Charles-
Paul, 167, 169

Borgondio, Jentile, 23, 75

Boyer, H.V., 94

Bruni, F.A. (Fidel), 23, 26, 31, 58, 65,
68, 77, 86

Bryulov, K.P., 30, 65, 77

Budberg, A.F., 165

Buffalo, Gaspar, Dom, 35

Bulgakov, A. Ya, 22

Bunsen, Charles, 77, 142, 155

Buturlin, M.D., 31, 47

Byron, George Gordon, 55, 57, 58, 98,
150

Cagliostro, G.B., 141

Camuccini, Vincenzo, 86

Capaldi, Marietta, 65, 69, 89

Catherine II, Empress of Russia, 116

Catherine (Ekaterina Pavlovna), Grand
Duchess, 20, 93, 96, 97, 104, 105, 114

Caulaincourt, A., Duc de Vicence, 107

Chaadaev, P. Ya., 26, 38

Chateaubriand, François René, 71, 97,
124

Cherkassky, V.A., 174, 175

Cimarosa, Domenico, 26

Cochelet, Louise de, 21, 118

Consalvi, Ercole, Cardinal, 17, 24, 28,
37, 122, 133–152

Constant, Benjamin de Rebecque, 58, 59

Contemporary (*Sovremennik*), 157
Correspondent (*Correspondant*), 154, 172
Crétineau-Joly, Jaques, 135
Curioni, Alberico, 139, 140

Dargomyzhsky, A.S., 53, 55
D'Azeglio, Massimo, 136, 137
Delaryu, M.D., 73
Delvig, A.A., 58, 70, 73, 159
Derzhavin, G.R., 33, 68
Descartes, René, 57
Devonshire, Elizabeth, Duchess Foster, 136, 148, 150, 151
Dibich, I.I., 125
Donizetti, Gaetano D., 60, 64, 65, 67
Durnovo, Alina P. (née Volkonskaya), 54, 57, 59, 123
Durnovo, P.D., 31, 33, 64

Ekaterina Mikhailovna, Grand Duchess, 155
Elena Nikolaevna, Grand Duchess, 155
Elagina, A.P., 50, 81
Elizabeth (Elizaveta Alekseevna), Empress of Russia, 58, 94, 126
Epistolary form: language and style, 37, 39–41, 53, 71, 80, 82, 83, 171, 174
Eugenia (Eugenie), Empress of France, 167, 169
European (*Evropeets*), 74
European Messenger (*Vestnik Evropy*), 171, 173, 174

Ferdinand IV, King of Naples, 140, 142
Ferreti, J., 78
Fesch, Joseph, Cardinal, 150
Fétis, François Joseph, 61
Fodor-Mainvielle, Josephine, 64, 65, 67
Franz Joseph, Emperor of Austria, 119
French Academy, Language Reforms (1740, 1762, 1798), 123, 124
French written by Russians, 37–39, 85, 130–132, 172, 174

Gaberzetter, I.I., 30
Galberg, S.I., 58, 68

Galitsyn, A.N. (see Golitsyn)
Genishta, I.I., 26
Gentz, Friedrich von, 140
Gerambe, Edouard, 102, 104
Gerambe, Ferdinand, 104
Gerbet, Olympe Philippe, Abbé, 34, 35
Glinka, M.I., 29, 31, 36, 53; Italian trip (1830–1832): 60, 61, 62; Italian composers and musicians, 58, 59, 61, 63, 64; Volkonskaya, 62, 63, 66
Gnedich, N.I., 159
Goethe, Johann Wolfgang, 19, 29, 57, 68, 77, 80, 82, 83, 100
Gogol, N.V., 32, 86–90, 157
Golitsyn, A.N., 98, 101, 113
Golitsyn, A.P., 44, 154, 172, 174
Golitsyn, S.M., 155
Golitsyna, Angéle, 40, 173
Golitsyna, M.A., (née Suvorova), 53
Golitsyna, A.I., (née Izmaylova), 44
Goncharov, I.A., 174
Gourief, Hélène, (Guryeva, E.D.), 46
Green Lamp (*Zelyonaya Lampa*), 159
Griboedov, A.S., 53, 76
Grigorovich, D.V., 174
Grossi, Tomaso, 91
Guéranger, Prosper (Dom), 34, 35
Gulyanov, I.A., 25
Guryev, N.D., 77, 113

Hoffman, E.T.A., 57
Hortense de Beauharnais, Queen of Holland, 21, 118
Hume, David, 57

Ingres, Dominique, 86
Iordan, F.I., 30
Isabella II, Queen of Spain, 168
Italinski, A. Ya., 134, 136
Ivanov, A.A., 86
Ivanov, N.K., 34, 60, 61, 63, 65, 66

Jomini, Henri Antoine de, 107
Journal of Debates (Journal des débats), 164, 175

Kamensky, S.M., 114
Kankrin, E.F., 82
Kant, Emmanuel, 17
Karamzin, N.M., 40, 43
Kaverin, P.P., 159
Kaysarov, P.S., 68
Khomyakov, A.S., 49, 50
Kiprensky, O.A., 30, 77, 86
Kireevsky, I.V., 26, 28, 50, 57, 62, 74
Kireevsky, P.V., 26
Kochubey, N.A., 155
Koloshin, S.P., 168–170
Kopp, J.H., 76, 79, 81, 85
Koshelev, A.I., 57
Kozlov, I.I. (1825–1826), 26, 37, 53–59;
    The Monk (Chernets), 56, 58; The
    Bride of Abidos (Abidosskaya Nevesta),
    56, 58; Princess Natalia Dolgorukaya,
    56, 58; poems to Volkonskaya, 53–55;
    on Benjamin Constant, 56, 58, 59; on
    Pushkin's Boris Godunov, 57, 59
Kozlova, A.I., 53, 59
Kozlova, S.A., 54, 59
Kozlovsky, P.B., 25, 44
Kraevsky, A.A., 62
Kurakin, A.B., 113, 116
Kutuzov, M.I., 44, 94

La Bédoyère, Charles Huchet, 21, 117,
    118
Lacordaire, Jean Batiste Henri, 34
La Fontaine, Jean, 113, 115
La Harpe, Frédédic César, 130, 132
Lamennais, Félicité-Robert, de, 34
Langeron, A.F., 22
Lanskaya, V.I., 47
La Rochefoucault, Sosthène de, 21, 24,
    118
Laval, A.G. (née Kozitskaya), 44, 47, 55
Leon XII (Annibale Della Genga), Pope,
    135, 150, 151
Letters to Volkonskaya classified as for
    content and style, 17, 35–39, 50, 78,
    79
Ligne, Charles Joseph, Prince, 20, 134,
    135

Literary Gazette (Literaturnaya Gazeta),
    29, 76
Lobanova-Rostovskaya, K.I. (née Bez-
    borodko), 33
Locke, John, 57
Louis XVIII, King of France, 97, 164
Louise, Queen of Prussia, 18, 93
Luquet, Abbé, 34, 35
Lutzov, R., 77

Marcello, Benedetto, 84
Marie-Louise, Empress of France, 167
Mars (Anne Boutet), 21, 24, 145
Mariya Fyodorovna, Dowager Empress,
    18, 93, 122, 135
Mattias, Maria De, 34, 35
Maykov, A.N., 155
Melgunov, N.A., 26, 61, 62
Mendelssohn-Bartholdy, Felix, 61
Mérian, André Josèf, 25
Mérimée, Prosper, 171, 172, 175
Merlini, Giovanni (Don), 35
Messenger of Europe (Vestnik Evropy),
    160
Metternich-Winneburg, Klemens, 98,
    111, 118, 121, 124, 134, 142
Mezzofanti, Giuseppi, 34, 77
Mickiewicz, Adam, 26, 50
Molière, Jean-Baptiste Poquelin, 26
Moreau, Jean Victor, 107, 112
Morning Dawn (Utrennyaya Zarya), 62
Moscow Observer (Moskovskii Nablyu-
    datel), 91
Moscow Telegraph (Moskovskii Tele-
    graf), 75, 160
Muravyov, A.N., 34

Napoleon I, Emperor of France, 18, 20,
    21, 43, 44, 48, 94, 100, 103–105, 107,
    109–111, 118, 133, 136
Napoleon III, Emperor of France, 165,
    168, 169
Naryshkin, A.L., 44
Naryshkina, M.A., 93, 97, 122, 123, 129
Naryshkina, Sofia, 98, 123, 129
Naumova, Avdotya, 22
Nesselrode, K.V., 134

Nicholas I, Tsar of Russia, 33, 34, 59, 81, 90, 101, 160
Nicole, Charles Dominique, Abbé, 22, 141
Nikolai Mikhailovich, Grand Duc, 93
Northern Flowers (Severnye Tsvety), 29, 52, 70, 72–74
Novosiltsev, N.N., 75
Nozzari, Andrea, 64–67

Odoevsky, V.F., 26, 57, 62
Okulova, Anna (Dyakova), 83–85
Okulova, Darya (Shipova), 83–85
Olloué, Major, 143, 144
Olsufyeva, M.V., 155
Orlov, V.G., 44

Pacca, Bartolomeo, 134
Paisiello, Giovanni, 23
Palloti, Vincenzo, 35
Paskevich, I.F., 160, 162
Pavey, Vladimir, 20, 28, 31, 34
Pavlishchev, N.I., 62
Pavlov, N.F., 28, 50, 62
Pavsky, G.P., 27, 29, 138
Pepe, G., 142
Philharmonic Society of Rome, 23, 66, 137
Pius VII (Gregorio Luigi Chiaramonti), Pope, 133, 135, 138, 142, 144, 147–149
Pius IX (Giovanni Maria Ferrelli), Pope, 35, 91
Pletnyov (Pletneff), P.A., 157
Pogodin, M.P., 49, 50, 61
Polevoy, N.A., 49
Pototskaya, Mariya, 77
Prim, Juan, 168
Protasova, A.A., 53
Pushkin, A.S., 17, 26–29, 32, 33, 36, 38, 41, 50, 57, 61, 62, 68, 70, 74–76, 145, 157; in Volkonskaya's salon, 26–29; poem to her, 27; attitude to Volkonskaya, 27, 28, 41; Ya. N. Tolstoy, 159
Pushkina, N.N. (née Goncharova), 38
Putyata, N.V., 49

Radetsky, Joseph, 105, 106
Raich, S.E., 50
Razumovsky, A.K., 44, 134
Remer, N.F., 66
Repnin, N.G., 22
Ricci, Mineato, 27, 28, 33, 65, 67, 79, 81, 83–85, 89, 91
Ricci, E.P. (née Lunina), 27, 33, 67
Rivas, Angel de Saaverda, 167, 168
Rossini, Gioacchino, 21, 23, 66, 68, 145
Rostopchin, F.V., 43
Royer-Collard, Pierre Paul, 164, 165
Rozhalin, N.M., 29, 57, 65, 68–70, 72, 74
Rumyantsev, N.P., 44, 96
Russian Discussion (Russkaya Beseda), 175

Sadan, General, 94
Sagan, Catherine W., Duchess of Curland, 117, 118
Samarin, Yu. F., 175
San Mazzano, Marchese, 134
Squance (Scassy/Scassi), 116, 121
Schelling, Friedrich Wilhelm, 57, 68
Schiller, J.C. Friedrich, 23, 57
Schwarzenberg, K.P., 105, 106
Scott, Sir Walter, 30
Shakespeare, William, 57
Shevyrev, S.P., 26, 28, 29, 50, 61–63, 68, 69
Shterich, E.P., 60, 63
Sobolevksy, S.A., 26, 29, 50, 60, 62
Sollogub, V.A., 172
Soymonov, A.N., 62
Spada, Antoine, 115
St. Aulaire, Louis Clair de Beaupoil, 70, 72, 73
Stackelberg, G.O., 134
St. Priest, Alexis Guignard, 140, 141, 148, 150
St. Priest, Armand, Count, 141
St. Priest, Sophie (née Golitsyna), 141
Staël-Goldstein, A.L. Germaine de (née Necker), Moscow (1812), 17, 18, 37, 43; St. Petersburg, 43, 44, 46; her posture toward Napoleon, 43, 44, 47;

interest to relationship with Volkonskaya, 44–46; *Corinne*, 44, 45, 73
Stein, Karl, Freiherr von, 44
Stendhal (Henry Beyle), 23, 41, 71, 74, 77, 137, 139
Stollberg, L.I., 103
Stroganov Academy, 45
Sverbeeva, E.A., 50
Suchtelen, Baron, P.K., 44
Szimanowska, Maria, 53

Talleyrand, Charles Maurice, 164
Thürnheim von, Lulu, 137
Titov, V.P., 57, 157, 158
Tolstoy, N.A., 109, 113, 116
Tolstoy, S.I., 168
Tolstoy, Ya. N., 159–170; early years in Russia, 165, 166; new political orientation abroad, 159–161, 165, 166; on French foreign policy and European events, 163–165, 167–169; Russian reforms, 161, 164–166, 170
Treletsky, Vladimir, 34, 35
Trubetskoy, S.P., 159
Tsvetaev, I.V., 29
Turgenev, A.I., 29, 37–40, 50, 70–74, 76, 78, 81, 84, 85, 87, 91; Rome (1832– 1834), 70–74; Pushkin's issue of *Northern Flowers*, 70, 72, 73; on Volkonskaya, 72–74
Turgenev, I.S., Baden Baden (1863–1868), 154, 171–175; Paris (1867), 172–174; "The Brigadier", 172, 174, 175
Turgenev, N.I., 122
Tyrwhitt, Sir Thomas, 112
Tyufyakin, P.I., 44

Union of Social Prosperity (*Soyuz Obshchestvennogo Blagodenstviya*), 159

Uvarov, S.S., 43

Valentini, G., 84
Vandamme, Dominique Joseph, 106, 107
Venevitinov, D.V., 26, 27, 50, 56–58, 62
Venevitinova, A.N., 31, 64

Vernet, Horace, 30, 61, 77, 86
Viardot, Louis, 171, 174
Viardot-Garcia, Pauline, 171, 172
Vielgorsky, I.M., 32
Visconti, P.E., 77
Vitberg, K.L., 120
Vladislavlev, B.A., 62
Vlasova, M.A. (née Beloselskaya), 28, 29, 32, 34, 36, 65, 67, 72–74
Volkonskaya, Louise (née von Lilien), 34, 158
Volkonskaya, M.N. (née Raevskaya), 27
Volkonskaya, S.G. (née Volkonskaya), 19, 31, 54, 57, 59, 64, 107, 108, 111, 113, 118, 123, 145–147, 149
Volkonskaya, Z.A. (née Beloselskaya): family, upbringing, 17, 18; at the court in St. Petersburg (1808–1810), 19, 44–47, 92–94; recurring mental depression, 18, 19, 23, 30, 33, 47, 94; following the army in the imperial suite (1813–1814), 19, 20, 94–96, 99–116; Paris, London (1814–1815), 20, 133; Vienna Congress (1815), 20, 21, 134; Paris, Rome (1815–1817), 21, 98, 117, 118; Russia (1817–1819), 21, 22, 119, 120, 134; Italy (1820–1823), 23, 135–151; Paris (1823–1824), 24, 25, 116–119; Russia (1824–1829), Moscow salon, 25–28, 50–52, 54, 55, 57, 58, 68, 75; visiting Goethe (1813, 1829), 19, 29, 68, 100; artistic activities, 21–24, 26, 27, 29, 31, 53, 54, 91, 116, 118, 134; literary work (prose and poetry in French and Russian), 22, 25–28, 45, 55, 70, 73, 78, 129, 178, 179, 183, 184, 187, 189, 190, 192, 193; music compositions, 21, 23, 27, 62; Rome (1830–1862) salon, 29, 30, 32, 61, 66, 67, 69, 74, 77, 78, 87, 89, 90; two trips to Russia (1836, 1840), 31, 32, 33; on the road to conversion, 24, 30, 31, 137, 138; after the conversion 32–36, 158

Volkonsky, A.N., 18, 22, 30, 31, 34, 35, 47, 68, 93, 94, 99, 103, 105, 107, 111, 112, 119, 127, 137, 145, 147, 154, 156–166
Volkonsky, G.P., 63
Volkonsky, N.G., 18, 19, 20, 22, 24, 31–34, 47, 48, 93, 94, 99, 103, 105, 107, 111, 112, 119, 127, 137, 145, 147, 154, 156–166, 169, 170
Volkonsky, P.M., 34, 59, 97, 98, 101, 111, 113, 115, 125, 126, 133, 134
Volkonsky, S.G., 27, 33, 59, 118, 155
Vyazemskaya, M.P., 81, 82, 155
Vyazemskaya, N.P., 82, 85, 155
Vyazemskaya, P.P. ("Pashenka"), 29, 76–82, 84
Vyazemskaya, V.F., 30, 76, 81, 155, 156
Vyazemsky, P.A., 26, 37, 39, 40, 42, 44, 49–51, 53, 55, 57, 59, 62, 71, 73; and

Volkonskaya, 23, 26, 29, 30, 37, 44, 75–81, 84; Stendhal, 77; Nicholas I, 81, 82; A.I. Turgenev, 81, 84, 85; first trip abroad, 75–85; abroad in 1858–1859, 154–158, 160
Vyazemsky, P.P., 78, 156

Wilhelm, Prince of Prussia, 126
Wellington, Arthur Wellesley, 124
Williams, Henry, 86
Wilson, Sir Robert Thomas, 44

Yazykov, N.M., 81

Zhukovsky, V.A., 32, 33, 37, 53, 58, 68–71, 74, 76, 79, 81–83; Rome (1838 1839), 86–91; and Gogol, 82–86; attitude toward Volkonskaya, 87, 91

List of Illustrations

Princess Zinaida Volkonskaya, around 1829 2

The poem by Pushkin dedicated to Volkonskaya 16

Princess Zinaida Volkonskaya 206

Princess Volkonskaya in the opera *G. d'Arco* 207

Prince A. M. Beloselsky-Belozersky 208

The Palace of the Beloselsky-Belozerskys 208

Prince N. G. Volkonsky 209

Princess Volkonskaya in Rome 209

Letter of Mme. de Staël 210

Tsar Alexander I on the battlefield at Leipzig 211

Short letter from Tsar Alexander I 212

Cardinal Ercole Consalvi 213

Short letter from Cardinal Consalvi 214

Letter from E. A. Baratynsky 215

Letter from I. I. Kozlov 216

Letter from A. I. Turgenev 217-218

Letter from Prince P. A. Vyazemsky 219

A. I. Turgenev and V. A. Zhukovsky 220

Zhukovsky's note to Princess Volkonskaya 220

Villa of Princess Volkonskaya in Rome 221

Two sketches depicting the villa 222

N. V. Gogol in the villa of Princess Volkonskaya 223

Church of Sts. Vinzenzo e Anastasio in Rome 224

Princess Zinaida Volkonskaya.
Fyodor (Fidel) Bruni

Portrait of Princess Volkonskaya in the title part in the opera *Giovanna d'Arco*
for which she wrote libretto and music.
F. Bruni, around 1826
Harvard University, Houghton Library

Prince Alexander Mikhailovich
Beloselsky-Belozersky,
Zinaida's father

The Palace of the Beloselsky-
Belozerskys in St. Petersburg,
corner of Fontanka and Nevsky

Prince Nikita Grigorièvich Volkonsky, husband of Zinaida.

Princess Volkonskaya in Rome around 1822 and 1855
etchings on glass and coral

Letter of Mme. de Staël
written to Princess Volkonskaya
in August 1812.
Harvard University,
Houghton Library

Tsar Alexander I on the battlefield at Leipzig, August 1813

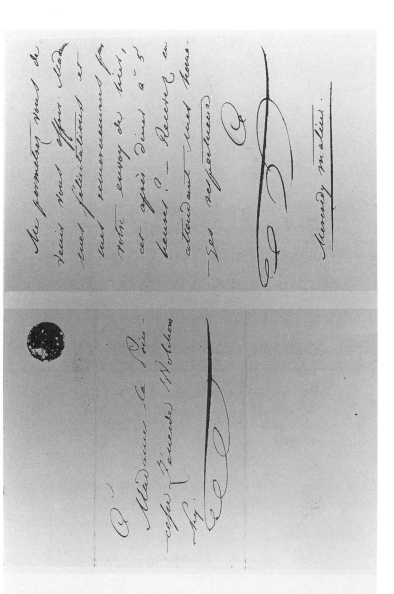

Short Letter from Tsar Alexander I to Princess Volkonskaya, August 1824.
Harvard University, Houghton Library

Hercules Consalvi Romanus S. Rotae Auditor,
Prothonotarius Apostolicus, et SS. D.N. PP. PII VII. Pro-Se
cretarius Status, S.R.E. Diacunus Card. creatus ab Eodem
in Consistorio secreto Palatii Quirinalis Feria II. Die 11. Aug.e 1800.

Cardinal Ercole Consalvi

Short letter from Cardinal Consalvi to Princess Volkonskaya, February 13, 1821.
Harvard University, Houghton Library

34.

Je suis pénétré de reconnaissance Madame pour tout ce que vous me faites d'obligeant sur ma petite nouvelle. Votre approbation serait plus que flatteuse pour moi, si je ne savais que vous êtes un critique aussi indulgent qu'éclairé. Ce n'est que ma mauvaise santé qui m'a empêché de me présenter chez vous et qui me privera encore demain de ce plaisir. Vous ne pouvez douter, Madame, que dès que je me tiendrai en état de sortir, je n'empresserai de vous présenter mes respects. S'il en était autrement je manquerais en même temps à mon intérêt et à mon devoir. J'ai l'honneur d'être

Madame

Votre très humble et très obéissant
serviteur

Eugène Baratynsky.

Letter to Princess Volkonskaya from E. A. Baratynsky, 1826.
Harvard University, Houghton Library

dont elle a pris ses chagrins qui a provoqué ce mal si douloureux
pour elle, si effrayant pour ses amis : j'espère que Dieu la tirera
pleinement d'affaire ; elle-même et sa charmante fille le méritent bien,
espérons et beaucoup. Le billet d'hier de la chère P. Aline est
très satisfaisant, et j'en rends grâce au Ciel. Parlez-moi de vos
occupations, chère Princesse ; que fait ce beau chant qui me vibre
encore dans le fond de l'âme ? On m'a lu des scènes de Godounoff,
il y a des choses tout à fait dignes de Shakespeare, c'est un véritable
génie.
   Veuillez dire à Viazemsky que je lui enverrai son exemplaire
par la poste prochaine. Ma femme et mes enfants se rappellent
à votre souvenir, et moi, je suis de cœur et d'âme avec un respect
sincère pour la vie

                              tout à vous

                              Jean de Kozloff.

Letter to Volkonskaya from I.I. Kozlov of November 25, 1826.
The last page of the letter which was dictated by Kozlov
to his daughter Alexandra was signed by the blind poet himself.
Harvard University, Houghton Library

... Demain dimanche, il n'est pas impossible de venir dîner avec vous. J'ai peu mis ailleurs et j'ai dû refuser M. S... mais après-demain, lundi, je suis à votre ordre. J'ai voulu passer chez vous et vous remercier de deux petits volumes que j'ai parcourus avec le plus grand plaisir. Je connais déjà le portrait et j'ai reconnu le pays aux beautés agrestes et portrait que vous en avez tracé dans les *fleurs du Nord*.

L'idée de la perle, qui doit nous rappeler une larme est mieux que une pensée; c'est un sentiment, et qui plus est ... cela d'une ...

L'observation sur la manière de tous les artistes et l'... sur les paysages est d'une force ... rare. Il y a de la vérité et de la poésie dans votre prose, chère Corinne, et si ...

Letter to Princess Volkonskaya from A. I. Turgenev (for dating
and attribution see pages 70-74).
Harvard University, Houghton Library

Letter to Princess Volkonskaya from A. I. Turgenev (for dating and attribution see pages 70-74).
Harvard University, Houghton Library

41

On vient de me remettre, princesse, votre billet au
moment où j'avois déjà fait ma tolette de voyage. Je
suis très peiné de ne pouvoir me rendre à vos ordres et
de n'avoir pas pris définitivement congé de Vous. J'ai
été toute la journée en l'air à cause de la noce de Himi-
nionets et je ne suis rentré chez moi que pour me mettre
en route. Voici la lettre pour Younowski que je Vous prie
de remettre au Comte Ricci en lui faisant agréer mes adieux
et l'assurance des sentimens distingués que je lui porte.
Quand au porte feuille ayez la bonté de me le faire envoyer
par la poste, ou de le faire remettre à mon homme d'affaires. Je prends aussi la liberté de Vous prier de dire mes
regrets aux demoiselles Ocoulott; je comptais les voir encore
avant mon départ, mais vraiment je n'ai pas eu la
tête à moi, ni ne l'ai pas maintenant. Vous devez
Vous en appercevoir au décousu et au désordre de
mon billet. Lisez le avec indulgence et agréez avec
bonté l'hommage de mes tendres respects et de mon
dévouement inaltérable. Wiazemsky.
ce dimanche.

The second letter from Prince P.A. Vyazemsky, April 12/24, 1835.
Harvard University, Houghton Library

Two profiles: A.I. Turgenev and V.A. Zhukovsky

Zhukovsky's note to Princess Volkonskaya of January 26/ February 7, 1839. Harvard University, Houghton Library

Villa of Princess Volkonskaya in Rome (Lateran) seen from the distance.
Colored lithograph by G. Vivian

Two sketches by V.A. Zhukovsky
depicting the villa of
Princess Volkonskaya with
N.V. Gogol shown on both

N.V. Gogol in the villa of Princess Volkonskaya.
Sketch attributed to F. Bruni

The Church of Sts. Vinzenzo e Anastasio in Rome
where Princess Volkonskaya was buried